C000255444

# THE COMPLETE BOOK OF
# TURKISH COOKING

# THE COMPLETE BOOK OF
# TURKISH COOKING

All the ingredients, techniques and traditions of an ancient cuisine

## Ghillie Başan

150 authentic recipes shown step by step in 800 photographs

With photography by Martin Brigdale

HERMES HOUSE

*For my brother and his delicious family:*
*Jamie, Liz, Toni, Lottie, Bruce and Lachlan.*
*Time to develop an adventurous palate!*

This edition is published by Hermes House,
an imprint of Anness Publishing Ltd,
Hermes House, 88–89 Blackfriars Road,
London SE1 8HA
tel. 020 7401 2077; fax 020 7633 9499

www.hermeshouse.com; www.annesspublishing.com

If you like the images in this book and would like
to investigate using them for publishing, promotions
or advertising, please visit our website
www.practicalpictures.com for more information.

Publisher: Joanna Lorenz
Senior Managing Editor: Conor Kilgallon
Project Editors: Lucy Doncaster and Felicity Forster
Copy Editors: Jan Cutler and Jeni Wright
Designer: Nigel Partridge
Home Economists: Fergal Connolly and Sunil Vijayakar
Stylist: Helen Trent
Production Controller: Don Campaniello

## ETHICAL TRADING POLICY

At Anness Publishing we believe that business should be
conducted in an ethical and ecologically sustainable way,
with respect for the environment and a proper regard to
the replacement of the natural resources we employ.

As a publisher, we use a lot of wood pulp to make
high-quality paper for printing, and that wood commonly
comes from spruce trees. We are therefore currently
growing more than 500,000 trees in two Scottish forest
plantations near Aberdeen – Berrymoss (130 hectares/
320 acres) and West Touxhill (125 hectares/305 acres).
The forests we manage contain twice the number of trees
employed each year in paper-making for our books.

Because of this ongoing ecological investment programme,
you, as our customer, can have the pleasure and
reassurance of knowing that a tree is being cultivated
on your behalf to naturally replace the materials used to
make the book you are holding.

Our forestry programme is run in accordance with
the UK Woodland Assurance Scheme (UKWAS) and
will be certified by the internationally recognized
Forest Stewardship Council (FSC). The FSC is a
non-government organization dedicated to promoting
responsible management of the world's forests.

Certification ensures forests are managed in an
environmentally sustainable and socially responsible
basis. For further information about this scheme, go to
www.annesspublishing.com/trees

© Anness Publishing Ltd 2007

All rights reserved. No part of this publication may be
reproduced, stored in a retrieval system, or transmitted
in any way or by any means, electronic, mechanical,
photocopying, recording or otherwise, without the prior
written permission of the copyright holder.

Previously published, in part, as *Turkish Cooking*.

## NOTES

Bracketed terms are intended for American readers.

For all recipes, quantities are given in both metric and
imperial measures and, where appropriate, in standard
cups and spoons. Follow one set of measures, but not a
mixture, because they are not interchangeable.

Standard spoon and cup measures are level.
1 tsp = 5ml, 1 tbsp = 15ml, 1 cup = 250ml/8fl oz.

Australian standard tablespoons are 20ml. Australian
readers should use 3 tsp in place of 1 tbsp for measuring
small quantities.

American pints are 16fl oz/2 cups. American readers
should use 20fl oz/2.5 cups in place of 1 pint when
measuring liquids.

Electric oven temperatures in this book are for
conventional ovens. When using a fan oven, the
temperature will probably need to be reduced by about
10–20°C/20–40°F. Since ovens vary, you should check
with your manufacturer's instruction book for guidance.

The nutritional analysis given for each recipe is calculated
per portion (i.e. serving or item), unless otherwise stated.
If the recipe gives a range, such as Serves 4–6, then the
nutritional analysis will be for the smaller portion size,
i.e. 6 servings. Measurements for sodium do not include
salt added to taste.

Medium (US large) eggs are used unless otherwise stated.

# CONTENTS

# INTRODUCTION

Diverse, endlessly fascinating and steeped in history, Turkey combines the ancient with the contemporary, the religious with the mystical, and boasts a peaceful landscape dotted with impressive mosques, ancient Roman and Greek ruins, colourful markets, and rustic villages full of cheerful children.

A country of contrasts, Turkey boasts ski resorts in the high mountains and luxurious yachts sailing in the blue waters of the south; old troglodyte cave dwellings and remote hilltop settlements; tea and cotton plantations; endless fields of roses and sunflowers; and olives, figs, almonds and pomegranates bursting from trees across the landscape.

## A MOVEABLE FEAST

Everywhere you turn in Turkey there is something delicious to eat, including street food such as bread rings covered in sesame seeds; deep-fried mussels with a garlic-rich sauce; warm roasted almonds and pistachio nuts; pastries bathed in syrup; divine milky desserts and chewy ice creams.

In the many restaurants and street cafés you can dine in style on whole grilled (broiled) fish served between two fat halves of a loaf of bread; aubergines (eggplants) stuffed, grilled or fried in endless ways; tangy salads; and yogurt dips strongly flavoured with garlic.

Every town and city has a market, where you will find a wealth of fresh, seasonal produce, such as plump olives and crunchy pickles, fresh figs, ruby-red pomegranates, juicy, ripe peaches, pungent spices, and fresh, leafy herbs, which are sold like bunches of flowers.

## SPANNING TWO CONTINENTS

With one foot planted in Europe and the other immersed in Asia, Turkey acts as a geographical and cultural bridge between the two continents, a fact that is vividly represented in the diversity of the cuisine. Within Turkey itself, the two continents are divided by the Bosphorus, the waterway that flows through the middle of Istanbul, one of the world's most exciting cities. Once the seat of the Ottoman Empire, it is still the centre of commerce and trade in Turkey, and is a vast melting pot of different cultures.

## ISTANBUL, THE CULINARY CENTRE

To get a taste of Turkey, Istanbul is the place to be. All roads lead to this majestic city and many Turks migrate here from all over the country, taking with them their own culinary traditions

*Above: A view of the Golden Horn and the Galata Bridge, Istanbul.*

and local flavours. As a result, the city is unique, never failing to surprise and tantalize, as it brings together ingredients, techniques and dishes from even the most far-flung corners of the country.

Day and night, Istanbul is intoxicatingly alive, with the endless street and water traffic, the honking of horns, the resonant call to prayer, and the alluring smell of food cooking in every street. Here, it is possible to taste red peppers from Gaziantep, tart green olives from Bodrum, dried apricots from Cappadocia, anchovy pilaff from Trabzon, spicy kebabs from Adana, the mildly hallucinogenic honey from Kars (from bees that feed on opium poppies), and a tempting array of soothing, creamy milk desserts and succulent, syrupy pastries, which originated in the Ottoman Palace kitchens and remain popular today.

## ANATOLIA, THE COUNTRY'S FOOD BOWL

The fertile heartland of Asian Turkey, Anatolia is surrounded by seas and is home to numerous lakes and rivers. The result of such extensive access to these bountiful waters is a wealth of freshwater and saltwater fish and shellfish, a fact that is much in evidence on the menus in seaside towns.

*Below: Turkey acts as a geographical and cultural bridge between Europe and Asia and the Bosphorus provides a sea route to Russia.*

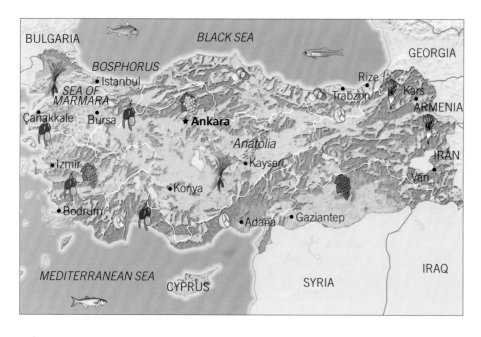

said that the country's turbulent history has also played a key role in shaping the cuisine.

Constantly in flux, the culinary traditions embody the many cultures that have had an impact on Turkish life over the centuries. These include ancient Persian and Arab practices that have been handed down from generation to generation; the influences of Islam and the Ottoman Empire; and today, the growth of urbanization and tourism.

In spite of these diverse influences, the culinary habits of the majority of the Turkish nation are based on Muslim practices. These include fasting during *Ramazan*, only eating *halal* meat, refraining from eating pork and drinking alcohol, and the consumption of traditional foods to celebrate religious days and rites of passage.

Other culinary traditions include the Ottoman "*hamam* party", an event that used to take place once a week but that is now, sadly, dying out. This event involved the women of each household visiting the public *hamam* (bath house) to wash, dance, sing and picnic on stuffed vine leaves, savoury pastries and olives. It just goes to show that, even when bathing, food has never been far from a Turk's mind!

*Above: Bustling boat traffic on the Bosphorus – an extremely pleasurable way to view both sides of Istanbul and visit the Princes Islands.*

Inland, the region is divided by high mountains and fertile central plains, where crops of fruit and vegetables are harvested, and there are rich grazing pastures for the cattle and sheep. Climatic variations in the region are striking, with long, cold winters gripping the east and hot summers scorching the south, and these conditions play their part in determining the type of food that can be successfully grown in each area.

## CULINARY TRADITIONS

While the food and cooking of Turkey is, inevitably, shaped by its diverse geography and climate, it could be

*Below: Fertile fields and nut trees in the heart of rural Anatolia.*

*Below: A young village boy grazing his sheep and goats among the ancient Greek ruins of the Temple of Aphrodite, western Turkey.*

# A CULINARY HISTORY

The early ancestors of modern day Turks originated in the Altay mountains in Central Asia, from where they drifted towards Anatolia, encountering and adopting different culinary traditions along the way. Some of these were based on the use of animal products, such as the milk and meat from horses as well as the many different wild animals that were hunted.

In common with other nomadic tribes of the period, the early Turks would also have made unleavened bread from wheat flour and would have drunk *ayran*, a yogurt drink, and *kımız*, a fermented liquor made from the milk of their mares.

When these nomads arrived in Anatolia around the 10th century, the region already had its own rich culinary heritage, influenced by the Hittites, the Romans, the Byzantines, the Arabs, the Mongols and the Crusaders who had passed through the region. The legacy of these influences was a cuisine that made use of the ready availability of beans, wheat and lentils, which were cooked with oil extracted from plants.

The early Turks adopted and further developed this cuisine, melding their own characteristics and culinary techniques with those already present in the region. Evidence of this early Turkish cuisine can still be found today among the Kazan and Tartar communities in central Anatolia. Here, many early dishes have survived, including *mantı*, a noodle dough, *yufka*, the thin sheets of flat bread, and *tarhana*, fermented dried curds that are used for making a traditional soup.

## THE IMPACT OF ISLAM

Following the death of the Prophet Muhammad in 632AD, a new Arab empire rose in the Middle East. As the Golden Age of Islam flourished between the 8th and 12th centuries, the Arabs invaded and conquered vast territories in Central Asia, imposing religious restrictions on all aspects of the cultures they encountered, including those of Turkey.

During this era there was a cultural awakening throughout the Middle East, as the seafaring Arabs brought back silk and porcelain from China, ivory and gold from East Africa, and spices from the East Indies. With the arrival of spices came a great deal of culinary creativity and the advent of instructive literature on recipes, etiquette and the health properties of certain foods, all of which had an impact on the cuisine of Turkey.

Around the same time, Mahmud al-Kashgari wrote the first important literary document, a Turkish-Arabic

*Above: Şiş Kebab is one of the recipes recorded by Mevlana Celaleddin Rumi.*

dictionary, which detailed and recorded aspects of the cuisine, such as the early nomadic Turks' love of yogurt, and their cooking methods for recipes such as *yufka* and *mantı*.

## THE SELJUK PERIOD

By the 11th century, the nomadic Turks had formed a warrior aristocracy, which resulted in the establishment of the Seljuk *(Selçuk)* Empire in Konya from where they ruled Greater Syria for most of the 12th century.

The culinary culture at this time was influenced by the sophisticated cuisine of Persia. Many important aspects of this food culture were recorded by the poet and mystic, Mevlana Celaleddin Rumi. Among the recipes listed in his works are dishes consisting of meat cooked with a variety of vegetables, such as leeks, spinach and turnip; *helva* made with grape molasses, *pekmez helvası*; the jelly-like, saffron dessert, *zerde*; and a number of pilaff and kebab dishes, all of which are still cooked to this day.

His writings also reveal the abundance of produce that was available at the time, such as marrows (large zucchini), celeriac, onions, garlic, chickpeas,

*Below: Nomadic Kurds maintain traditional techniques and culinary customs by milking their sheep to make yogurt and ghee, in Erzurum, eastern Turkey.*

*Above: The* Mevlana tekke, *tomb of the poet and mystic Mevlana Celaleddin Rumi in Konya. Rumi documented many aspects of Turkish cuisine in the 12th century.*

*Above: Garlic was one many ingredients in use during the Seljuk period.*

lentils, apples, quince, melons and watermelons, dates, walnuts, almonds, yogurt and cheese. Wheat flour was used to make *tutmaç*, traditional noodles that are cooked with yogurt or meat; *yufka*, the thin sheets of flat bread; *börek*, the savoury pastries and pies that the Ottoman Palace chefs later developed into wondrous creations; and *çörek*, small ring-shaped buns.

It was around this time that the Turks began to understand and record the importance of eating healthily, devising a system of balancing the warming and cooling properties of certain foods, based on the ancient Chinese principles of yin and yang.

## THE MEVLEVI ORDER

Following the death of Mevlana in 1273, the Mevlevi Order (of whirling dervish fame) was founded. They established strict rules of kitchen conduct and table manners, most of which are still adhered to in modern Turkish society. In their teachings, the kitchen was regarded as a sacred hearth and it was there that new apprentices matured and learned under the Guardian Master Cook, the Sheikh Cook, and the Sheikh Stoker.

In order to join the Order, the apprentices had to be prepared to shed their social upbringing and pride, and spend long hours in the kitchen, which was regarded as a temple in which every individual had a clearly defined role, such as the sherbet-maker, the pickle-maker, the bread-maker, even the dish washer.

Mevlana's personal cook, Ateş Baz-ı Veli (the original Guardian Master Cook), was considered so important that he was buried in an impressive mausoleum, a privilege usually reserved for royalty. Now a shrine for gastronomic pilgrims, it is said that if you remove a pinch of the salt from around the mausoleum, your cooking will be blessed.

*Below: A vivid array of spices displayed at the the Egyptian Bazaar in Istanbul. Many of these spices are the legacy of the Arab traders from the 8th to the 12th centuries.*

## THE OTTOMAN PERIOD

The most significant change in Turkish cuisine came about during the Ottoman (*Osmanlı*) Empire. Lasting for 650 years, the Empire was first established in Bursa in the 14th century by a Turk called Osman, the son of a pagan chief. It later spread and at the height of its power, it controlled much of south-eastern Europe, the Middle East and north Africa.

Once Constantinople (now Istanbul) was conquered by Mehmet II in 1453, the Topkapı Palace became the centre of the Empire and all culinary activity. By this time, the Turks had developed a sophisticated cuisine, which merged traditional nomadic traditions with new techniques and ingredients from Persia.

Mehmet II was a gourmet of the highest order with a penchant for indulging in lavish feasts, prepared in the Palace kitchens by carefully selected chefs from Bolu. These kitchens were divided into four main areas. The most important of these was the *Kuşhane* – the birdcage kitchen – named after the small cooking pots in which food for the Sultan was prepared in small quantities. The second most important kitchen was the *Has Mutfak*, where food was prepared for the Sultan's mother,

*Below:* Iznik *tiles decorate the* harem *quarters at the Topkapı Palace, Istanbul.*

*Above: Most grand houses, such as these ones overlooking the Bosphorus in Istanbul, would have employed a highly skilled chef.*

the princes, and privileged members of the *harem*. The remaining two kitchens produced the food for the lesser members of the *harem*, the chief eunuch, and the other members of the Palace household. The head butler of the Palace was responsible for the kitchens and each one had its own head chef.

During the reign of Mehmet II, the Palace kitchens boasted a huge staff of specialist chefs, such as the *börekçi*, the maker of savoury pastries; the *baklavacı*, the maker of sweet pastries; the pickle-maker, the *helva*-maker, the meatball-maker, the pudding-maker, the yogurt-maker, the bread-bakers, and so the list goes on.

The tradition of specialization in the kitchen that was launched by the Mevlevi Order in Konya reached its height during this period, as each chef strove to produce the most exquisite and tasty dish imaginable, resulting in a plethora of sophisticated and creative dishes that became known as the Palace (*Saray*) cuisine.

## COOKING AS AN ART FORM

As the Ottoman Empire expanded its territories during its six-century rule, it also increased its culinary repertoire by flamboyantly adopting and adapting the recipes it encountered in the Balkans, the Mediterranean region, North Africa and much of the Arab world. During the reign of Süleyman the Magnificent, creations from the Palace kitchens reached such heights of indulgence that various dishes with sensuous names emerged – such as "young girls' breasts" *(kız memesi kadayif)*, "ladies' navels" *(kadın göbeği)* and "ladies' thighs" *(kadınbudu köfte)* – dishes that are still part of Istanbul's cuisine.

While the culinary creativity of the Palace was at its peak, a similar level of industrious ingenuity was taking place in every Ottoman *yalı*, the grand houses inhabited by the distinguished members of Ottoman society, and in every wealthy household that could afford a chef. There was even an element of competition in the streets, as the *kelle-paçacı*, the maker of sheep's head soup, and the *gözlemeci*, the pancake-maker, vied for trade and praise among all the other makers of sweet buns, rice dishes, meatballs and Turkish Delight.

This was a time when cooking was regarded as an art form and eating was a pleasure, a legacy that is at the root of Turkish cooking today.

## NEW FOODS, HIGH STANDARDS

In the 16th and 17th centuries, the Ottomans persuaded the Spaniards, the other key players on the world stage at that time, to return from the New World via the North African coast, so that new ingredients, such as chilli peppers, tomatoes and maize, could be brought into Constantinople. These new ingredients were quickly absorbed into the sophisticated Palace cooking, from where they filtered throughout the Empire, shaping a large proportion of the Mediterranean cuisine.

While the Ottomans ruled, the very best ingredients were brought to Istanbul, ensuring high standards of food at every level. When the Ottoman Empire collapsed after its defeat in World War I, its culinary influence remained evident to the west of Constantinople but, as the Empire had never really penetrated eastwards into the heart of Anatolia, the local dishes managed to survive there unaffected by the Ottoman influence.

## MODERN CUISINE

The contemporary cuisine of modern Turkey is a divided one, founded on both its ancient Anatolian traditions

*Above: Ladies' Navels,* kadın göbeği, *a classic Palace dessert.*

*Above: A street vendor selling stuffed mussels, Istanbul.*

and its sophisticated Ottoman heritage. In addition, the Turks themselves are divided: there are those who do not sway from the traditional recipes and methods while there are others who, bursting with creative flair, have a desire to come up with something new. In essence, that is what Turkey is all about: constantly developing, but never forgetting tradition.

There has always been room for creativity and the generation of new ideas about ingredients and techniques – the Ottomans were fine examples of

that – and the moveable feast of Turkey is no exception, continually evolving and reinventing itself. With such a rich and diverse culinary culture, shaped by the movement of peoples and empires, exploring the cuisine of modern Turkey is a journey in itself.

In the tradition of its Ottoman ancestry, Istanbul remains one of the best places to sample the best of Turkish cuisine. Almost every regional variation of a dish can be found somewhere in this vast, vibrant city, ranging from the simple spicy tastes of Anatolia to the more elaborate dishes from the Ottoman Palace kitchens.

If you travel elsewhere in Turkey, you will notice the marked difference in the dishes from different regions. For example, in Amasya the *acı ezmesi* (fresh tomato and chilli relish) can be so hot it blows your head off, whereas in Bursa the chilli taste in the same dish may be much milder.

Everywhere you go in Turkey, whether it's a village on a mountaintop, or a busy marina in a coastal resort, there will be a family or a group of friends seated in a courtyard, a doorway, a balcony, by the beach or beside the road, anywhere they can set up a table to balance a few dishes upon. One of life's little pleasures is to sit by the Bosphorus in Istanbul, listening to the calls to prayer resounding across the water, as you savour every morsel laid before you. For that magical moment, you can live like a Sultan!

*Below: The splendid Topkapı Palace – the seat of the Ottoman Empire – perched above the sea of Marmara and the Golden Horn, Istanbul.*

# TURKISH CUISINE

The Turks are masters at combining several of the most important things in life: food, family and friends. Hospitality is high on the agenda and comes naturally to most Turks. The idea of sharing is very prominent when friends, relatives, or even strangers, come to the home. Guests usually arrive with a gift of something sweet, but whatever there is to eat in the house is shared. The concept of visiting and eating, or hosting and eating, is such an important part of the social culture that there are numerous proverbs centred around it, such as "Guests must eat what they find, not what they hope for!" or "Greet a Turk and be sure you will eat."

The history of hosting and eating amongst the Turks is vividly recorded in Medieval documents, which reveal that

some of the feasts would last for as long as forty days and forty nights. In addition to the traditional wedding and circumcision feasts, there were many others hosted by statesmen, noblemen, and the rulers of the Ottoman Empire. These elaborate meals would generally take place at long or u-shaped tables. These were laid with silver and gold candlesticks, urns and pitchers, some of which were decorated with jewels, and large bowls of fresh grapes, plump figs and pomegranates.

There were specific table seating arrangements and a regular flow of dishes, such as a sour soup, roasted legs of lamb with peas and plain pilaff, stuffed savoury pastries, sweet pastries, clotted cream and sweetmeats. Feasts were not entirely exclusive to the

wealthy though, as the very same hosts would also provide food for ordinary folk, presenting them with a wide selection of meat dishes, savoury pastries, stuffed vegetables and omelettes.

## THE ROLE OF *HELVA*

During the Ottoman period, the sweetmeat, *helva*, played such an important role in feasts and social gatherings that there were specific *helva* parties dedicated to its consumption. Particularly popular during the winter months, these parties were a form of entertainment for family, friends and neighbours, who would congregate in each other's houses to eat a variety of foods, such as stuffed chicken, savoury pastries, pancakes, and poached apricots filled with cream. The end of an evening always culminated in a bowl of *helva*, usually made with flour or semolina.

The guests would also bring a gift of *keten helvası*, which was similar to candy floss. To contrast with the sweetness, pickles would often be served with the *helva* and, to end the meal, coffee would be served.

A great deal of merriment was had by all at the parties, as games were played, songs were sung, stories and proverbs were recited, and the adults conversed late into the night – this was termed "*helva* conversation", *helva sohbeti*, which was also the name given to the parties. During the reign of Ahmed III (the Tulip period) the *helva sohbeti* were so popular that the wealthy households transformed them into large-scale entertainment with professional musicians and comedians.

## TRADITIONAL MEALTIMES

The early Turks of Central Asia ate on a leather sheet, a *kenduruk*, which was spread out on the floor, or on the ground if eating outside. In the 11th century this ground sheet evolved into a large tray, *tergi* (*tepsi* in modern Turkish), made out of wood, copper or silver, which was raised on a stone or a wooden trestle to make a low, round table. All meals were eaten at this table and the family would gather to sit around it on cushions.

*Below: This 19th-century painting depicts the elaborate table setting in the Yıldız Palace, Istanbul, that was typical of the Ottoman period.*

Before eating, a large jug of water and a hand-washing bowl would be placed by the low table to ensure everyone washed their hands. The mother of the household would then place the food on the table in bowls and copper dishes.

In a wealthy home, a servant would bring in the food and the family meal would usually begin with a soup,

### Feeding the poor

An important Ottoman tradition was the feeding of the poor. This took place at *imarets*, which were places of charity often attached to mosques, where students, travellers and poor people would come in their hundreds and thousands to eat.

Simple foods, such as loaves of bread, plain pilaff, soups, *aşure* (a pulse and grain pudding), and *zerde* (a jellied saffron and rice pudding), were served daily at the *imarets*, which housed a kitchen and dining hall. Next door there was often a *tabhane* (an alms house), which provided basic accommodation for the elderly and weak, as well as for travellers or migrants seeking work.

*Below: The Nilüfer Hatun Imareti, Iznik, was built as a soup kitchen in the 14th century.*

*Above: A traditional seating arrangement, with a low table and cushions, Istanbul.*

followed by a savoury pastry or pilaff, and a vegetable dish. In a poorer household, there might have been only one dish. At the end of the meal, the water jug and hand-washing bowl would appear once again, and the men would then be left to enjoy tobacco and coffee or tea. In rural Anatolia, families still eat in this manner but, in the modern homes, the table arrangements mirror those used in homes all over Europe.

Communal meals were traditionally the domain of men during the Ottoman period, and were eaten in institutions such as the military, dervish lodges, or rest houses. A bowl of soup with some bread or boiled rice would be placed in the middle of the low table and each diner would use a spoon to dip in. Since the soup was the main dish, it had to be wholesome and nourishing enough to sustain everybody for the day. The meal would end with a prayer and a pinch of salt on the tongue to thank God for the food.

Traditional culinary customs still play an important role in parts of rural Anatolia, but among the modern Turks many of these customs are dying out.

*Above: A Turkish man using three fingers to carry bread to his mouth.*

### RULES OF ETIQUETTE

In a traditional Turkish household it is polite to follow various rules of etiquette. These include washing your hands before and after the meal and respecting the prayer that will be recited before and after eating.

Two hands are used to break bread and only three fingers are used to pass the food to the mouth. Knives are rarely present at tables – most dishes have been prepared in a manner that avoids the necessary use of one – and an individual never passes a knife to another without spitting on it first, otherwise it is believed a fight will ensue. Any coughing, sneezing, or picking of teeth with a toothpick must be done with the head turned away from the table and a hand covering the mouth.

A pinch of salt is often eaten before and after the meal. It is also polite to compliment the hostess on her food after you have finished eating, by saying *"elinize sağlık"* ("health to your hands"); the idea being that one acknowledges that gifted hands have produced a stunning spread, and long may that last.

# THE ROLE OF *MEZE*

The sight and smell of the array of small dishes that are called *meze* is incredible: heavenly, garlic-flavoured, smoked aubergine (eggplant) purée; springy cracked wheat salad with tomato, mint and flat leaf parsley; crushed green olives with coriander seeds; small green (bell) peppers stuffed with aromatic rice, pine nuts and currants; spicy walnut purée with pomegranate syrup; artichokes and broad (fava) beans in olive oil; a sweet, tangy *tahin* and lemon purée; light, crisp, cigar-shaped pastries filled with white cheese, mint and dill; plump mussels coated in a beer batter and deep-fried; tiny, tasty fish *köfte* flavoured with cinnamon and dill; thin strips of warm, grilled aubergine and courgette (zucchini) served with a cooling, garlic yogurt; and whole juicy mushrooms cooked with pine nuts, spices and fresh herbs. Each and every plate of temptation is classed as *meze*.

## TITBITS FOR A "PLEASANT TASTE"

The wonderful thing about *meze* is that there really are no rules. Traditionally, a table of *meze* would be laid out to accompany the alcoholic drink, *rakı*,

with the aim of achieving a "pleasant head", not to fill one's belly but to delight one's palate. It was originally a custom enjoyed by men, often traders and travellers, but over time it has evolved into a family affair. Often loosely translated as *hors d'oeuvre*, an appetizer, or a snack, the versatility of *meze* enables it to be all of these things and much more besides.

The literal translation of *meze* is a "pleasant taste" and that is just what it is: something tasty. There are those who insist that only a bowl of nuts, olives or small pieces of fresh or dried fruit constitute the true *meze*, whereas many others feel that almost anything and everything qualifies, from warm, freshly toasted pumpkin seeds to small, succulent lamb kebabs, or even some street food, such as freshly peeled, salted cucumbers.

*Above: Simple* meze – *a bowl of green plums,* erik, *that are dipped in salt.*

## FRUIT *MEZE*

For those who insist that *meze* should consist of just one fruit, each season offers its own special gems, such as fine slices of fresh quince with a squeeze of lemon, the unripe, firm, tart-tasting green plums *(erik)* that are dipped in salt, and the large, ruby pomegranates dripping in juice.

Fresh watermelon, cherries, apricots and figs are also popular *meze* fruits, but throughout the tradition of *meze*, the most widespread fruit to accompany the popular drink, *rakı*, has always been

*Below: A* meze *spread consisting of Smoked Aubergine with Yogurt Purée; Salad of Feta, Chillies and Parsley; Grated Beetroot and Yogurt Salad; and bread.*

### The history of meze
Dating back to the ancient Greeks, Romans and Persians, as well as medieval Arabs and Ottomans, the tradition of *meze* has a long history. Until relatively recently, it was a custom enjoyed by men alone – traders, travellers, noblemen, kings and Sultans.

The word *meze* is thought to have originated from the Persian word *maza*, which means "relish" or "taste", and is the word used in Syria and Lebanon, whereas in other parts of the Middle East the word is *mezze*. All these words traditionally referred to small morsels, or portions, of flavoursome food served to accompany a spirit or wine.

*Above: Marinated olives with oregano and lemon make a tasty* meze *dish.*

*Above: Made from puréed chickpeas mixed with sesame seed paste, garlic and lemon juice, hummus is an extremely popular* ezme *dish.*

a sweet, juicy melon cut into golden chunks and served on its own, or with cubes of white cheese.

## SALADS AND SIMPLE *MEZE*

*Meze* and salads go hand in hand, as many salads are served as *meze* and some dishes are called "salad", even if they do not resemble one.

The most primitive form of *meze* is a small plate of *çerez*, which usually consists of a dainty serving of dried fruit, such as white mulberries, or plump olives with a squeeze of lemon juice, or even just a selection of nuts, roasted pumpkin seeds, salted sunflower seeds, or roasted chickpeas *(leblebi)*, the traditional accompaniment to the drink, *rakı*. Full of protein and minerals, and delicious when freshly roasted, nuts have long been eaten as appetizers because they are reputed to increase one's toleration of alcohol.

Another simple form of *meze* is the popular *ezme*, which consists of ingredients that are beaten, crushed, mashed, pounded, puréed, or pressed into a paste. An *ezme* dish should be of a consistency that is perfect for scooping up with bread and, in some cases, for

treating as a dip. Not all dishes that are pounded or puréed are called *ezme* – some have their own names like hummus, made with chickpeas, *tarama*, made with fish roe, and *fava*, a dish of puréed broad beans; others come under the umbrella title *salata* (salad).

## WHAT MAKES A *MEZE* TABLE?

The *meze* table is not regulated by time or order, just the understanding that the food should be served in small quantities to be savoured and shared at a leisurely pace and that one should rise feeling contented and comfortable, not stuffed. With this in mind, many Turks tend to enjoy *meze* in the evening when time is not pressing and a glass of cloudy *rakı* can be enjoyed at leisure. Traditionally, the relaxed partaking of *meze* was often accompanied by feelings of peace and serenity, even deep meditation.

A *meze* spread can consist of a myriad of miniature foods; sometimes they may even be a miniature version of a main dish, such as *fistic lahmacun*,

miniature Anatolian pizzas, or *cizbiz*, small grilled (broiled) meatballs. Incredibly versatile, *meze* and salads are suited to the Western way of eating, as a small assortment can be served as nibbles with a drink, or a wide choice can be prepared for a buffet spread.

*Right: A street vendor roasting chickpeas,* lablebi, *an accompaniment to* rakı.

# RELIGIOUS DAYS AND FESTIVALS

Following the conversion to Islam in the 9th century, all aspects of Turkish culture underwent dramatic changes, as Islam introduced the practice of observing holy days, as well as imposing restrictions on the consumption of certain foods and alcohol. The new customs and rituals gathered families together to cook and celebrate, lending certain foods a sacred significance.

Food for special occasions remains an important feature of Turkish culture. In fact, most social and religious events would be unthinkable without some sort of gathering around food and drink.

Perhaps enforced by the Koranic verse "To enjoy sweets is a sign of faith", there seems no limit to the capacity and creativity of pudding- and sweet-making in the name of religious or social duty. *Helva* is prepared for commemorative occasions, such as births and deaths, as well as moving house, graduating from school, the commencement of military service, and many harvests and festivals.

*Zerde*, a jelly-like, saffron-scented rice pudding, *helva* and *baklava* are traditionally prepared for weddings and circumcision feasts in the belief that by eating something sweet, a sweet life will be ensured.

Even visits to the *hamam* (the public bath house) can involve food in some parts of Anatolia, as women and children gather together to bathe and eat picnic food. In fact, it is safe to say that at any form of social gathering in Turkey, whether it is visiting the home of a friend or joining a family for a meal, it is deemed polite to bring a gift of something sweet.

The principal religious events in Turkey are *Ramazan*, the month of fasting, *Ramazan Bayramı*, a three-day festival at the end of the month-long fast, *Kurban Bayramı*, a festival to mark the near sacrifice of Isaac, and *Muharrem*, the first month of the Muslim calendar. The other social events and ritual ceremonies involving food and feasting include circumcisions,

*Above: Semolina* helva *with pinenuts is prepared for festive occasions.*

weddings, childbirth, funerals, and various local gatherings, such as the celebration of the spring harvest.

## RELIGIOUS RULES

In the holy book of Islam, the Koran, there are four categories of food that are strictly forbidden: any animal that died in a manner other than by having its throat cut (non-*halal* meat); the blood from an animal's body; all forms of pork; and the meat of an animal that is sacrificed in the name of any other god. The consumption of other creatures, such as reptiles and beasts of prey, are not restricted in the text but Islamic scholars consider them harmful so they are not on the culinary menu. Although it is considered lawful to "fish in the sea and consume the catch", only a small proportion of Turks tuck into shellfish.

The Koran also forbids any form of alcoholic drink, although the text refers to "wine", providing the opportunity for argument among those who wish to consume *rakı*, or other local spirits. The words of the Prophet Muhammad are: "That which causes any form of inebriation is wine and any kind of wine is forbidden." However, these restrictions are waived on the rare occasion of severe hunger or thirst, or an illness that occurs in a situation where it is impossible to stick to the strict Islamic rules.

*Left: The beautiful Blue Mosque, Istanbul, is decorated with blue tiles.*

*Right: A skilled maker of* kadayıf *swirls pastry dough on a revolving stove top.*

## RAMAZAN

The ninth month of the Muslim calendar, which follows the lunar year, is called *Ramazan* (Ramadan) in Turkey. This is the month of fasting that is observed by all Muslims. Fasting during *Ramazan* is regarded as an act of piety – this means that no food or drink may pass the lips during the period between the early morning meal, *Sahur*, eaten an hour before the morning prayer, and the call to the evening prayer, when the *Itfar* meal can be enjoyed.

In some neighbourhoods and villages, there is a festive atmosphere during *Ramazan* as friends and relatives visit each other and share in the ritual meals. However, modern life requires that business carries on as usual, so tempers can run wild during the daytime, especially if *Ramazan* falls during the hot season. The only exceptions to the rule of fasting are infants considered too young to undergo the rigours of fasting, pregnant women, the sick and elderly, and travellers.

## ITFAR AND SAHUR

Traditionally, the *Ramazan* fast was broken at the end of day by first taking a little breakfast before the ensuing *Itfar* meal. This breakfast would normally consist of special breads, such as *Ramazan pide* or *simit* (the round bread

rings), accompanied by various jams, cheese and olives, as well as cups of blessed water.

The *Itfar* and *Sahur* meals of *Ramazan* generally consist of light soups, seasonal vegetables cooked in olive oil, stuffed vine leaves and peppers, meat stews, *baklava*, and flat breads such as *pide* and *güllaç*, the paper-thin sheets soaked in milky rose-flavoured syrup. The *Sahur* meal is generally lighter on the stomach and always ends with fresh fruit or a fruit compote, *hoşaf*, to leave the mouth refreshed rather than thirsty for the long day ahead.

### RAMAZAN BAYRAMI

When the month of fasting draws to a close, it is time to celebrate with another festival, *Ramazan Bayramı*, a three-day feast! Again families and friends visit each other, but the streets are festive, too, with an abundance of street sellers, merriment and fireworks. In addition to the savoury dishes, this festival is celebrated with a myriad of sweet dishes, such as *baklava* and *kadayıf*, as well as *helva* and *lokum* (Turkish Delight) and other forms of

*Left: On the way to market, a man and his sheep walk through a street in Urfa.*

confectionery, including sugared almonds and boiled sweets (candies). Children are given sweets wherever they go, and boxes of *lokum* are presented to guests, hosts and friends when people visit one another.

For such events some people will drive to the other side of a city to get the freshest *baklava* from a famous *baklavacı* that uses ghee or a high-quality butter in the pastry, or they will fetch the creamiest milk dessert from the most reputed milk-pudding shop, *muhallebici*, and they search for the most moist *helva* from the *helvacı*. The sweet dishes and confectionery flow in abundance at this festival, which is also known by its popular name, *Şeker Bayramı*, the Festival of Sweets.

### KURBAN BAYRAMI

The holy festival of *Kurban Bayramı* is another important event in the Muslim calendar across the Islamic world, as it marks the near-sacrifice of Isaac. At *Kurban Bayramı* sheep are herded through streets, villages and markets, where families gather to buy one to take home and sacrifice it ritually. The family will then choose cuts of meat and offal (innards) to make special dishes to mark the event and give the rest to the poor in the neighbourhood.

### Back to the Ark

The fruit and grain dessert *aşure* is associated with the legend of Noah's Ark. It is believed to have evolved when provisions ran low on the Ark and Noah suggested that all the remaining dried fruit, nuts and grains should be boiled together. Following tradition, it is made in bulk so that it can be shared with everyone.

*Below: Noah's Dessert.*

The prepared dishes will include *işkembe çorbası*, the traditional tripe soup that is served with a splash of vinegar or pickles; *kavurma*, which involves frying the meat in its own fat; a pilaff made with the liver; *köfte* and kebabs, *kıkırdak poğaçası*, a delicacy made by boiling the fat tail; and *bumbar dolması*, a dish of grilled intestines stuffed with liver, onions, spices and currants, which is similar to the street specialty, *kokoreç*.

### MUHARREM

On the tenth day of *Muharrem*, which is the first month of the Islamic calendar, the martyrdom of Hüseyin, the Prophet's grandson, is commemorated with prayers in the mosques and the sharing by families and friends of *aşure*, a magnificent fruit and grain dessert.

The preparation and sharing of *aşure* can take place at any time from the tenth day onwards, as it is made in vast quantities and is time-consuming to make. Each household prepares a large bowl of the dessert using nuts, grains and dried fruits of their choice, and shares it with friends and neighbours. Sometimes particular members of the family are appointed to make this dessert every year, as their version is unbeatable.

### KANDIL

There are five religious feast nights called *Kandil* nights, when the minarets of the mosques are illuminated. The dates and months of these nights are determined by the Arabic calendar, which follows the lunar year.

On the twelfth night of the third month, *Rebiülevvel*, it is the Prophet Muhammad's birthday; the first Friday of the seventh month, *Receb*, marks the Prophet's conception and is particularly significant as it is the night that people believe their prayers will be answered; the twenty-seventh night of the seventh month, *Receb*, marks the Prophet's ascension to heaven; the fifteenth night of the eighth month, *Şaban*, is the Night of Privilege, when the angels note and consider the future actions of individuals for the ensuing year; and the twenty-seventh night of the ninth month, *Ramazan*, is the night of Power, when the Koran was revealed to the world.

This last night, known as *Kandil Gecesi*, is the most celebrated and joyous of all the *Kandil* nights, as people gather in the streets to enjoy fireworks and festive foods. Perhaps because it occurs towards the end of the month of fasting, devout Muslims are usually in the mood to feast extensively and have fun. *Kandil* foods include *lokma*, pastries soaked in syrup, *baklava* and *helva*.

### HIDRELLEZ

The spring festival, *Hıdrellez*, takes place in some regions of Turkey. Generally, it is an occasion for families to gather in the countryside and celebrate with picnic food, such as stuffed vine leaves, *kuru köfte*, and pilaff dishes containing chunks of meat. A great deal of merriment is had by all as the women prepare the picnic, the men cook the meat on the *mangal*, the children run about and play in the woods and fields, and the whole family dance and sing after eating.

### CIRCUMCISIONS

In modern Turkish society, circumcision remains an important event which usually takes place when a boy is between the ages of five and eight years old.

*Below: In preparation for their circumcision, three boys are dressed in the traditional white suits and capes, and receive sceptres.*

Proud parents dress their boys in a white jacket, trousers and a cape and often a group of boys will face the circumcision together. Before the event, the boys are sometimes marched through the streets to the beat of a drum and, after their ordeal, which is carried out by a religious person or a doctor, they lie on a bed in the middle of a room, often in some degree of discomfort, while the family and friends gather to feast and dance. All the guests bear gifts of sweetmeats, money, and good-luck talismans for the boys. Plenty of sweet dishes are served at these feasts, as well as stuffed vine leaves, meatballs, pilaff, and *keşkek*, a porridge-like mixture of bulgur wheat and meat.

During the Ottoman period, the circumcision feasts of princes lasted for days, even weeks and, on occasion, these celebrations would be combined with the marriage festivities of the princesses. Guests would arrive from faraway corners of the Empire to be met by high standards of hospitality. When Mehmed IV had his sons Mustafa (Mustafa II) and Ahmed (Ahmed III) circumcized, he also arranged the marriage of his sister, Hatice Sultan, who was only seven years old at the time. The celebrations for this occasion lasted for almost one month and involved thousands of dishes, including 50,000 chickens.

## WEDDINGS

In both urban and rural Turkey, no wedding would be complete without a great deal of feasting and dancing. Depending on the region, the bride may be transported to her wedding on the back of a donkey, in a horse-drawn cart, or in the family car, and she is almost invariably dressed in white.

Many of the wedding dishes are associated with other social events, such as births and religious festivals, but among the wealth of meatballs, stuffed vine leaves, savoury pastries and vegetables on offer, there will always be rice in the form of a pilaff, sometimes served in a ceremonious mound or encased in pastry, *perdeli pilav*, and in the traditional pudding, *zerde*.

*Above: A family preparing a daughter for marriage in a village in rural Anatolia. The bride is wearing the traditional white dress, brightened with vivid splashes of orange.*

Some of the dishes are prepared to welcome the bride into the groom's household or, as in the case of *içli köfte* (mother-in-law meatballs), to ensure the bride's lips are sealed with discretion. Others, such as the rice grains in pilaff and the seeds of a pomegranate, symbolize fertility and the birth of many children – with hope for a boy first! Trays of confectionery, such as sugared almonds and Turkish Delight, as well as *helva* and *baklava* will be offered by the hosts and brought by the guests to ensure a sweet life for all.

Before and after an Ottoman wedding, confectionery was served to women in the *harem* and to men in *selamlık*. At the end of the ceremony, the guests would be splashed with rose water and served a fruit or almond sherbet in silver goblets. The ensuing banquet would be lavish, with every type and shape of bread, rice piled in a dome dripping with butter, and whole roasted lamb, or leg of lamb with almonds. The day after the feast, the women would gather for *paça günü* ("sheep's hooves day"), at which they would eat sheep's hooves in a soup or stew sent to them by the groom. The bride would wear a special dress for the occasion, at which musicians and dancers performed.

## BIRTHS

On the second or third day after the birth of a child, a sweet red drink, *lohusa şerbeti*, is prepared to mark the joyous occasion. Flavoured with cloves and coloured with cochineal, this drink is served to visitors who come to congratulate the mother and bring gifts for the baby. In some traditional households, a *kına gecesi*, a henna night, is still held on the seventh night after the child is born. Traditionally, this was when neighbours and friends were invited to dine, play music and sing.

## FUNERALS

Death is regarded as part of life by Muslims, who are taught by Islam to be resigned to it. When someone passes away, neighbours prepare simple food, such as savoury pastries, pilaffs, and meat stews, for the family of the deceased during their period of mourning. On the day of the funeral, however, the grieving family prepares a *helva* made with semolina and pine nuts, *irmik helvası*, to offer to visitors who have come to pay their respects. In some Anatolian households, the family may also prepare *helva* or *lokma*, fried pastries soaked in syrup, to offer to the spirit of the deceased.

# COOKING IN TURKEY

*With a blend of Ottoman creativity and Anatolian tradition at its foundation, the Turkish kitchen is a unique tapestry of exciting tastes. Life revolves around food, and with daily markets bursting with vegetables and fruit, bunches of herbs and baskets of pungent spices, crates of gleaming, fresh fish, and cheeses stacked into towers next to buckets of yogurt, it is easy to see how food has become an obsession. Cooking in Turkey is a passion and most of the dishes are wonderfully versatile and simple.*

# THE TRADITIONAL KITCHEN

Much has been learned about the practices of early Turks from the many cooking utensils that have survived and are now exhibited in museums. We know, for instance, that communal meals were prepared in huge cauldrons, and that spoons were of such great significance that they were included in proverbs, such as "Fate turns up in the spoon". Available in different shapes and sizes, everyday spoons were carved out of wood or tortoiseshell, while grander ones were made of silver, gold or mother-of-pearl, often set with precious gems.

## THE CENTRE OF THE HOME

The traditional kitchen was split into two sections: the pantry and the cooking area. The pantry was usually dark and ventilated, so that the goods remained fresh for days or even months. Jars of jam, honey, *pekmez*, pickles and cooking oils were placed on a stone step along the base of one of the walls, and the *pastırma*, *sucuk*, onions and garlic hung from hooks along the wall. Fresh fruits were also hung in muslin (cheesecloth) bags for storing and preserving.

The dry goods, such as flour, sugar and bulgur wheat, were stored in sealed copper and earthenware pots to keep the ants and weevils at bay. As these foods were used daily, they would be placed somewhere accessible, such as near the doorway connecting the pantry to the cooking area.

Inside the cooking area you would normally find a basin and a fountain for washing, shelves for the storage pots,

*Above: Cooking pots of various shapes are used in Turkish kitchens.*

pans and crockery, and a wire-mesh meat safe, used for keeping flies off the cooked dishes.

Located in the same part of the kitchen, near the kitchen hearth or stove, you would find a wide, round wooden board or low table. Surrounded by cushions and sited in the optimum spot for the swift transferral of pastries to and from the oven, this table would be required for rolling out huge wheels of *yufka*. This difficult art is still practised today, but can really only be successfully achieved by using an *oklava*, a long, thin rolling pin designed for the purpose.

Nearby, stacks of round, shallow baking tins (pans), *tepsi*, would be at hand, ready to be lined with the sheets of *yufka* to make the varied savoury and sweet pastries so enjoyed by Turks.

## STOVES AND OVENS

A *mangal* (a charcoal stove) would be used for cooking a wide range of dishes in a traditional kitchen, while a coke-fed stove (*maltız*), or a hearth, was used for dishes that required an intense heat. As the *mangal* was portable, it could be used in the open doorway, or outside in the courtyard. Sometimes the *mangal* would be outside the kitchen in the yard, and today it is often taken on picnics in the countryside.

*Below: Preparing traditional pastry –* yufka *– using a long, thin rolling pin called an* oklava *in the hearth area of a kitchen in rural Turkey.*

*Above: Traditional, dainty tulip-shaped glasses used for drinking tea.*

Any bread-baking or roasting would take place in the family *tandır*, a pit dug in the earth, or in the village *fırın*, a large communal oven. For some festive occasions, a whole sheep or goat would be cooked on a spit over the family *tandır*, to be shared among friends.

## KITCHENS TODAY

When you step into the village kitchens of central and eastern Anatolia very little has changed since ancient times. Only basic tools are used, such as wooden spoons, deep ladles, heavy enamel pans or tin-lined, copper pots. Earthenware casserole dishes (*güveç*), or concave roof tiles (*kiremit*), are used for roasting and baking cuts of meat and fish in the communal oven.

*Left: A mangal being used to cook sardines at a country picnic in Anatolia.*

*Right: Mortars and pestles of various sizes are used frequently in Turkish cooking.*

A copper yogurt urn lined with tin is still used to make yogurt whenever it is required. As Turks consume a lot of yogurt, this can be on a daily basis. Depending on the region, these yogurt urns can be very attractive, such as the elegant tulip-shaped ones from Trabzon, or rather mundane, such as the stout, bucket-shaped urns used in Van.

A sturdy mortar and pestle, usually made out of stone, brass, or iron, is used for crushing spices and lighter, wooden ones, often with a convenient handle, are used for crushing garlic with salt to create a creamy mixture that is beaten into yogurt and other dishes.

Brass coffee grinders and the long-handled *cezve* are the necessary equipment for making Turkish coffee, while the double-tiered tea-pot system and dainty tea glasses, which are often shaped like tulips, are the required utensils for making tea. Almost every household, office, bank, shop, café and restaurant is equipped with these traditional utensils for making coffee and tea all day long.

Long metal, copper, or aluminium skewers for grilling meat can be plain or elaborate, depending on the location and the wealth of the family. Some are decorated with the Turkish symbol – the star and sickle moon motif – while others display designs of tulips, or a pomegranate with seeds to symbolize prosperity and fertility.

Long, thick kebab swords are also a feature of kitchens in the southern region of Turkey, where fiery kebabs are cooked as the sheath to the sword.

## RURAL AND URBAN PRACTICES

Kitchens and cooking practices differ slightly in towns and the countryside. Many urban dwellers have fairly simple kitchens at the back of the house in which the family meals will be cooked, but, unlike in villages, little baking is done, as urban dwellers rely on the

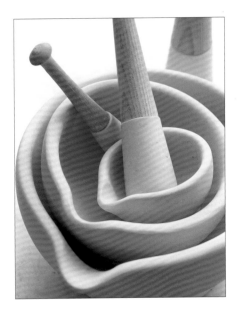

neighbourhood specialist bakers for their selection of breads and pastries. In the city, apart from for festive occasions, puddings are rarely homemade, as urban Turks enjoy going out to the pudding shops and pastry houses for their sweet snacks.

Wealthy Turks in the cities rarely cook; instead they dine out frequently in their favourite restaurants and clubs and, when at home, they often have cooks to prepare the meals for them.

## COOKING AS AN ART

Whether the cook is in the kitchen of a rural or urban home, most preparations for Turkish food are carried out by skilful hands and nimble fingers. Recipes are handed down from mother to daughter and the cooking is done from memory and taste. Recipe books are not required and the seasons or holy days often dictate the dishes.

The chefs in many restaurants and specialist shops, particularly those trained in the Palace cuisine, are usually men. In these busy kitchens, more sophisticated utensils are often required, as well as accurate oven temperatures and cooking times, crucial for the milk puddings, *helva*, sweet pastries, and Turkish Delight *(lokum)*. There are several cooking schools in the main cities but the one in Bolu has had a long and successful history for producing chefs of the Palace tradition.

# VEGETABLES

Because the Turks are fascinated with the health properties of the food they eat, vegetables play an extremely important role in their culinary culture. For example, aubergines (eggplants) are believed to be beneficial for fighting infections of the ovaries, courgettes (zucchini) for combatting intestinal parasites, onions for ulcers, cabbage for stomach pains, and garlic for blood circulation and overall good health. As a result, it is not unusual to find baskets of dried medicinal herbs and vegetables, their seeds and roots, beside piles of fresh vegetables in the markets.

Throughout the Seljuk and Ottoman periods, many vegetable recipes were based on the ancient Chinese yin and yang theory that some vegetables "warm" the blood whereas others "cool" it. As a result, Turkish cooking possesses more healthy vegetable dishes than most other cuisines, and many of these are to be found in the broad spectrum of *meze*, salads and vegetarian dishes.

## MARKET-FRESH VEGETABLES

Visiting the market is very much part of the day's activities in most households. Choosing the vegetables for lunch or supper can be quite time-consuming and a lot of fun, while the cooks pick over the vegetables on display and haggle with the sellers. Often the vegetables available will dictate the meals of the day, as there might be an unexpected selection of fresh broad (fava) beans bursting from their pods, or the regal-looking, young globe artichokes artfully prepared for cooking.

Cucumbers are often peeled at the markets and sold as a refreshing snack, or they are taken home, cut into strips and lightly salted, to be served as a nibble with a drink. Similarly, giant cos lettuces are taken home, where they

*Below: There are many types of aubergine, including striped, purple ones.*

are placed in a jug of water on the table, so that everyone can help themselves to a crunchy leaf and sprinkle it with a little salt. Green salads usually consist of cos lettuce, young spinach leaves, springy lamb's lettuce and beet leaves.

## AUBERGINES/EGGPLANTS *(PATLICAN)*

Sometimes referred to as "poor man's meat", aubergines are cooked in numerous ways in Turkey. During the Ottoman period, the Palace chefs were known to have prepared aubergines in at least 40 different recipes, and some Turks claim there are at least 200 aubergine dishes in the country.

Generally, the aubergines of the region are purple, or almost black, in colour and range from the large, bulbous ones that are shaped like boxing gloves, and the long, slender variety that are ideal for *dolma*, to the small teardrop-shaped ones, which taste lovely smoked.

Smoking aubergines is common practice in Turkey, where the distinctive-tasting flesh is bound with olive oil and plenty of freshly squeezed lemon juice and made into a variety of delicious *meze* dishes, such as *patlıcan ezmesi* and *patlıcan salatası*, or it is beaten into a cheese sauce to make the unique dish, *beğendi*.

*Left: A village woman carefully selecting vegetables from a stall at a rural market in eastern Anatolia.*

## Smoking aubergines (eggplants)

To smoke aubergines easily and effectively, you need to have a gas cooker or a barbecue or charcoal grill.

**1** First, place the whole aubergine directly over the gas flame, or over the hot charcoal. Leave the aubergines to soften, turning from time to time. Over a gas flame the skin will become charred and flaky, whereas the heat from the barbecue or charcoal grill toughens the skin like leather.

**2** When the aubergine is soft (that is, so that you can press it down easily with your finger), place it in a plastic bag to sweat for a few minutes.

**3** To extract the smoked flesh, you can slit the aubergine open lengthways and scoop it out, or you can hold the aubergine by its stalk under a running cold tap and peel off the skin using your fingers – if you do the latter, make sure you squeeze out the excess water at the end.

### Dried and pickled aubergines

Every part of an aubergine is used in Turkey, including the skins, which are hung up to dry in the sun and then threaded on to strings and sold in the markets. Reconstituted in water, the skins are stuffed in the winter with an aromatic pilaff or spicy bulgur wheat mixture, or poached in a little olive oil and lemon juice to make a dish that is a speciality of the *güney* cuisine from Gaziantep and Antakya.

Another speciality from that region is jars of pickled aubergines stuffed with hot peppers, and if you travel westwards along the coast to Adana, you will come across a most unusual jam made with baby aubergines.

### Frying aubergines

Prior to frying, whole aubergines are generally partially peeled in stripes, a little bit like the markings of a zebra, and then submerged in a bowl of salted water for 30 minutes.

Similarly, aubergine slices or cubes are soaked in salted water first and then drained. The idea here is to draw out any indigestible juices that may be present and to soften the flesh slightly. Both the whole aubergines and the slices must be thoroughly drained and, in some cases, squeezed of any excess water before they are dropped into the hot oil.

### BEETROOT/BEET (PANCAR)

The most popular way to enjoy beetroot in Turkey is to pickle it in a mixture of vinegar, garlic and salt. Baby beetroot are pickled whole and the large ones are sliced. Slices of beetroot are added to jars of pickled turnip to colour it a pretty shade of pink. Beetroot is also often enjoyed as a *meze* dish mixed with yogurt.

### CARROTS (HAVUÇ)

The south of Turkey is one of the few regions where you can still find red- and purple-skinned carrots, which have a slightly peppery taste, more akin to a radish than a regular orange carrot. These special carrots are best appreciated as a grated salad, dressed in a little lemon juice.

The orange colour of most carrots is due to the high content of betacarotene and these carrots also contain a fair amount of natural sugar, making them both pretty to look at and sweet to taste. A popular vegetable in the Turkish kitchen, the long, tasty orange carrots add a splash of bright colour to many dishes. They are grated or chopped and combined with yogurt, or tossed in salads and pilaffs, such as *kaşgar pilav*; cooked with lentils, beans, or other vegetables in stews; sliced and pickled, steamed and puréed to make *ezme* or *köfte*; and poached with sugar to make a sticky *helva* and a delectable jam.

### CELERY (KEREVİZ)

Celery stalks are mainly braised with meat or they are grated and combined with coconut in the refreshing southern salad, *kereviz salatası*. The celery root, on the other hand, is employed in a number of meat and fish dishes. Generally it is diced and cooked with potatoes and carrots, to which it adds its own distinctive flavour.

### COURGETTES/ZUCCHINI (KABAK)

The courgette is an immature marrow (large zucchini), which is believed in Turkey to be cooling to the blood and,

*Below: Pale, marble courgettes and slender green ones.*

therefore, requires balancing with warm herbs, such as dill and mint. The young, fresh, bright-green courgettes are crisp and slightly perfumed, and are best tossed raw in salads or cooked very lightly. At the beginning of the season, young courgettes are often sold with their papery, yellowy-orange flowers attached, and these can be stuffed with aromatic rice or bulgur wheat.

The courgettes in the Turkish markets are always green or creamy coloured with a marbled effect. They are rarely much longer than 18cm (7in), as they should be firm and tender, not large and spongy, or watery. They are often cooked with tomatoes in stews or egg dishes; alternatively they can be deep-fried and served with a nut sauce, *tarator*, or garlic-flavoured yogurt; stuffed with aromatic rice in a similar manner to aubergines; or combined with white cheese in the mint- and dill-flavoured patties, *kabak mücver*.

The larger marrows, on the other hand, tend to be more watery and are stuffed with minced (ground) meat, or cooked in stews. The seeds of the marrow are roasted and eaten like pumpkin seeds or nuts.

### CUCUMBERS *(SALATALIK)*

Generally, the cucumbers of Turkey are much the same size as courgettes – short and stubby and almost seedless. The skin is quite bitter, so they are usually peeled, or partially peeled, before eating. One of the most

*Below: Cucumber sprinkled with a little salt makes a refreshing snack.*

refreshing street snacks is a freshly peeled cucumber dipped in salt. Strips of cucumber sprinkled with salt is also a popular *meze* dish. When not being devoured on their own, most cucumbers are sliced or chopped and added to salads, such as the cooling yogurt and mint dish, *cacık*, that can be served as a salad or as a cold soup.

### GLOBE ARTICHOKES *(ENGİNAR)*

In botanical terms, the artichoke is really just a rather splendid-looking thistle that happens to be edible. The tall plants are cultivated throughout the Middle East and Turkey, where the regal-looking globe is regarded as a delicacy. Turks rarely eat the scales; instead, the globes are trimmed down to their hearts, or bottoms. In the markets, the fresh artichokes are sold on their stems so that they can be stood in a bucket of water, like a bunch of flowers, until ready to use.

When preparing the globes, they need to be rubbed with lemon juice and plunged into cold water to prevent them from discolouring. The most traditional method of cooking artichokes is to poach them in olive oil, either on their own with dill, or with broad (fava) beans, almonds and tomatoes, both of which are called *zeytinyağlı enginar*. Another version involves stuffing the artichokes with aromatic rice and wrapping them in vine leaves before poaching in olive oil. Ready-prepared artichoke hearts, or bottoms, are available frozen in some supermarkets.

### LAMB'S LETTUCE *(SEMİZ OTU)*

The Turkish lamb's lettuce is fairly thick and fleshy. Its principal role is in a simple salad dressed with garlic-spiked yogurt,

*Above: Lamb's Lettuce Salad is a popular dish in Turkey.*

*semiz otu salatası*, which is served as a *meze* dish or as an accompaniment to grilled (broiled) meat and savoury pastries. Otherwise, it is braised with minced meat, or sautéed with beans.

### LEEKS *(PIRASA)*

In Turkish markets, the leeks are as long as hockey sticks and feature in the expression *"pırasa bıyıklı"*, which means "whiskered like a leek" in reference to the Turkish men with long, bushy moustaches that droop down the sides of their chins.

Leeks have been used in cooking since the Turks migrated from Central Asia and remain very popular to this day. They are employed in a range of soups, stews, patties and savoury pastries. They are also cooked on their own in olive oil, *zeytinyağlı pırasa*, and they are stuffed with a rice and minced meat mixture in *pırasa dolması*, which is usually served with an elegant egg and lemon sauce.

### OKRA *(BAMYA)*

Fresh okra is cooked on its own, lightly sautéed with lemon, or added to meat, poultry and vegetable stews. It is usually widely available in Middle Eastern, African and Asian stores, as well as many supermarkets.

When choosing okra, look for pods that are firm, unblemished and bright green in colour. The tiny dried okra pods are grey-green and slightly hairy.

*Above: Okra is widely available in Middle Eastern stores and larger supermarkets.*

They need to be rubbed in a cloth to remove the hairs before using. They are used primarily in soups and stews originating from the south-eastern region of Turkey, where the dried pods are enjoyed for the tart flavour they impart to the dish. Strings of dried okra hang in the markets alongside strings of dried aubergines and (bell) peppers.

## ONIONS *(SOĞAN)*

All types of onion are usually available in the markets in Turkey, from the round and bulbous varieties in their varying shades of red, purple and gold, to the pearly, white onions, pink shallots and long, mild-tasting spring onions (scallions).

*Right: Onions and garlic are key ingredients in many Turkish dishes.*

*Right: Mildly perfumed* çarliston biber *are delicious grilled.*

Large white onions are often hollowed out and then stuffed with an aromatic mixture of rice and minced lamb before being baked in the oven.

Golden onions are used for making a popular cumin-flavoured marinade for meat and fish. First, the peeled onion is grated and crushed to a pulp, which is sprinkled with salt and left to weep; the pulp is then pressed in a sieve (strainer) to extract the onion juice, which is generally mixed with crushed cumin seeds and spread over the meat or fish.

Purple and red onions are particularly favoured for salads and *meze* dishes, as they are slightly sweet, and shallots are used in stews or threaded on to kebabs. The long onion tops are specially cut to sauté in butter with a squeeze of lemon, or to use in an omelette.

## PEPPERS *(BIBER)*

The most common peppers used in Turkish cooking are small and green. These slightly tart peppers are the immature fruit of the capsicum pepper plants, and they are often favoured for use in stuffed dishes such as *zeytinyağlı biber*, and for slicing raw into salads.

The more mature, sweet, red capsicum peppers are used in vegetable or meat stews or they are grilled, skinned and marinated in olive oil. They are also dried in the sun, threaded on to long strings and sold in the markets.

These dried peppers are ground to a fruity powder, which we know as paprika; softened in a bowl of warm water to be stuffed with rice or bulgur wheat in the winter; or pounded with hot red pepper, olive oil and salt to form a thick paste, which is used in some *meze* dishes, soups and stews, and is also enjoyed simply spread thinly on a piece of bread.

The other commonly used pepper in Turkey is the long, thin, twisted, light-green variety, *çarliston biber*, which resembles a Turkish slipper. Mildly perfumed and sometimes slightly hot, these pretty peppers are generally grilled or fried and served whole as a *meze* dish or as an accompaniment to kebabs.

### Hot peppers

Alongside the slipper-shaped peppers in the market, you will also find a darker-green, thinner, twisted pepper, which is – make no mistake – a hot chilli. Rarely cooked in dishes, it is often chopped or sliced and used raw in salads and *meze* dishes, such as the "gypsy rice", *çingene pilavı*, and the fresh, fiery relish, *taze ezmesi*.

Even hotter are the tiny, green matchstick chillies, which occasionally appear in meat dishes, but are more often preserved in vinegar to make a fiery pickle.

The other hot pepper used in the Turkish kitchen is the red, horn-shaped chilli, which is generally dried and used as the ubiquitous spice, *kırmızı biber*, in many dishes.

*Above: Pumpkins and squash are enjoyed in sweet and savoury dishes.*

### PUMPKINS *(BAL KABAĞI)*

Autumn, the season of pumpkins, heralds the arrival of the pumpkin-seller in the streets of villages and cities, his cart laden with the bright orange, gourd-like fruits. These he skilfully peels and cuts for the traditional syrupy dessert, *bal kabağı tatlısı*, in which succulent blocks of pumpkin are poached in a clove-scented syrup. Other pumpkin dishes include soup, stews, pilaff, savoury pastry, jam and *baklava*, but the most impressive of all is baked pumpkin stuffed with a

jewelled pilaff, which consists of pine nuts, pistachio nuts, currants, orange peel, and apricots, or with an aromatic lamb pilaff. In some Anatolian villages, the hollowed-out pumpkin is used as a cooking vessel for soups and stews (although it can only be used once). Pumpkin seeds are roasted and eaten as a snack wherever you go in Turkey.

### FRESH BEANS *(TAZE FASULYE)*

Runner beans, string beans and green (French) beans all come under the banner "fresh beans" *(taze fasulye)*. Only fresh barlotti and broad (fava) beans have their own names – this may be because they are used in their dried form too. All the fresh green beans are cooked in the same way, the principal and most delicious method being to cook them in olive oil with a little tomato and dill, *zeytinyağlı taze fasulye*.

### SPINACH *(ISPANAK)*

Medieval records show that spinach was originally used as a herb and was not regarded as a vegetable until the Arabs introduced it into the Turkish cuisine. In Turkey it features in a number of vegetable or meat stews, but its most popular role is when it is combined with

*Above: Fresh spinach leaves feature in a number of Turkish dishes.*

butter or a cheese sauce and used as a filling for savoury pastries and flat breads. It is also very popular as a *meze* dish, served warm or cold, with garlic-flavoured yogurt. The spinach roots are often sautéed in butter with beans or poached in lemon juice.

### TOMATOES *(DOMATE)*

One of the 16th-century New World arrivals in the region, tomatoes are so entrenched in the cuisine of Turkey that it is difficult to imagine how the Turks and other tribal peoples of Anatolia managed without them. The tomato harvests are abundant and the bright-red fruit come in a variety of shapes and sizes, all exceedingly tasty, as they benefit from being ripened in the sun.

Generally, tomatoes are skinned and seeded before being added raw to salads or cooked in infinite ways. Whole tomatoes are stuffed with rice, bulgur wheat, or minced (ground) meat, in the same manner as (bell) peppers. Ripe tomatoes are crushed to a pulp, which is poured into trays and thickened in the sun to form a paste, whereas the unripe, green fruit is pickled.

*Left: Turkey is one of the biggest producers of tomatoes in the world – ruby red, juicy and delicious.*

Firm plum tomatoes are also poached in syrup to make a delicious jam that is spooned on to fresh, crusty bread. Turkey is one of the largest producers of tomatoes and exports them fresh, as well as dried and in cans of commercial paste.

## VINE LEAVES *(YAPRAK)*

Fresh vine leaves are usually sold stacked in piles in the markets, as well as being preserved in brine in packets, jars and cans. The leaves have a slightly malted taste and are used for wrapping around poached or grilled (broiled) fish, cheese and stuffed artichokes. Their most famous role, though, is the *dolma*, in which the leaves are filled with an aromatic rice mixture, or one made with minced meat and rice, and then rolled into logs and poached.

### Preparing vine leaves

If you are using fresh vine leaves, you need to plunge them into boiling water for 1 minute to soften them, then drain and refresh them in cold water. Preserved leaves, on the other hand, have already been softened, but they need to be soaked several times in boiling water to rid them of salt. Place the leaves in a bowl and pour boiling water over them, making sure it gets between the layers. Leave them to soak for about 15 minutes, drain and repeat. Make sure the leaves are thoroughly drained before use.

*Below: Prepared fresh vine leaves, ready for stuffing.*

*Above: Artichokes with Beans and Almonds is a* zeytinyağlı *dish.*

## SPECIAL COOKING METHODS

The Turks possess several unique ways of cooking vegetables, aside from deep-frying in sunflower oil and grilling over charcoal. When a variety of different vegetables are cooked together, they are ofen baked in an earthenware dish *(güveç)*, or they are packed tightly in layers with meat and cooked gently to make a *bastı*. This attractive dish is usually tipped upside down on a plate, so that the bottom layer of meat in the pan lies on top of the vegetables on the serving plate.

Some vegetables lend themselves to being hollowed out, then stuffed with minced meat or rice, or a mixture of the two, to make a *dolma* or *orturtma* dish – both of which refer to a cooked, stuffed vegetable. The most unique of all is the *zeytinyağlı* dish, in which the vegetables are poached in olive oil.

### Zeytinyağlı

The *zeytinyağlı* (olive oil) dishes are an exquisite legacy of the Palace kitchens. The traditional method involves poaching the vegetables, some of which may be stuffed,

*Above: Baked Stuffed Apples are served as a vegetable dish.*

in a generous quantity of olive oil combined with a little lemon juice so that they are deliciously moist and tender. The vegetables are then left to cool in the oil and are served at room temperature. The flavoured oil at the base of the pan is very much part of the dish and should be spooned over and around the vegetables when they are arranged on the serving plate.

### Dolma

The word *dolma* is used for vegetables that are stuffed. In fact, it is used for anything that is stuffed, such as fruit and fish, and the famous *dolmuş*, the Turkish taxi stuffed with people! If there isn't a natural cavity to stuff, the Turks will create one, even in an aubergine without splitting it open – a great deal of gentle bashing and massaging expertly forces the aubergine to spit out its innards through a hole at one end, so that the skin can be stuffed.

Fruits, such as apples, plums and prunes, are stuffed and served as a vegetable dish, and vine leaves and cabbage leaves are wrapped around rice fillings to make *dolma*. The most traditional fillings for log-shaped *dolma* consist of an aromatic rice with pine nuts and currants, or minced beef or lamb with rice and herbs.

# FRUIT

Although seasonal fruit – such as juicy, ripe melons, soft peaches, delicate figs, jewel-like pomegranates and sweet grapes – is mainly eaten fresh, there are several desserts that feature fresh and dried fruits; for example, *hoşaf*, a refreshing compote of apricots, sultanas (golden raisins), almonds and pine nuts; and *ayva tatlısı*, fresh quince poached in a clove-scented syrup (a recipe that is also used with pumpkin). Apricots, plums and figs, both in their dried and fresh forms, are often filled with cream or nuts and soaked in syrup, and fresh sour cherries are cooked with sugar and poured over baked bread to make *vişne tiridi*, also known as *vişneli ekmek tatlısı*.

Other fresh fruits that are commonly consumed on their own when ripe include mulberries, apples, oranges, watermelon, Galia and honeydew melons, green plums and lemons. Unripe fruits, on the other hand, are sought after for making into jam.

*Above: Seasonal fruits, such as watermelons, grapes, figs, pomegranates and lemons, on display at a market stall in Istanbul.*

### APRICOTS (KAYISI)

Although the soft-skinned, sun-ripened fresh apricots are often eaten fresh as a snack, many will be dried on the flat roofs of central Anatolian villages, destined for many inspired dishes. Fresh apricots are also poached in sugar to make a delicious, scented jam, while dried apricots are poached in

*Below: Poached Apricots in Scented Syrup with Buffalo Cream.*

syrup so that they are soft enough to stuff with almond paste or clotted cream, as in the delectable dessert, *kaymaklı kayısı*.

Dried apricots are also stuffed with a savoury rice and minced (ground) lamb filling; they are added to lamb and chicken stews, and they are combined with other dried fruits and nuts in pilaffs and fruit compotes, such as *hoşaf*. Naturally sun-dried apricots are coffee-coloured with a hint of caramel in their intense fruity flavour, whereas the commercially dried fruit is treated with sulphur dioxide to retain its bright orange colour.

*Below: Fresh, ripe figs are a treat.*

### FIGS (İNCİR)

Fresh figs really need to mature on the tree under a hot sun to be at their best: moist and very sweet. A variety of figs grow in Turkey, where they are enjoyed fresh when ripened – the skin of the most common fig should be slate-grey tinged with purple, and the fruit should be plump and tender, as if it is about to burst open to reveal its vermilion or pink seeds. However, figs are also picked when they are small and green, as they are perfect for a delectable jam, *yeşil incir reçeli*, which resembles gleaming jewels floating in syrup and tastes like honey.

### Jams *(reçel)*

Exquisite and colourful, the jams of Turkey are out of this world. Both ripe and unripe fruits are sought after for making jam. Even some unripe vegetables, such as tomatoes, are destined for the syrupy conserves that are such a feature in Turkish culinary life.

The delicious jams are served for breakfast with warm bread and slabs of moist white cheese; drizzled over freshly baked cakes and doughs as a sweet snack; or spooned on top of creamy yogurt. They range from the delicate, scented taste of steeped rose petals, to the honey-tasting, whole green figs. Other conserves are made from quince, peach or apricot, mulberry and sour cherry, watermelon, plum tomato with almonds, and, quite remarkably, whole baby aubergines.

Jars of genuine Turkish jam are usually available in most Middle Eastern stores and some delicatessens and supermarkets. Remember that the consistency of Turkish jam is more akin to a syrupy conserve than a thick, spreadable jam, so a spoon rather than a knife is required to transfer it to your bread.

*Below: Dried Fig Jam with Aniseed and Pine Nuts.*

*Above: Juicy lemons and limes to squeeze over many Turkish dishes.*

With huge harvests every year, figs are also dried in the sun until the skin hardens and lightens in colour. These have a chewy texture and crunchy golden seeds. Turkey is one of the largest exporters of dried figs, along with dried apricots.

### GRAPES *(ÜZÜM)*

The grape vine and its fruit have had many culinary uses since ancient times. Turkey is one of the principal producers of the table grape, but there are many other varieties, too – some of which are specially grown to produce dried fruits; others for making wine.

In general, the table grapes are green or reddish-purple, very sweet and juicy, and enjoyed just as they are. Tart green grapes are sometimes added

*Below: Thick, syrupy* pekmez, *the popular grape molasses.*

to stews, but can be substituted with the sour green plums *(erik)*. Fresh grapes are also puréed and dried to make popular "leathers" and they are pressed for their juice, which is boiled and reduced to form a useful fruit molasses called *pekmez*.

The dried fruits, in the form of raisins and sultanas (golden raisins), are used in sweet dishes, such as Noah's dessert, *aşure*, and the tiny black currants, which are known as *kuş üzümü* (bird grape), are used in many savoury dishes, such as pilaffs and *köfte*, as well as in sweet dishes. Raisins and currants are also used in the production of *rakı*, the distilled aniseed-flavoured, alcoholic drink that many Turks prefer to wine.

### LEMONS *(LİMON)*

Before the arrival of lemons in Turkey, the juice of sour pomegranates, the fermented juice of sour grapes, and ground sumac berries were used as souring agents. Nowadays, though, juicy, thin-skinned lemons are harvested in abundance and are used in dressings, marinades, a refreshing sherbet drink, and the syrup for *baklava* and other sweet pastries and doughs.

Another very Turkish tradition is to serve lemon wedges with practically every dish, not simply as a garnish, but to squeeze over the food before you eat to give it a refreshing lift and, at times, to enhance the flavour. This practice is particularly effective when the fresh juice is squeezed over chunks of fruit, such as sweet melon or succulent watermelon, most vegetable and rice, bean or grain dishes, and the tasty liver dish, *arnavut ciğer*.

*Above: Sweet, juicy slices of watermelon make an ideal snack.*

---

### Fruit leathers

In the dried-fruit-and-nut sections of Turkish markets, you will usually come across long, coloured strips hanging from hooks like rigid ribbons. These are fruit leathers, which are primarily made from apricots, grapes, mulberries, pomegranates, apples and sour cherries.

First, the fresh fruit is pounded and sieved (strained) to a smooth purée, which is spread very thinly and evenly in flat trays and left to dry in the sun. Once the sun-dried purée is firm enough to lift out of the tray, it is cut into thin strips, which are hung in the markets or rolled up to store.

These leathers are especially popular with children, who like to chew on them in the same way other children might enjoy sweets (candies), and they can also be melted in a little water to be used as a concentrated purée in stews, sauces and desserts.

---

## MELONS *(KAVUN)* AND WATERMELONS *(KARPUZ)*

Although not of the same family, melon and watermelon are sold beside one another in the markets and are enjoyed fresh and ripe, when the juice dribbles down your chin with every bite. Both fruits are enjoyed as a snack at any time of day, cut into cubes at the start of a meal, or sliced into wedges to be served at the end. Golden cubes of honeydew, Galia or Casaba melons are perhaps one of the most traditional forms of *meze*. A popular way to enjoy them is with cubes of feta, as the sweetness of the juicy melon perfectly complements the salty, firm texture of the cheese.

In the southern regions of Turkey, where many unusual jams seem to be concocted, the unripe flesh of both the golden varieties and the watermelon is poached with sugar to make interesting conserves.

When choosing sun-ripened melons in the markets, the simplest test of ripeness is to press the end opposite to the stem to see if it yields, or to smell it for its perfume. The flesh of ripe watermelons should be a vibrant reddish-pink when cut open, with a sweet, fresh taste and not over-watery.

## POMEGRANATES *(NAR)*

With its leathery skin and jewel-like seeds, the pomegranate is believed to be a symbol of beauty and fertility, as well as beneficial to the soul, as it purges it of anger, hate and envy.

During the Ottoman period, there were white-skinned and purple-skinned pomegranates available, in addition to the more common red- and pink-skinned fruit that can be found in abundance in the markets today. Generally, the fruit stalls separate the sweet pomegranates for eating from the sour ones for cooking and marinating, although the latter are mainly used for sherbets and molasses *(pekmez)* in modern Turkey, as lemons have taken over the "souring" role of pomegranates.

Fresh pomegranates are mainly enjoyed as a dessert fruit, as they are so deliciously juicy and sweet when ripe. On occasion, a bowl of gleaming, ruby-red seeds may be presented as a dessert, or as a palate-cleanser, all laboriously separated from skin and pith and then chilled – an exquisite and refreshing treat that is sometimes enlivened with a few fresh mint leaves. The fresh seeds are also combined with other fresh or dried fruit in exotic compotes sprinkled with rose water, or they are scattered over *meze* dishes, salads and pilaffs.

Pomegranate "leathers" are dark in colour and slightly sour-tasting, as is the molasses that is used to flavour several stews and roasted poultry, as well as the medieval walnut and red pepper dip, *muhammara*.

*Below: Pomegranates can be enjoyed on their own or in a number of sweet and savoury dishes.*

*Above: Quinces are at their best when they are cooked.*

## QUINCES *(AYVA)*

Related to the apple and the pear, the quince is similar in appearance although larger and lemon-yellow in colour. The flesh is firm, mildly perfumed, and slightly tart. When consumed in any quantity, it has a tendency to stick your tongue to the roof of your mouth.

The fruit really comes to life though when cooked, as it emits a delightful floral fragrance and lends a honeyed taste to the dish. Although quince is often cooked with lamb or poultry and

*Below: Sour cherries can be used to make a wonderful jam, as well as the summer dessert,* vişne tiridi.

stuffed with rice and minced (ground) lamb, it is at its most flamboyant when it is shredded and transformed into a syrupy, golden jam, or when it is poached with sugar and cloves to make the stunning Palace dessert *ayva tatlısı*, in which the fruit turns a pretty shade of pink and the syrup becomes jelly-like because of the pectin in the fruit and pips. Topped with a rolled log of *kaymak*, this is a seasonal treat.

## SWEET AND SOUR CHERRIES *(KİRAZ* AND *VİŞNE)*

The height of the season for the sweet cherry *(kiraz)* is relatively short – roughly the month of July – so the juicy, ripe fruits are passionately devoured in quantity for breakfast, for a little refreshment at any time of day, and for dessert.

The sour cherry *(vişne)*, however, has a number of culinary uses. Poached with sugar, sour cherries can be easily transformed into a delicious jam, *vişne reçeli*; a

popular summer dessert, *vişne tiridi*; and a wonderful purple syrup that is used as the basis of a refreshing sherbet drink. Sour cherries are also puréed and dried to make "leathers", and they are dried whole to preserve them for stews and pilaffs. The kernels of the black *malep* cherries are ground to a powder (also called *"malep"*), which is used for flavouring biscuits (cookies) and cakes.

*Below: Sweet cherries are delicious eaten raw during their short season.*

### Fruit molasses *(pekmez)*

To make a fruit molasses, the juice is first extracted from the fruit before it is boiled and reduced to create a dark, fruity syrup, *pekmez*. In its crude form in some Anatolian villages, the *pekmez* is slightly fermented and is used in place of sugar or honey in many dishes. As it is of pouring consistency, *pekmez* lends itself for use as a natural sweetener in cooking, and can be drizzled over yogurt or flat breads. It is also used in some *helva* recipes, or is combined with sesame paste to make *tahin pekmez*, a sweet, nutty mixture that is enjoyed on bread. A variety of fruits, such as mulberries, sour cherries, sour pomegranates (this *pekmez* is slightly tart), and carob pods can be used to make *pekmez*, but the most popular one in Turkey is made from the juice of grapes.

# NUTS AND SEEDS

A wide variety of nuts play an important role in both the Palace and Anatolian culinary traditions. Hazelnuts grow along the Black Sea coast, pistachio nuts flourish in the Mediterranean and south-eastern regions of Turkey, chestnuts grow in abundance around Bursa, and almond and walnut trees can be seen almost everywhere. Regarded as healthy and nourishing, children are encouraged to snack on nuts, and specialist nut and dried-fruit sellers entice people to buy them by roasting the nuts on their makeshift stalls or in their shops.

### ALMONDS *(BADEM)*

In the spring, unripe almonds are picked while still green and velvety, to be dipped in salt and eaten as a snack. Ripe almonds are blanched or roasted, then find their way into numerous pilaffs and meat or poultry dishes, as well as desserts and sweetmeats, such as *keşkül*, a traditional Palace milk dessert made with almonds and marzipan.

Blanched almonds are also coated in sugar and bought as gifts to celebrate births and circumcisions, and they are sold at the sweet festival, *Şeker Bayramı*. Blanched almonds are also bound in muslin (cheesecloth) and

poached to extract their creamy milk, which is used to make a delicate syrup for a refreshing sherbet drink. Almond trees have been regarded as a symbol of beauty since ancient times and are often depicted on Turkish ceramic tiles and crockery.

### CHESTNUTS *(KESTANE)*

Dried and roasted chestnuts are used in a variety of lamb and vegetable stews, as they often take the place of potatoes. However, the best time to enjoy chestnuts in Turkey is in the winter when they are roasted in the street at makeshift stalls and sold piping hot in a funnel of newspaper, or when they are tender and succulent, having been poached in sugar syrup as a delectable sweet treat, *kestane şekeri*, which is often taken as a gift when visiting someone's home.

### HAZELNUTS *(FINDIK)*

If you drive along the Black Sea coast in September, you will see carpets of freshly picked hazelnuts drying in the sun by the roadside. Destined for many Turkish biscuits (cookies) and sweetmeats, such as *helva* and *lokum*, tons of these nuts are also sent abroad, as Turkey is one of the largest exporters of hazelnuts.

Hazelnuts are often pounded to make *tarator*, the popular garlicky nut sauce that can also be made with almonds, pine nuts or walnuts. They are roasted and crushed for use in several savoury dishes and, as they contain high levels of protein, children are encouraged to eat them, so they appear in almost every type of chocolate and in chocolate spread, and they are preserved in honey with pistachio nuts.

*Left: A woman shelling almonds in the street in a small, rural village in south-western Turkey.*

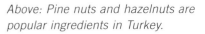

*Above: Pine nuts and hazelnuts are popular ingredients in Turkey.*

### PINE NUTS *(ÇAM FISTIK)*

Perhaps the most frequently used seeds of all, tiny, creamy pine nuts find their way into numerous savoury and sweet dishes in Turkey. They emit a subtle smell of pine and have a mild resinous taste, and, when they are roasted and golden, they are both nutty and pretty to look at.

As a result of both their visual and gastronomic attractiveness, pine nuts are often scattered over *meze*, pastries and desserts as a decoration, and they are an important component of fish and meat *köfte* as well as the rice filling that is stuffed into every *dolma*.

As they go well with just about anything, pine nuts are often poached or soaked with fruit, such as in the traditional dessert, *hoşaf*. They are also added to a variety of sweetmeats, in particular the celebratory *helva* dishes: *un helvası*, prepared for births and marriages, and *irmik helvası*, which is offered at funerals.

*Below: Fresh chestnuts are encased in hairy shells.*

*Above: Shelled pistachio nuts can be used to make a variety of dishes.*

## PISTACHIO NUTS *(ANTEP FISTIK)*

Freshly roasted pistachio nuts, still warm from the pan, are absolutely delicious and are often consumed on their own as a snack. They are also used in many sweet pastries and sweetmeats, such as *kadayif*, the delectable shredded pastry filled with pistachio nuts and bathed in syrup, and pistachio marzipan, which is a lovely shade of green. Pistachio slivers are used to decorate a number of desserts because of their pretty colour, and they are added to rice and bulgur wheat pilaffs.

Pistachio nuts grow profusely in the southern region around Gaziantep and are, therefore, known as *antep fıstık*.

A speciality from this region is a minced (ground) meat kebab containing whole pistachio nuts.

## SESAME SEEDS *(SESAM)*

The tiny, but flavoursome, sesame seeds are sprinkled over savoury pastries and breads, particularly *simit*, the ubiquitous bread rings you often see being sold at markets or carried through the streets on long poles and, occasionally, artfully balanced in a pile on top of a young boy's head. The seeds are also ground for their distinct oil, which is used in cooking in some parts of Anatolia.

### Tahini *(tahin)*

The other key role of sesame seeds is when they are ground to a fine, oily paste called *tahin*. This is used in several traditional recipes, such as *humus*, and is combined with grape *pekmez* (a fruit molasses) to make a thick sweet mixture that is enjoyed on chunks of bread for breakfast, or for a quick snack during the day.

## SUNFLOWER SEEDS *(GÜNEBAKAN)*

Bright yellow sunflowers grow all over Turkey, and the heads are gathered and left to dry in the hot sun, either in wooden carts or by the side of the road, until the small seeds burst out of the pods.

The seeds, which are contained in black, or black-and-white striped, edible husks, are often roasted and eaten as a snack, or they are added to *köfte* and pilaffs instead of pine nuts. The seeds are also pressed to make a light, general-purpose cooking oil, which is the preferred oil for deep-frying and is used for all manner of cooking where olive oil is too expensive.

*Left: Shelled walnuts are used to make traditional* tarator *sauce.*

## WALNUTS *(CEVİZ)*

Regarded as the king of nuts, walnuts are used in many savoury and sweet dishes, such as *muhammara*, a spicy *meze* dish made primarily with pounded walnuts; Turkish red pepper *(kırmızı biber)* and pomegranate syrup; and in the moist walnut sponges soaked in syrup, called *kalburabastı*.

The walnut is the most traditional nut to be used in the Palace cuisine of Istanbul, epitomized in the classic *baklava* – although modern versions often use pistachio nuts or a mixture of the two. It is also the preferred nut for the traditional version of *tarator*, the nut sauce, when it is served with shellfish, such as deep-fried mussels, *midye tavası*. Walnut trees grow throughout Turkey and many of them are quite ancient, yet still produce a good crop.

*Below: Tahini and sesame seeds are key ingredients in many Turkish recipes.*

# FISH AND SHELLFISH

Bounded by sea on three sides – the Mediterranean, Aegean and the Black Sea – and with the Sea of Marmara and its waterways, the Bosphorus and Dardanelles, in the north, Turkey has over 7,000km (4,350 miles) of coastline. The plentiful fishing waters provide daily catches of bluefish, red and grey mullet, swordfish, sea bass, tuna, bonito, turbot, plaice, mackerel, sardines, anchovies and all manner of shellfish.

Regarded as a symbol of fertility, fish is much enjoyed in the coastal regions of Turkey. Inland, though, in the heart of Anatolia, where various species of carp are fished from the rivers, fish is not eaten so regularly, perhaps because it is invariably grilled (broiled), or fried, and so it can become monotonous. It must be pointed out that fish cuisine is relatively new to the carnivorous inland Turks who, until the advent of tourism, were not tremendous consumers of fish or shellfish. For this reason the variety of fish dishes is more limited in Turkish cuisine than that of the much-loved meat and poultry. The exception to this is the Black Sea region, where anchovies have played an important culinary role for a long time.

In most of the coastal regions, fish is bought very fresh, straight off the boats at the daily fish market, where some of

*Above: Fishermen with the day's fresh catch from the clear blue waters of the Aegean at the harbour in Ayvalik, western Turkey.*

the smaller species are still swimming around in buckets, while others are beautifully arranged on ice, with bright eyes and gleaming skins. Sloshing about in rubber boots, the fish sellers will usually help to select and prepare the fish for your chosen dish. Among

the many favourite varieties on offer, you will be able to purchase fresh red mullet for grilling (broiling) over charcoal, swordfish for making kebabs, mackerel for stuffing or adding to stews, bonito for stews or grilling, and anchovies for poaching in vine leaves.

*Below: Sardines are delicious when they have been cooked whole over charcoal.*

*Below: Fresh fish is artfully displayed to entice passers-by at the busy fish markets along the Golden Horn and the Bosphorus in Istanbul.*

*Above: Fresh anchovies are a feature of Black Sea cooking.*

*Above: Fresh mackerel is enjoyed in salads, stews, grilled and stuffed.*

*Above: Sardines grilled or baked with vine leaves are very popular.*

### ANCHOVIES (HAMSI)

The Black Sea coast differs from the rest of Turkey in that it has its own unique fish cuisine, mainly revolving around the anchovy. This small, oily fish is celebrated in song and poetry as well as in many recipes, such as *hamsi sarması*, in which the anchovies are poached in vine leaves; *hamsi pilavı*, an impressive-looking mound of rice encased in anchovy fillets; and anchovy bread. There is even said to be an anchovy pudding and anchovy jam!

### BONITO (PALAMUT)

Another firm-fleshed fish, bonito is popular baked whole with bay leaves, or with freshly squeezed lemon and a variety of fresh, leafy herbs. Its most traditional role, though, is in the classic *pilâki*, where the fish is baked, or poached, with diced carrots, potatoes and celeriac.

### MACKEREL (USKUMRU)

Richly flavoured mackerel is a very popular fish in the recipes of Istanbul and Izmir, where it is often cooked in olive oil and served at room temperature.

An oily fleshed fish, mackerel lends itself particularly well to grilling and baking and is also versatile in a number of stews.

A rather decadent dish, *uskumru dolması*, that originated in the Palace kitchens involves stuffing the mackerel. For this traditional recipe, the fresh fish is pummelled and massaged to loosen the flesh from the skin so that the flesh can be squeezed out of an opening and then fried with nuts and spices before being stuffed back into the skin. Baked or grilled, this stuffed mackerel dish is

*Below: Red mullet is traditionally grilled and served on a bed of rocket leaves or flat leaf parsley.*

very impressive and can sometimes be found as a speciality on Istanbul restaurant menus.

### RED MULLET (BARBUNYA)

Once the favoured fish of the Romans, red mullet could be said to be one of the most prized among the Turks, too. It is a pleasing fish to look at, with its dappled pink skin. Since it is quite a meaty fish for its size, it is very rarely tampered with and is generally served fairly plain so that its natural flavour can come through. Grilled or fried, sometimes rubbed with garlic and served with lemon is the best way to enjoy the sweet flesh of red mullet.

### Cooking methods

The *pilâki* recipes are the most distinctive of the Turkish fish dishes. These are made by sautéing onion, garlic, carrot and celery (or celeriac) in olive oil. The fish is then added with salt, water and sugar, and cooked until tender (all *pilâki* dishes, including those made with beans or mussels, are cooked the same way). One dish that seems to have disappeared from the culinary scene is oyster *pilâki*, an old Ottoman favourite.

Chunks of firm-fleshed fish are sometimes cooked in earthenware pots with vegetables, spices or herbs to make a stew, or they are marinated and threaded on to kebab sticks and chargrilled. Along the Black Sea coast, the concave roof tiles are often used as cooking vessels for baking, as they are perfectly shaped for a whole fish.

Small fish, such as anchovies and sardines, are gutted and cleaned, then salted and dipped in flour before being fried on both sides until golden brown. The joy of these little fish is that they can be popped straight into your mouth and eaten whole. Generally, most fish are grilled over charcoal, or fried. Prior to grilling or frying, the fish is marinated in onion juice and, once cooked, it is invariably garnished with parsley, dill or rocket (arugula) leaves.

*Below: Mackerel pilâki.*

*Right: Sea bass are popular in Turkey, where the fillets are often sliced into chunks and threaded on to skewers to make fish kebabs, which are grilled on a barbecue or under a hot grill.*

### SARDINES *(SARDALYA)*

Small sardines are often wrapped in vine leaves and poached or grilled (broiled) or, like anchovies, they are dipped in flour and deep-fried. The large, fleshy sardines are juicy and lend themselves to being baked with tomatoes and herbs, or to being stuffed with herbs and spices and grilled. They are also dried and used in stews and stocks.

### SEA BASS *(LEVREK)*

Like sea perch, sea bass is extremely versatile as the tender flesh is firm and sweet and suited to being cooked in a number of ways. Popular among these is to bake the fish whole, encased in salt, or on a concave tile with a simple sauce of tomatoes and herbs. It is also used in stews and fish *köfte*, and is threaded on to kebab skewers with tomatoes and peppers.

### Preserving fish

Ancient methods of preserving fish are still adhered to. Small fish are gutted, split open and hung up on a line to dry. Dried fish is generally reconstituted in soups, stock and stews. Sardines and anchovies are also preserved whole in vinegar or brine. Pickled anchovies are particularly popular on the Black Sea coast, where the fish is abundant.

*Below: Sardines hung out to dry on lines in Çanakkale on the Dardanelles Strait.*

## SEA PERCH *(LÜFER)*

This fish, also known as blue fish, is firm-fleshed and extremely versatile. It is one of the most popular fish for grilling (broiling) and baking, and is often used in stews, such as the classic *lüfer yahnisi*, which is flavoured with cinammon and a dash of vinegar.

## SWORDFISH *(KİLİÇ)*

The traditional way of cooking swordfish is to grill (broil) it on a skewer, as in *kiliç şiş*, a popular dish in fish restaurants. The firm flesh lends itself well to marinades.

*Below: Mussels are delicious stuffed.*

*Left: Fresh prawns are often stir-fried or baked.*

## TUNA *(ORKİNOS)*

Generally, tuna fish is seared and served with dill, or the raw flesh is marinated in lemon juice and served as a cold *meze* dish. As the Japanese over-fish the waters around Turkey for tuna, it is becoming quite expensive and more difficult to find in the markets.

## SHELLFISH AND CEPHALOPODS

Istanbul and the towns along the coast of the Aegean and the Mediterranean are the main areas where shellfish, squid and octopus are enjoyed. Prawns (shrimp) are stir-fried with garlic and cumin, or baked with peppers and onions. Some restaurants offer prawn kebabs, and prawns are added to rice dishes.

Whole mussels stuffed with rice are a favourite in Istanbul and Izmir, and they are also used in a *pilâki* dish. Squid rings and mussels are deep-fried in batter and often served with a garlicky sauce. Baby squid are stuffed with rice and herbs, and octopus is grilled (broiled) and served with olives and (bell) peppers.

*Below: Squid is often deep-fried.*

### Preparing squid

**1** Hold the body of the squid in one hand and grasp the head with the other. Tug off the head, taking most of the innards with it. Take out the backbone and then remove any remaining innards.

**2** Peel off the thin outer membrane by gripping one end firmly and the pulling hard with the other hand. Rinse the sac inside and out, and pat dry.

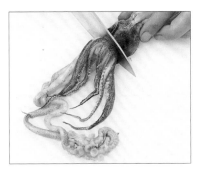

**3** Trim the head of the squid by severing the tentacles just above the eyes. Discard the eyes but keep the top of the head with the tentacles attached.

# MEAT AND POULTRY

Ever since the early Turks of Central Asia herded sheep to new grazing grounds, lamb or mutton has traditionally formed part of their daily diet. The fat-tailed sheep are the most highly prized, as the fat stored in the tail acts as an emergency supply for the beast in arid conditions, but also provides many Anatolian Turks with their favourite cooking fat.

In the early history of Anatolia, beef was rarely eaten, as the cattle were raised for milk and for tilling the fields, but, in modern Turkey, beef is available for those who can afford it and is often cooked in stews and minced (ground) for fillings and köfte in place of lamb. Wild game, such as rabbit, deer and bear, featured in the diet of the early hunters and was also sought after by various Ottoman sultans, but it rarely turns up on the modern Turkish table.

Meat dishes perhaps form the largest culinary group in Turkish cooking as there is seemingly no end to the number of stews and the variety of kebabs. Apart from on festive occasions, when a whole sheep or large joints of lamb are roasted, meat is seldom cooked on its own. Instead, the Turks cube or mince tender cuts of meat and combine it with herbs, spices and vegetables. Even the classic kebabs often have pieces of tomato or pepper threaded on to the skewer with the meat, which is then served with yogurt and some pide.

This tradition of cooking meat with vegetables, particularly in stews, such as the yahni, güveç and kapama dishes, can be traced right back to the influence of the Chinese on the Turkish ancestors of Central Asia. However, unlike the Chinese, the Turks prefer their meat well-done with no trace of blood, which can result in some of the grilled (broiled) and seared dishes being rather dry.

## BEEF (DANA)

The use of beef is relatively new in Turkish cuisine and, although it is fairly widespread now, often it has simply been substituted into recipes that would have been designed for the more traditional lamb.

*Above: Beef steak (top) and minced beef (above).*

The well-hung beef sold in most markets is obtained from animals that are under two years old. As the calves have been reared naturally, the meat is pinkish-red and very lean. Beef, or veal, is generally used in stews, or in grilled and seared dishes, such as dana pirzola, a dish of seared veal chops with oregano and lemon.

Beef is also combined with onions, parsley and spices for use in meatballs, such as köfte, which require the beef, or lamb, to be passed through the mincer twice. The spicy tartare meatballs, çiğ köfte, from the south-east of Turkey are generally made from beef and are reputed to contain thirty different spices. They are so well-kneaded that the raw meat is almost undetectable; the spice is cut by the bunches of leafy parsley eaten with the köfte.

In eastern Anatolia, the male tradition of eating bull's testes still exists. Invariably grilled and sprinkled with Turkish red pepper, the village men

*Below: Minced meat kebabs on traditional skewers sizzling enticingly over a charcoal stove are a frequent sight in streets and homes in Turkey.*

gather around the *mangal* to devour the tender testes with *rakı*, or a locally brewed spirit, in the belief that their virility will be enhanced!

## LAMB *(KUZU)*

When Turks talk about meat, they primarily mean lamb and mutton. For all religious and celebratory dishes, the traditional lamb or mutton, rather than beef, is cooked. This is evident at *Kurban Bayramı*, the festival to mark the near-sacrifice of Isaac, for which the whole sheep is ritually sacrificed. At this event, every part of the sheep is used in a variety of dishes – some of the meat will be prepared in a stew with fruit, while some will be simply fried in its own juices. Known as the *kavurma* method, the podgy tail will be boiled and eaten with bread, and the intestines will be simmered in a soup, *işkembe çorbası*, or stuffed with a mixture of chopped offal, onions and spices and grilled in a traditional dish called *kokoreç*. When a ram is sacrificed, the testes are also usually consumed, often grilled or cooked in a stew.

A whole lamb or, sometimes, a kid goat, is spit-roasted for communal feasts. The most traditional method is to suspend the spit over the hot embers in a pit dug in the ground. In some regions, several lambs are roasted at once, hung lengthways from a spit, in a large communal oven.

Other forms of spit-roasting include a brick-lined pit, *biryan*, into which the lambs are lowered on a spit and then sealed in with an iron lid, so that the meat roasts and steams at the same time.

In eastern Anatolia, the use of the *tandır* is widepread. Related to the Indian *tandouri* and the Persian *tennur*, the *tandır* can be a fairly primitive affair, made out of earth or clay and sealed with an earthenware or stone lid, with a pipe at the bottom or a chimney on top to control the air flow. The cooked lamb from the *biryan* and *tandır* is normally extremely tasty, tender and moist.

## CHICKEN *(TAVUK* OR *PİLİÇ)*

Undoubtedly, chicken is the most widespread kind of poultry consumed in Turkey, although traditionally wild duck and quails are eaten in some areas and in some kebab houses.

*Above: Chicken can be spit-roasted, grilled, stewed, stuffed or shredded.*

Eaten almost as often as lamb, chicken can be cooked in many different ways, including spit-roasted whole, cut into chunks, threaded on to skewers and grilled as kebabs, or stewed with vegetables. Chicken can also be used in *köfte* and soups, or oven-roasted.

When it is roasted, the cavity of the chicken is often stuffed with almonds and apricots. It even appears finely shredded in the classical pudding, *tavuk göğsu*, a creation originating from the Ottoman Palace kitchens.

Chicken livers are also enjoyed, sautéed with garlic and served with lemon, or combined with aromatic rice and pine nuts in a delicious dish called *iç pilavı*, which is particularly popular in Istanbul.

## DUCK *(ÖRDEK)* AND QUAILS *(BİLDİRCİN)*

Medieval recipes include lavish dishes of duck stuffed with olives and figs, or even aubergines (eggplants) stuffed with quails, but neither of these dishes makes a frequent appearance on modern Turkish menus.

Wild duck is still enjoyed in some rural regions, where it is generally roasted in the oven with herbs and honey, and some modern kebab houses offer duck kebabs.

*Left, clockwise from top: Lamb chops, diced lamb and minced (ground) lamb.*

*Above: Quails are commonly butterflied and grilled at picnics.*

Roasted, stuffed quails are a feature of some kebab houses, but the most common venue for spit-roasted quails is at countryside picnics.

## KEBABS

Kebabs are perhaps the best-known meat dish from Turkey. Among the more popular are *döner* and *şiş* kebabs, although kebabs come in a variety of guises, some grilled (broiled), others roasted or baked in paper or earthenware pots. This is because they evolved out of a practical need to cook small chunks of meat simply and quickly while retaining their moisture.

Throughout Turkey, the majority of kebabs are prepared with lamb, mutton or chicken. Many popular kebabs are served on *pide* with yogurt or tomato sauce, and the fiery kebabs from the *güney* kitchen are often made of minced (ground) meat and plenty of Turkish red pepper *(kırmızı biber)*. Many of the grilled kebabs on skewers are distinguished by the types of vegetables used, or by the region they originated from, such as *Adana kebab* and *Tokat kebab*.

## *KÖFTE*

Made with minced meat, these traditional meatballs are an economical way of using meat. Because the minced meat is combined with breadcrumbs, onions, herbs and spices, a small amount of meat goes a long way. The meatballs are kneaded to bind them and moulded into a variety of shapes. The exception is the Palace dish, *kadınbudu*, the descriptively named "ladies' thighs", as the meat is combined with rice and then flattened and dipped in batter before frying.

*Left: Minced meat and herb kebabs and diced meat kebabs with red onions and green peppers.*

Generally, most meatballs can be grilled or fried, although the classic *kuru köfte* are always fried in olive oil, as they are designed to be eaten cold while travelling or on picnics.

## OFFAL/INNARDS

Apart from chicken livers, the offal in Turkish cooking is generally extracted from the sheep, although ox liver is sold in some areas. Liver is enjoyed lightly fried and cooked in a special sausage called *bumbar dolması*; the intestines are cooked in soup or stuffed and grilled; and the brain is poached in water and vinegar and served sliced as a cold *meze* dish.

In addition to these more commonly consumed innards, there are a couple of specialities that fall into this category: sheep's head and hooves. The sheep's head is often cooked in a soup with the hooves, or it is baked on its own and served either hot or cold. Once all the meaty parts of the head have been eaten, the prized brain is released from the skull and then offered to a guest, or to the head of a household.

When the earthy sheep's hooves are prepared on their own, they are simmered in water for a number of hours and then the tender meat is placed on lightly toasted bread and covered in a yogurt sauce.

*Below: Classic Turkish* köfte *is made with currants and pine nuts.*

*Above:*
*Fresh, prepared tripe.*

During the Ottoman period, street vendors specialized in selling offal in both its cooked and its raw form. Some of these offal vendors still exist today, and the aroma of grilled stuffed intestine, *kokoreç*, draws the hungry Turks from their roadside perches or shaded doorways. In most markets and urban butchers, offal is still sold separately from other meats.

## COOKING METHODS

There is a wide range of cooking methods when it comes to meat. Spit-roasting, grilling (broiling), stewing, frying, steaming, stuffing, sautéing and pressing minced (ground) meat into balls *(köfte)*, are all popular cooking techniques. Traditionally, meat is cooked in small pieces combined with other ingredients, as is clearly demonstrated in the many stews and kebabs on offer in Turkey.

Cooking whole cuts of meat is a rare event and usually reserved for a celebratory occasion. *Yahni* is a traditional meat stew with onions, but the stew can also incorporate fruit, such as green plums or apricots, with the meat. The Anatolian *güveç* dishes refer to meat or poultry cooked in earthenware pots, or curved tiles, resulting in a moist combination of meat or poultry with vegetables or pulses, such as the chicken and okra dish *güveçte piliçli bamya*.

Traditional spit-roasting is a communal event, as it requires a fire pit to be dug in the ground over which a whole lamb or goat, rubbed with salt and spices, is cooked slowly over the glowing embers, producing an extremely tasty meat.

In the Anatolian villages, large cuts of meat are usually cooked in the *tandır*, the communal clay oven, and throughout Turkey everyone has a *mangal*, a small outdoor charcoal stove, which can be conveniently set up on a city balcony or transported to the beach or the woods for a countryside picnic, and is ideal for grilling small cuts of meat, fish, corn on the cob and chicken.

## CURED MEATS

There are two types of cured meats in Turkey: *pastırma*, the cured fillet of beef, and *sucuk*, the spicy sausages that resemble salami. Both hang in bunches at the markets and be can be bought whole or sliced. The *pastırma* can be eaten just as it is, or it can be cooked with other ingredients, but most of the cured *sucuk* require cooking.

### *Pastırma*

This is a cured, air-dried fillet of veal or beef coated in a thick paste made from ground cumin, fenugreek, *kırmızı biber*, and garlic, known as *çemen*. Generally, *pastırma* is finely sliced and eaten on its own with bread, or with olives and pickles, as a *meze*. It is also cooked with pulses and eggs, and is used as a filling in savoury pastries.

### *Sucuk*

Shaped like a horseshoe, *sucuk* is a cured sausage made with lamb or beef and flavoured with garlic and cumin. In rural areas, people make their own *sucuk* with a variety of spices and hang them outside to cure.

Clusters of *sucuk* horseshoes are easy to recognize at markets and most families buy several *sucuk* at once, as they can be sliced and eaten as a snack, cooked with pulses or eggs for their wonderful flavour, or they can be grilled on the *mangal* and enjoyed with slices of bread.

*Below: Thin slices of* pastırma *coated in flavoursome* çemen.

# DAIRY AND EGGS

The existence of dairy products in the diets of the Turks can be traced right back to the first millenium BC. At this time, the milk of mares was regarded as superior to the milk from other animals and was used to make yogurt and cheese and a fermented drink, *kımız*.

Milk from ewes was used to make a rancid-tasting butter, as well as yogurt and cheese. Fresh milk was rarely drunk; instead it was usually curdled in order to preserve it. It is thought that this may have led to the discovery of how to make yogurt, and how to use it for curative purposes.

For a nation who claim to have a low tolerance for flowing milk, the Turks gain plenty of minerals and vitamins through their vast consumption of yogurt, cheese, and a delicious selection of milky puddings.

*Below: Sheep graze everywhere in Turkey, including among the ruins of a fortress in the countryside, as here. Their milk is used to make a range of dairy products.*

## CHEESE (PEYNİR)

In Turkey there are many varieties of white cheese, most of which are made from cow's or sheep's milk.

### Beyaz peynir

The principal, everyday white cheese, *beyaz peynir*, is fairly solid and is sold in blocks, which are often stacked like building bricks in the market stalls. Stored in brine, the cheese ranges in colour from pearly white to a pale yellow. The salt content varies from cheese to cheese, so the first thing a Turkish cook does is to immerse it in water to draw out the salt and keep it in a cool place.

*Beyaz peynir*, which can be substituted with feta cheese in the recipes in this book, is eaten for breakfast with olives, bread and jam.

*Above: Blocks of* beyaz peynir *are matured in brine for at least six months.*

It is used in salads and savoury pastries and is also served by itself as a *meze* dish, cut into cubes and drizzled with olive oil and a sprinkling of dried oregano and Turkish red pepper *(kırmızı biber)*, or paprika.

*Beyaz peynir* is made in a similar way to *köy peyniri* but it is made in blocks, which are left to dry out. These are then stored in salty water for at least six months to mature. The correct amount of salt is determined by a simple egg test: a pan containing enough water to submerge the cheese is brought to the boil and an estimated amount of salt is added. An egg is then cracked into the water – if it starts to sink more salt is required but, if it floats, the salt content is deemed accurate. The salty water is then left to cool before it is poured over the cheese in a container which must be kept in a cool place. During the maturing process, the cheese will harden and absorb the salt.

When choosing one of these cheeses at the market, the women often try a nibble from several blocks to determine which one suits their palate in both salt content and texture.

### Dil peyniri

A mild-tasting cheese, *dil peyniri* is pulled apart in stringy strips and enjoyed with pickles as a snack. When cooking with *dil peyniri*, particularly in the traditional dessert *künefe*, you can use Italian mozzarella as a substitute, as it is mild-tasting and melts with the same stringy consistency.

*Below:* Dil peyniri, *a popular stringy cheeese.*

*Above:* Kaşar peyniri *is ideal for grating and cooking.*

---

### Making *köy peyniri*

MAKES ABOUT 350G/12OZ

2 litres/3½ pints/9 cups full-fat (whole) or semi-skimmed (low-fat) milk
15ml/1 tbsp salt
60ml/4 tbsp rennet, or lemon juice

**1** Pour the milk into a deep, heavy pan and heat it gently. Stir in the salt and rennet or lemon juice, and continue to heat until just below boiling point – don't bring the milk to the boil.

**2** Turn off the heat, cover the pan with a clean dish towel and leave it overnight, or for at least 6 hours, to separate into curds and whey. (If using lemon juice, this will happen immediately, so you don't need to leave it to separate.)

**3** Line a colander with a piece of muslin (cheesecloth), and place it in a bowl. Pour the mixture into the middle, gather up the edges of the muslin and tie it to a rod suspended over the sink or a bowl. Leave the curds to drain overnight, or for at least 6 hours, so that you are left with a ball of soft, creamy cheese. Eat with bread, or combine with herbs and use as a *meze* dip.

---

### Kaşar peyniri

The hard and tangy *kaşar peyniri* is used in cooking and grated on top of dishes. (A tangy Cheddar with no added colouring or Italian Pecorino can be used as substitutes in the recipes that follow.)

### Köy peyniri

A slightly softer, creamier white cheese is *köy peyniri*, "village cheese", which is made every week in rural areas. Regional variations are much sought after in the markets.

### CLOTTED BUFFALO CREAM *(KAYMAK)*

One of the delights of a traditional *muhallebici* (a milk-pudding shop), is *kaymak*, a particularly thick clotted cream made from the milk of water

*Below:* Kaymak *is thick clotted cream made from buffalo milk.*

buffalo. *Kaymak* is left to set in a flat tray before it is cut and rolled into neat, spectacular-looking logs.

These gleaming rolls of pearly white cream are piled on top of sticky desserts, stuffed into poached fruit and pastries, or eaten on their own with a dusting of icing (confectioner's) sugar.

Nowadays, *kaymak* is also often made from cow's milk and is sold unceremoniously in tubs at supermarkets – and this can be substituted with a thick, commercial clotted cream – but the traditional pudding shops stick to the original method, created by the Palace chefs, using buffalo milk to which a little *mastika* is sometimes added for texture.

### YOGURT *(YOĞURT)*

The Turks are one of the world's largest consumers of *yoğurt*, which they generally prefer to be full-fat and made from the milk of ewes.

In rural parts of Anatolia today, ancient methods of curdling milk and yogurt-making are still used. These techniques include using a fig branch to curdle milk in the mountains, as the sap from the branch separates the curds from the whey; and some of the nomadic communities elsewhere collect the eggs of a particular kind of ant, which they then crush and use as a yogurt culture.

Once a staple of their ancestors in Central Asia, the Turks love yogurt so much that it is served with almost everything, providing an easily digestible

*Above: Thick, creamy* süzme *yogurt is available in most Turkish stores.*

source of calcium and antibiotic properties, as well as numerous vitamins and minerals.

Eaten on its own as a snack, thick, creamy yogurt is often dusted with icing (confectioner's) sugar, or drizzled with a generous spoonful of amber honey. It is served in dollops with many vegetable and kebab dishes, or mixed with the mashed or grated pulp of cooked vegetables to make soothing dips. Beaten with crushed garlic and a splash of lemon juice or vinegar, it is spooned over deep-fried or grilled (broiled) vegetables and poached eggs.

Everyday yogurt recipes include *cacık*, a bowl of diced cucumber, yogurt, garlic and dill, which is often served as an appetizer or as an accompaniment to savoury pastries and kebabs; *haydari*, a very thick yogurt dip spiked with garlic and fresh or dried mint; and *ayran*, the cooling, national yogurt drink, enjoyed with spicy food or as a thirst-quencher on a hot day.

The standard, everyday yogurt, *sıvı tas*, is thick, light and creamy, whereas the solid yogurt, *süzme*, which is required for particular dips and desserts, is strained through a piece of muslin (cheesecloth) for about six hours, so that it is so thick you can stand a spoon in it. For the recipes in this book, choose the live, set yogurts,which are available in supermarkets, or make your own.

### Making *sıvı tas*

When making yogurt you need to use live yogurt to start off the process. The standard ratio for yogurt to milk is 30ml/2 tbsp live yogurt to 600ml/1 pint/2½ cups full-fat (whole) or semi-skimmed (low-fat) milk. To make a thicker yogurt, you can add 15–30ml/1–2 tbsp powdered milk to the milk that is boiling in the pan.

**1** First, bring the milk to the boil in a large, heavy pan. When it starts to boil, reduce the heat and leave it to simmer for 2–3 minutes.

**2** Turn off the heat and leave the milk to cool to a temperature that is bearable to dip your finger into and to leave it there for a count of ten.

**3** Beat the yogurt with a wooden spoon in a large, deep bowl and strain a little of the milk into it, beating all the time. Strain the remainder of the milk into the bowl and beat well until everything is thoroughly combined.

**4** Cover the bowl with clear film (plastic wrap) and cover the whole bowl with a piece of blanket or a thick cloth, tucking the edges around it to keep it warm.

*Above:* Ayran *is refreshing on a hot day.*

**5** Place the wrapped bowl in a warm place overnight, or for at least 6 hours – it should have fermented and thickened a little during this time.

**6** Unwrap the bowl and place it in the refrigerator for 2–3 hours, or until it has set. This yogurt can be used in many dishes, spiked with garlic and spooned over vegetables, or mixed with finely sliced cucumber to make *cacık*.

### Making *süzme*

This extra-thick strained yogurt makes a good dip or can be used for making Turkish desserts.

**1** Line a colander with a piece of muslin and tip the freshly made *sıvı tas* into the middle.

**2** Gather together the corners of the muslin and tie them around a rod, or a long wooden spoon, placed over the sink, a wide bowl or a bucket to catch the fluid.

**3** Leave the yogurt to drain for 4–6 hours, or until it is the consistency of cream cheese.

*Left:* Süzme *is traditional strained yogurt.*

*Above: Fresh eggs
can be used in many dishes.*

*Above:* Menemen, *a ragoût of onions
and peppers with eggs.*

---

### Making *ayran*

Serve this refreshing drink with
spicy food or as a cooler for a
hot day.

SERVES TWO

300ml//½ pint/1¼ cups thick,
  creamy yogurt
300ml/½ pint/1¼ cups cold water
a pinch of salt
dried mint, to garnish

**1** In a jug (pitcher), whisk the
yogurt with the water, until it
becomes foamy. Season with a
little salt to suit your taste.

**2** Pour the mixture into glasses
and scatter the surface with a little
mint. If it's a very hot day, add
extra salt and some ice cubes.

---

### EGGS (*YUMURTA*)

There are several egg dishes in modern
Turkish cuisine that are worth
mentioning, such as *menemen*, a
ragoût of (bell) peppers and tomatoes
topped with eggs; *çılbır*, poached eggs
served with garlic-flavoured yogurt; and
eggs cooked with spinach, *pastırma*,
the cured fillet of beef, and *sucuk*, the
spicy cured sausage.

*Right: Chickens for eggs are bought and
sold at markets across Turkey.*

*Menemen* is often regarded as street
food as it is cooked on small stoves at
bus stations and markets, but it makes
a good supper dish. *Çılbır* is another
classic. Traditionally, the eggs are
poached in water that is boiling with a
gentle roll and a dash of vinegar, but
some cooks take a short cut and fry the
eggs lightly so that the yolks are still soft.
The combination of hot, runny eggs and
garlic-flavoured yogurt is delicious. It is
often topped with melted butter that
sometimes contains *kırmızı biber*, the
Turkish red pepper, or dried sage.

During the Ottoman period, eggs
were stuffed in the same way as many
vegetables, including aubergines
(eggplants) and peppers, and poached
eggs were frequently served with a
dressing of olive oil and lemon juice,
but these dishes never appear on
menus anymore.

Today, many creative new recipes
are being devised in homes across
Turkey, including a dish in which
poached eggs are dressed with olive oil
and some chopped dill, making a very
flavoursome meal.

# GRAINS AND PULSES

The Turks eat rice, bulgur wheat, and dried pulses (peas, beans and lentils) every day, but it has not always been that way. Bulgur wheat and beans were established in the early history of Anatolia, but rice is relatively new.

## GRAINS *(TANE)*

Wheat is one of the oldest cultivated cereals and still remains the staple grain in Anatolia. More expensive than bulgur wheat and couscous, rice continues to play second fiddle to the other wheat grains in parts of Anatolia, but it is the principal grain used in Ankara, Istanbul, Izmir and much of western Turkey.

### Rice *(pirinç)*

The migrating Turkic tribes would have taken rice to Persia from China and India, but it did not really make an impact on Anatolia and Constantinople until the Ottoman era, when the wealthy imported large quantities of the grain from Egypt. Many rice dishes quickly evolved, and today rice is widely used in much of Turkey.

Long grain rice from Iran, Syria and Turkey itself is preferred; shorter grains are reserved for the aromatic savoury fillings that are stuffed into vegetables and fruits, and for sweet desserts, such as the popular *sütlaç*.

The Turkish concept of *pilav* is thought to have originated from the Persian tradition of *pulaw* dishes, but has since developed into a class of its own, which spans all social divides.

*Below, from left to right: Short and long grain rice are used in Turkish dishes.*

### Cooking rice

The cooking of rice is regarded as an art. The grains must be soft but still have a bite to them, as well as having absorbed the flavours in the dish. As a rule, the grains and other ingredients are cooked in a little butter, ghee or oil before adding the water. Once the water has been absorbed, a clean cloth, followed by the lid, is placed on top of the pan and the rice is left to steam off the heat, until the grains are cooked but still firm.

Depending on the grain, the ratio of rice to water is either equal, or the volume of water is one-and-a-half times that of the rice.

### Rice flour

Fine, powdery white rice flour, slaked with a little water, is a necessary component of the much-loved traditional milk puddings, as it helps to set them. Traditionally, this was achieved by first soaking rice in water and then grinding it to extract a milky substance called *sübye*, which was a vital tool for the *muhallebici*, the maker of milk puddings.

Rice flour works as a modern substitute, but some traditionalists stick to the more sophisticated method of their Ottoman ancestors.

### Bulgur wheat *(bulgur)*

Bulgur wheat is the freshly harvested wheat that is parboiled, drained and rubbed to remove the bran. The wheat is then crushed into coarse, medium or fine grains. The most commonly used grains are the coarse and medium

*Above: Rice flour is a key ingredient in various milk puddings.*

varieties – the fine grains are mainly used in fillings for stuffed vegetables, such as the dried aubergine shells, and for making the south-east Anatolian version of *kısır*, a bulgur wheat, tomato and herb salad, which requires the mixture to be moulded into balls and served in small lettuce leaves. They are also sometimes used in *içli köfte* the infamous mother-in-law's meatballs, which involve stuffing a bulgur wheat shell with a spicy mixture and then sealing it closed before cooking. On presenting these to her new daughter-in-law, the message is clear – her lips must now be sealed with discretion, like these meatballs!

Generally, bulgur wheat is served as a pilaff, combined with meat, vegetables or nuts and dried fruits, such as *Arap pilavı*, or it is served plain. One of the most popular snacks in eastern Anatolia is a bowl of bulgur wheat, which is tipped on to a plate and then has a hole made in the centre, into which yogurt is spooned, and then melted ghee is poured over the top. Everyone takes a spoon and dips in.

## PULSES *(BAKLİYAT)*

The word *bakliyat*, meaning "pulses" in Turkish, derives from the Arabic word *bakli*, which means vegetable. The main pulses in Turkish cuisine are dried haricot (navy), soya and borlotti beans, chickpeas, red and green lentils, black-eyed beans (peas), split peas, and fresh and dried broad (fava) beans. Regarded as vegetables, pulse dishes are popular in Turkish cookery, served as snacks,

*Above, clockwise from top: Black-eyed beans (peas), chickpeas and borlotti beans.*

meze dishes, as meals on their own with bread, or they can be used in place of rice as an accompaniment.

In the poor rural areas, pulses are often cooked as the main staple in place of meat. Considered to be "food of heaven", beans are held in such high regard that there is a Turkish saying, "He thinks he is as blessed as a bean", meaning that he puts on airs.

## Broad beans/fava beans *(fava)*

Like chickpeas, broad (fava) beans are also regarded as a staple of the poor, as they are so meaty and versatile. The season of the fresh green broad bean is short, so it is enjoyed in summery pilaffs, tossed in salads, and poached with artichokes. Fresh ones really need to be eaten on the day of purchase as the sugars in the beans alter the taste and texture after a few days.

Dried broad beans are available in supermarkets and Middle Eastern stores, and are added to stews and soups. One of the broad bean specialities of Turkey is the meze dish *fava* (named after the bean), a purée of broad beans which is dressed in olive oil and fresh dill.

## Chickpeas *(humus)*

Often referred to as the "food of the poor", chickpeas are cultivated in Turkey and the Middle East to be used

in a variety of stews and soups, as well is in the well-known, garlicky purée, *humus*. The Turks also cook them in pilaffs and in an unusual Armenian dish, *topik*, in which puréed chickpeas are bound with mashed potato to make a parcel that is filled with a spicy currant and nut mixture.

Earthy and meaty, they are ideal for cooking with strong flavours and they fill the belly in households where there is not much meat on the table. Dried chickpeas are readily available everywhere and require soaking in plenty of water for at least six hours before use. During the soaking period, they will double in size. Roasted chickpeas are tossed in salt and served as a nibble, or they are coated in sugar and enjoyed as a sweet snack.

## Lentils *(mercimek)*

Legumes of antiquity, lentils are regarded as a cheerful food. The most common varieties in Turkey are the tiny

*Below: Dried green lentils are used in soups, stews and vegetable dishes.*

red ones, which are sometimes referred to as Egyptian lentils, and the larger matt-green ones. A little soaking in water helps to soften the larger lentils before cooking, but the smaller ones don't need this.

Cooked lentils have a sprout-like taste and a good bite to them, unless they are cooked to a pulp for soup or a purée. Filling and nourishing, they are packed with protein and cheap to buy. Baskets of different coloured lentils, split peas, dried beans and grains make an attractive display at the market stalls. The best known lentil dishes in Turkey are soups, lentil and vegetable dishes, pilaffs, and lentil patties.

## Soaking and cooking pulses

If you are using dried beans or peas you will need to soak them before cooking. Rinse them well under cold, running water and then transfer them to a bowl. Cover with plenty of cold water and leave to soak overnight. (If you are in a hurry, the beans can be soaked in boiling water and left for one to two hours.) Black-eyed beans (peas) do not need to be soaked, and neither do lentils.

Some beans contain toxins that must be removed by boiling rapidly, uncovered, for 10 minutes before simmering until tender. Soya beans, however, need to be boiled rapidly for 30 minutes before simmering.

*Below: Dried chickpeas need to be soaked for six hours before using.*

# BREAD, PASTRIES AND PASTA

The first cereal crops are believed to have been grown in Anatolia since before 7000BC. There are early records of baking in central Anatolia, where flat breads were made with wheat and often flavoured with spices. Primitive layered breads emerged at this time but it wasn't really until the Ottoman period that more sophisticated bread and pastry doughs were developed.

The industrious experimentation in the Palace kitchens resulted in wondrous creations that employed layers of thin flat bread dough to make divine pastries such as *baklava*. Noodle dough, on the other hand, is known to have come from China, as records of this dough can be traced there along the route travelled by the early, nomadic Turkish ancestors.

## BREAD *(EKMEK)*

A gift from God, bread is treated with great respect in Turkey. In traditional households, bread is broken into pieces by the hand, as the act of cutting it with a knife would be like raising a sword against God's blessing.

Regarded as the food of friendship, the Turks buy bread daily, straight from the baker's hot oven. Torn apart with fingers, it is shared among friends and family and eaten with practically every meal. Day-old bread is used in soups, *köfte*, garlicky nut *tarator*, and it is soaked in syrup and poached fruits to make popular puddings. If bread is dropped on the ground or has to be thrown away, it is first kissed and held to the forehead as a mark of respect.

Bread is eaten as a snack, or with jam (jelly) and white cheese for breakfast. It is also indispensable at every meal, where it serves as a scoop or a mop for all the tasty flavours and juices, enhancing the pleasure of each mouthful. In many households, a meal without bread is unthinkable.

Generally, the harvested grains are ground between two heavy, flat stones to obtain flour. This can be seen in small rural villages and remote homesteads, as the country people very often grind small quantities of wheat or barley for basic flat breads and pancakes. As the dough for flat bread simply consists of

ground flour and water, sometimes with the addition of a little ghee, it is easy to prepare and cooks quickly on a flat stone or metal sheet placed directly over a wood fire. For urban dwellers, life is easier when it comes to bread, as the baker's shops and markets are well-stocked with different breads and sacks of coarsely, or finely, ground flour.

Both leavened and unleavened breads are popular in Turkey. The standard crusty leavened loaves, found in every village and town throughout the country, are similar to French baguettes in texture, but are shaped like kayaks. In the rural villages, leavened bread is cooked in the communal oven, the *fırın*, which can also be used for some flat breads by sticking the dough to the inside or outside walls of the hot oven. In small villages, where there may only be one *fırın*, certain days will be allocated for the communal baking.

In the larger villages and small towns, there are neighbourhood bakers, who often bake batches of bread twice a day – in the early morning and again in the evening. The tempting aroma of freshly baked bread lures you to the door, whether you were intending to buy bread or not.

In the cities, there are many types of leavened loaves and specialist bakers that cater for their own communities, such as the Jews and Armenians. In these bakeries, you will find a variety of wholemeal (whole-wheat) and rye loaves and rolls, sweet buns, and bread made with egg-based dough. There are several types of savoury and sweet buns, but the most popular are the sesame covered rings, *simit*, which are sold by street-sellers who carry them through the crowds stacked on long poles, or on wide, circular trays balanced on their heads.

### Flat breads

The principal flat breads are the paper-thin sheets of *yufka* and the soft, spongy *pide*, with or without a hollow pouch. The local *yufkacı* is greatly valued for its daily supplies of freshly griddled *yufka*, ready for wrapping

*Below: A variety of leavened and unleavened loaves are baked daily at the local* fırın *or are available at bakeries in larger villages, towns and cities.*

*Above: A boy selling freshly baked* simit, *the popular round bread rings coated in sesame seeds.*

around fillings to make savoury pastries, or for layering a dish with the filling between them like Italian lasagna.

Making *yufka* is an art, since each tiny ball of dough is shifted from hand to hand, stretching it as it goes, until it is so big it has to be shifted from outstretched arm to arm, continually stretching but keeping it taught and circular, until it resembles a large wheel that is as thin as paper. As the genuine article is difficult to obtain outside Turkey, it has been substituted in the recipes with filo pastry.

### Pide

There are many types of *pide* available at the local *fırın*, such as the delicious, sweet *helva pide*, which melts in your mouth, and the sesame-sprinkled *Ramazan pide*, which is eaten to break the fast during the month of *Ramazan*. In some of the recipes, pitta breads, which are available in supermarkets and Middle Eastern stores, can be subsituted, but if you have time to make fresh *pide* it is worth it.

### Making *pide*

This is an easy recipe for a tasty and very practical *pide* that can be enjoyed with any savoury dish in this book. Hot from the oven, it is also delicious drizzled in honey. The charred flavour and aroma of the tiny, black nigella seeds scattered over the surface of the *pide* give it its unique taste.

MAKES 2 MEDIUM-SIZED *PIDE*, OR 1 LARGE

15g/½ oz fresh yeast, or 7g/¼ oz dried yeast
2.5ml/½ tsp sugar
about 150ml/¼ pint/⅔ cup lukewarm water
450g/1lb/4 cups unbleached strong white bread flour
5ml/1 tsp salt
30ml/2 tbsp olive oil, plus extra for greasing
30ml/2 tbsp thick, set natural (plain) yogurt
1 egg, beaten
15ml/1 tbsp nigella or sesame seeds

**1** Preheat the oven to 220°C/425°F/ Gas 7. Put the yeast and the sugar into a small bowl with 45ml/3 tbsp of the lukewarm water. Set aside for about 15 minutes, or until it froths.

**2** Sift the flour with the salt into a large bowl. Make a well in the centre and pour in the creamed yeast with the oil, yogurt and the remaining water. Using your hands, draw in the flour and work into a dough, until it leaves the side of the bowl – add more water if necessary; the dough should be sticky but pliable.

**3** Knead the dough on a lightly floured surface until it is smooth and light.

**4** Punch the dough flat, then gather up the edges into the middle, then flip it over.

**5** Splash a few drops of oil in the base of large bowl, roll the ball of dough in it, and cover with a clean, damp dish towel. Leave to rise in a warm place for a few hours, or overnight, until it has doubled in size.

**6** Knock back (punch down) the dough to release the air, and knead it again for a few minutes. Lightly oil one large circular, or rectangular, baking tray, or two smaller ones, and place in the oven for 2 minutes.

**7** Place the dough on a floured surface, divide it into two pieces, if you like, and flatten with the heel of your hand. Use your fingers to stretch it from the middle, creating a thick lip at the edges.

**8** Indent the dough with your fingertips and place it on the baking tray. Brush with a little beaten egg and scatter the nigella or sesame seeds over the top.

**9** Bake the dough in the hot oven for about 20 minutes, or until the surface is crispy and golden. Transfer the *pide* to a wire rack and serve warm.

*Above: A stack of paper-thin sheets of*
yufka, *ready to be used to make various sweet and savoury pastries.*

### Yufka

Extremely versatile, flat sheets of *yufka* can be rolled up like a tortilla and filled with anything you like – cream cheese, honey, pickles, charcuterie – and eaten as a snack called *dürüm*.

The thin pastry can also be cut into strips, rolled into cigars with a filling of cheese and herbs, and deep-fried *(sigara böreği)*; or it can be layered in a flat dish with a minced (ground) meat, chicken, cheese or spinach filling and baked in the oven *(tepsi böreği)*.

It takes years of practice to learn how to make the very wide wheels of paper-thin *yufka* and, ideally, you need a long, slim rolling pin called an *oklava* to do it. You can, however, use a standard rolling pin, and it is worth trying to make smaller rounds of the pastry at home. Alternatively, you can substitute *yufka* with filo pastry.

### PASTRIES

The Ottomans left a wonderful legacy of savoury and sweet pastries in Istanbul. During the reign of Sultan Mehmet II, the Palace pastry chefs took their role very seriously and the pastry cooks of the city had to adhere to their recipes and methods, otherwise they risked being punished.

Today, both savoury and sweet pastries form a large category of dishes that are popular in Turkish cuisine. Some pastries are made using flat bread dough, others employ specially made doughs that resemble the flaky and puff pastries of French cooking.

### Börek

There are about a dozen types of *börek*, which are a unique category of Turkish savoury pastries and flat breads. They vary in shape and size, with regional variations on the fillings. The most common fillings found throughout Turkey include mashed white cheese with fresh herbs; spinach and onions;

---

### Making *yufka*

MAKES 12 GOOD-SIZED *YUFKA*

115g/4oz/1 cup strong white
  bread flour
25g/1oz/¼ cup strong wholemeal
  (whole-wheat) bread flour
2.5ml/½ tsp salt
100–120ml/3½ –4fl oz/
  scant ½ –½ cup lukewarm water

**1** Sift the flours with the salt into a bowl. Make a well in the centre and gradually pour in 100ml/3½ fl oz/ scant ½ cup of the water, drawing in the flour from the sides. Add more water, if necessary, to make a firm dough. Knead the mixture well.

**2** Divide the dough into 12 pieces and roll each of these into small balls. Leave the balls to rest on a lightly floured surface under a damp dish towel for 30 minutes.

**3** Flatten the balls with the heel of your hand and roll them out into wide circles, as wide and as thin as you can without tearing them. Dust them with flour if they become sticky.

**4** Heat a griddle and quickly cook the *yufka* sheets for about 30 seconds on each side – they will brown in places.

**5** These sheets of cooked dough can now be stacked and kept in a dry place until required.

**6** If eating them the *yufka* plain, you can sprinkle them with a little water to soften the sheets, or you can toast them on a heated griddle. If using them as a pastry sheet as part of a dish, they may need to be softened with a little water so that they are pliable for rolling out and shaping.

*Right: Layered Minced Meat and Pine Nut Pie,* Tepsi Böreği, *is a delicious baked dish made with* yufka.

*Above: Thin strands of* kadayif *pastry are used to make many desserts.*

and one made with finely minced lamb or beef and onions. Regional specialities can include puréed pumpkin or potato; baked aubergine (eggplant) and cheese; or fish mixed with herbs.

The doughs range from the rounds of *yufka*, which can be substituted with filo pastry, to the more complex doughs, which are similar to the Western flaky and puff pastries.

*Su böreği* falls somewhere in between a pastry and dough, forming a link between the two. Layered like Italian lasagna, the sheets of boiled pastry are layered and baked in the oven. *Kadayif* is long, finely shredded strands of pastry used for desserts.

## PASTA

Having arrived in Anatolia with some of the migrating Turks who came all the way from the northern borders of China, pasta (or noodle) dough is widespread in Anatolia. Early records show that a variety of pasta dishes were prepared with the meat of sheep and horses.

In central and eastern Anatolia today, the most popular pasta dishes are those made with *mantı* or *erişte*, a ribbon-shaped pasta that can be combined with various ingredients, such as spinach, tomatoes, herbs, spices or minced meat.

*Right: Cheese-filled Pastry in Lemon Syrup,* Künefe, *is made using* kadayif.

### Mantı

Falling somewhere between a noodle and a dumpling, *mantı* is an early form of pasta that takes its name from the Chinese word *mantu*. The Tartar Turks who settled around Kayseri are renowned for their skills at making *mantı*, and today the ancient dish has become fashionable in the restaurants of Istanbul and Ankara.

The most traditional way to prepare *mantı* is to stuff the little noodle squares with minced lamb, crushed chickpeas, or chopped nuts, and pinch the edges together to form little pouches.

These pouches are then baked in the oven until they are golden brown in colour, when they are submerged in a bowl of vegetable or chicken stock.

*Above:* Mantı *are dumplings that can be served with yogurt sauce.*

The cooked noodle parcels are left to absorb the flavours of the stock for a few minutes, then they are served immediately with a garlic-flavoured yogurt sauce or with a tomato sauce, or with a mixture of the two, as in Chickpea Parcels.

# Olives, Pickles and Cooking Oils

Turks never stray too far from a bowl of olives or pickles, as they are regarded as refreshing snacks or *meze*. Olives are an important part of the traditional sweet and salty breakfast, and pickles quench the thirst on a hot day. Olives also have their use in the production of olive oil which, along with sunflower oil, is the main cooking oil in Turkey

### OLIVES *(ZEYTIN)*

The Turks enjoy olives throughout the day, kicking off with a handful for breakfast to accompany a slab of *beyaz peynir*, the ubiquitous white cheese, followed by a few plucked from the market stall while shopping, to a bowlful of marinated, plump ones as a snack or *meze* dish in the middle of the day, and again in the evening.

The hardy olive trees manage to grow in poor soil in varied climates, which means that olives are grown all over Turkey, producing a wide variety of colourful fruits, in shades of purple, red, green, brown and black.

When the young black olives are harvested, they are immersed in salt for a week, so that the skin crinkles and the flesh softens. Rinsed of salt and stored in olive oil, these wrinkled black olives are the most popular for breakfast and for snacking on.

As a *meze* dish, olives are often served with lemon to squeeze over them to enhance their flavour. Olive stones have a purpose, too: once they have been cleaned and polished until smooth, they are threaded on to strings to make the prayer beads, *tespih*.

*Above: There are many different types of olive available in markets.*

### PICKLES *(TURŞU)*

There is such a variety of pickles in Turkey that they take on a whole new meaning. Pickles are not just things to tuck into a sandwich or to snack on. A kaleidoscope of colour, the jars stacked in pickle shop windows beckon people to stop and buy their favourite pickle by the kilo, or to quench their thirst with a glass of *turşu suyu*, pickle juice.

In the autumn, the market stalls are stocked with rock salt, bushels of garlic and bunches of celery stalks – the chief elements for pickle making. Small, unripe vegetables and fruit are destined for pickling, as their acidity contributes to the fermentation process and they retain the desired crunchiness.

Brine, or wine vinegar, are the standard pickling agents but in the past pickle merchants used fresh grape juice, which inevitably turned to vinegar during the fermentation. Yeast, provided by a few chickpeas or mustard seeds, or by a slice of stale bread wrapped in muslin (cheesecloth), is sometimes added to the pickling jar to speed up the process.

Recipes like *patlıcan turşusu*, stuffed aubergine pickle, are ancient and unchanged in method since the 15th century and are always a delight on the *meze* table. Other traditional pickles include white or red cabbage leaves; firm, green tomatoes; turnip with a little beetroot to colour it pink; long, twisted

*Below: A range of pickles are available at stalls in markets.*

*Right: Olives are served as* meze *and with cheese for breakfast.*

## Making *armut turşusu*

This recipe for pickled pears with saffron, honey and spices is popular in the agricultural regions around Bursa, where the orchards provide plentiful harvests of pears every year.

When making your own Turkish pickles, store them in glass jars or stoneware crocks. You should taste the vinegar during the fermentation process to make sure it has retained its acidity.

SERVES 4

120ml/4fl oz/½ cup water
400ml/14fl oz/1⅔ cups white wine,
   or cider, vinegar
175g/6oz aromatic honey
2 cinnamon sticks
8 allspice berries
a fingerful of saffron threads
4 firm, medium-sized pears, cut in
   half lengthways with the stalks
   intact, or 8 whole small,
   firm pears

**1** In a large, heavy pan, heat the water and vinegar with the honey, cinnamon sticks, allspice berries and saffron.

**2** Bring the liquid to the boil, stirring all the time, until the honey has dissolved. Reduce the heat and slip in the pears.

**3** Poach the pears gently for 15–20 minutes, or until they are tender but still firm. Lift them pears out of the liquid and arrange them in a sterilized jar or crock. Pour the liquid over them and leave to cool.

**4** Cover the jar and store the pickled pears for up to 6 months in a cool place, or in the refrigerator. Serve them chilled, or at room temperature with grilled (broiled) or roasted meats, or with a selection of cheeses.

green chilli peppers, as well as the tiny, fiery ones and vast quantities of pungent garlic and unripe fruit, such as apricots, melons and pears, which are often combined with immature, green almonds.

### *Armut turşusu*

Most Turkish pickles are sour or piquant to taste, but there are several sweet-and-sour ones that are a delicious accompaniment to roasted and grilled (broiled) meats.

### COOKING OILS

Olive oil, sunflower oil, butter, ghee (clarified butter), and sheep's tail fat are the principal cooking fats employed in Turkish cooking.

Ghee and sheep's tail fat are the oldest and most traditional of the fats used for cooking in Anatolia. Olive oil has only been used in Turkish cooking since the Ottoman period, when the Palace chefs devised a plethora of dishes involving vegetables being gently poached in the fruity oil. Prior to that olive oil was used as a lighting fuel in the mosques.

*Right, clockwise from top right: Ghee, standard butter, clarified butter.*

*Left: Olive oil is used for marinating, basting and poaching.*

### Ghee

In parts of rural Anatolia, ghee (clarified butter) is used for soup, meat and rice or bean, pea and lentil dishes. The ghee from some villages can be quite rancid in taste, and it is often melted and poured over dishes, particularly plain rice or bulgur wheat.

### Olive and sunflower oils

For cooking, olive and sunflower oils are used intermittently, or even in combination. Olive oil is almost always used in dishes where the flavour of the oil contributes to the flavour of the dish, such as the Ottoman *zeytinyağlı* vegetable dishes, which involve poaching the vegetables in the oil and then leaving them to cool to room temperature before serving – wedges of lemon are always served to squeeze over these dishes in order to cut the oil.

Depending on the region of Turkey, olive oil is used in most salads, as well as for marinating and basting meat, poultry and fish, whereas sunflower oil is the preferred oil for frying.

### Sheep's tail fat *(kuyrukyağı)*

Many Turks and Kurds of the eastern region enjoy the flavour of sheep's tail fat, which is literally the fat from the podgy tail of the sheep. It is an aquired taste, as it never loses the odour of the animal. The tail is burned to release the fat, which is collected in a jar and stored for use.

# SPICES, HERBS AND FLAVOURINGS

During the Golden Age of Islam, between the 8th and 12th centuries, with Mecca as the religious centre and Baghdad as its capital, the cooking of the Middle East flourished. Arab ships sailed to China for silk and porcelain and to the East Indies for spices. The cooking of the region as a whole soon altered as these spices and flavourings arrived at the markets of Egypt, Constantinople and Venice. Empires traded with one another, or imposed their tastes on the lands they conquered.

As the ancient yin and yang theories of China filtered through to the Seljuk Empire, a belief in balancing the warming and cooling properties of certain foods developed in the traditional Turkish kitchen and set the course for many dishes.

Warming spices such as cumin, cinnamon, allspice, cloves and Turkish red pepper *(kırmızı biber)* are believed to induce the appetite and aid digestion; generous quantities of fresh herbs, particularly mint, dill and flat leaf parsley, are often mixed together as a warming triad to balance the cooling properties of some vegetable dishes and salads; and pungent garlic, which is used liberally in eastern and southern Anatolia but is added in subtle amounts to Ottoman Palace dishes, is believed to be beneficial for the healthy circulation of the blood.

*Below: Cumin seeds and ground cumin are frequently used in Turkish cooking.*

## ALLSPICE *(YENİ BAHAR)*

Dried reddish-brown allspice berries originally came to Constantinople from the New World during the Ottoman-Spanish alliance and are, therefore, known as *yeni bahar*, "new spice".

They are used whole in marinades and pickles, and crushed for some stews, but their principal role is to flavour the aromatic rice that is used to stuff vegetables, fruit, mussels and small poultry. Sold ready-ground for this purpose the spice is commonly known as *dolma bahar* (*dolma* refers to any dish that is stuffed). The ground spice, which has a taste that is reminiscent of cloves and cinnamon, also features strongly in a number of ready-prepared spice mixtures.

## CINNAMON *(TARÇİN)*

Brought to the region from the Spice Islands by Arab traders, cinnamon quickly became absorbed into the Turkish culinary culture. Sold in bark or ground form, the spice is pungent, warming, and lends itself to sweet and savoury dishes.

The Turks use ground cinnamon in a number of minced (ground) lamb dishes, such as *köfte* and *musakka*, and in several Anatolian fish and vegetable stews. It is also used to flavour rice dishes, such as *iç pilavı*, and is one of the warming spices used in ready-prepared spice mixtures. A principal spice in many sweetmeats, sweet pastries and breads, cinnamon is also sprinkled over milk puddings and the hot orchid-root drink, salep.

## CORIANDER SEEDS *(KİŞNİŞ)*

Fresh coriander (cilantro) seldom features in the cooking of Turkey, apart from in some traditional

*Above: Coriander seeds are used to flavour stews, soups and pickles.*

Circassian dishes, such as *çerkez tavuğu*. The dried seeds, however, are used to flavour a number of stews, soups and pickles, but tend to feature more in the cooking of central eastern Anatolia than in the Palace cuisine of Istanbul. Along with cumin and cinnamon, ground coriander is one of the main spices incorporated in the ready-made spice mixtures that are mainly used for flavouring *köfte* and some *pilaff* dishes.

## CUMIN *(KIMYON)*

When roasted, cumin seeds emit a nutty aroma, and they have a distinctive taste. They are best stored in seed form and then ground when needed, as the ready-ground spice loses its pungency fairly quickly.

Believed to aid digestion, cumin is used in a number of dishes that might cause a degree of indigestion or flatulence, such as pulse dishes and some vegetable stews. Cumin is also one of the principal flavourings of *sucuk*, the cured sausage, and it is combined with fenugreek and *kırmızı biber* in *çemen*, the paste that coats the cured beef fillet, *pastırma*.

## DILL *(DEREOTU)*

With long feathery fronds, fresh dill is used both as a garnish and a traditional flavouring in many Turkish dishes. Chopped, it is added to a number of *meze* and vegetable dishes, such as the Palace *zeytinyağlı* dishes in which

*Above: Fresh dill is used both as a flavouring and a garnish.*

various vegetables, such as artichokes, are poached in olive oil and served at room temperature.

Dill is often combined with mint and flat leaf parsley in the traditional herb triad which is used in many vegetable and bean or pea dishes, as well as in the cheese filling for savoury pastries. It is also the most traditional flavouring for grilled (broiled) fish and shellfish, either by adding it to the marinade or dressing, or by scattering the herb over the fish.

---

### Garlic and nut sauce *(Tarator)*

SERVES 4-6

6 cloves garlic, peeled and chopped
salt
50g/20oz walnuts, roughly chopped
2–3 slices day-old bread, soaked
  in water and squeezed dry
45–60ml/3–4 tbsp olive oil
juice of half a lemon
ground black pepper

**1** Using a mortar and pestle, pound the garlic to a paste with a little salt. Add the walnuts and pound them to a coarse paste.

**2** Add the soaked bread and slowly pour in the olive oil, beating all the time to form a thick, pulpy mixture. Beat in the lemon juice and season with salt and pepper.

---

## FLAT LEAF PARSLEY (*MAYDANOZ*)

Large bunches of flat leaf parsley are stacked high at the Turkish market stalls, since it is the most ubiquitous herb of all. Coarsely chopped, it is added to numerous *meze* dishes and salads, such as the popular shepherd's salad, *çoban salatası*, and it is often served on its own with fish or meat kebabs, particularly *çöp şiş*, where it plays an integral role. Parsley is also married with dill and mint in the traditional herb triad, which flavours many vegetable dishes, and the cheese filling for savoury pastries.

When it is used as a garnish, flat leaf parsley is generally intended to be eaten to heighten the appetite, or temper the flavours, and small bunches of parsley always accompany fiery dishes with the idea that you chew on the leaves to cut the spice. It is even, on occasion, served as a salad to cleanse the palate, dressed with a drizzle of olive oil and a little lemon juice. Curly parsley does not have the same intensity of flavour, nor is it as juicy and refreshing.

## GARLIC (*SARMISAK*)

In both its fresh and dried form, garlic is used liberally in the cooking of Anatolia but sparingly in the Palace cuisine. Jars of pickled garlic bulbs, however, are a common sight in the markets and pickle shops throughout Turkey, and whole bulbs are often threaded on to kebab skewers and grilled with sheep's tail fat in central and eastern Anatolia.

Crushed garlic is used in many *meze* dishes and is frequently combined with creamy yogurt to spoon over a wide range of vegetable and meat dishes. It also adds a pungent kick to the various *tarator* sauces that are made with pounded nuts and served with deep-fried shellfish and fried or steamed vegetables, and it is the principal flavouring in the bread-based sauce *sarmısaklı sos*, a popular accompaniment to the deep-fried mussels in Istanbul and Izmir.

In addition to its flavouring role, garlic is well known for its healing properties and it is also hung in doorways as it is believed to ward off the evil eye.

### *KIRMIZI BİBER*

In essence, *kırmızı biber* is a red pepper, a type of horn chilli that came originally from the New World, but has grown in Turkey for several centuries and is regarded with pride. In fact, you could say that it is the national spice. Quite unlike any other spice of its nature – such as chilli, or paprika, both of which work as substitutes – it is in a class of its own. Even in Turkey it confuses people, as it is available in varied strengths and forms.

Roughly chopped, crushed and flaked, or ground into a powder, it ranges from vermilion in colour to a deep, blood red, and is almost black when roasted. At its hottest it is known as *pul biber*, which is very finely ground and used sparingly. The best quality form is sold ready-oiled, so that it imparts its flavour immediately, even in uncooked dishes.

The red chilli peppers are recognizable in the markets as fresh and dried forms, threaded on to strings and hung up. The spice is inseparable from the *güney* cuisine, the cooking of southern Turkey, and is used liberally in Gaziantep. Nothing tastes quite like the real thing but, in the recipes that follow, this "Turkish red pepper" can be replaced by paprika or fresh red chilli.

*Below: Pul biber, the red chilli powder, is one of the national spices.*

*Above, clockwise from top: Sumac, mastic crystals and cinnamon sticks.*

### MASTIC *(MASTIKA)*

This is the aromatic gum from a tree (*Pistacia lentiscus*) that grows wild in the Mediterranean region of Turkey. The blobs of sticky gum are collected from the tree, often with ants still attached, and used for the delicious resinous flavour and chewy tang they impart to the dishes.

Traditionally, the gum was used in a number of savoury and sweet dishes but, nowadays, it is mainly used in the Palace milk desserts and in the famous snowy-white, chewy ice cream from Istanbul. The gum crystals can be chewed as gum but, when using them for culinary purposes, they must first be pulverized with a little sugar, using a mortar and pestle.

### MINT *(NANE)*

Both the fresh and dried leaves of mint are used in *meze* dishes, salads, vegetable dishes and pilaffs, such as *Sultan Reşat pilavı*, the delicious aubergine rice dish with cinnamon and lots of mint. One of the traditional "warming" trio, along with flat leaf parsley and dill, fresh mint leaves are sold in large bunches, like flowers, and used in liberal quantities for their distinctly refreshing taste.

The dried leaves are used in tea, in the traditional soup, *yayla çorbası*, and in several thick *meze* dips such as *haydari*, a popular yogurt, mint and garlic dip; and *tahin tarama*, a mixture of sesame paste and grape syrup.

### NIGELLA *(ÇÖREOTU)*

In Turkey, nigella is most commonly associated with *çörek* (hence the name *çöreotu*), a sweet bun that is eaten during the Sweet Festival, *Şeker Bayramı*. The little black seeds look like tiny charcoal teardrops and have an aromatic, peppery flavour, which gives a lift to many breads and buns, such as *pide*. Due to their unique flavour, they are occasionally tossed in salads and sprinkled over cheese.

### OREGANO *(KEKIK)* AND THYME *(DAĞI KEKIK)*

Fresh oregano leaves are sometimes scattered over white cheese or tossed in salads but, generally, the herb is sun-dried and crumbled or finely chopped. It is the favourite herb to scatter over roasted or grilled (broiled) lamb, and bowls of dried oregano are a frequent sight at kebab houses, where they are placed on the tables alongside bowls of sumac and *kırmızı biber*, the three traditional condiments.

*Right, clockwise from top: Dried mint, oregano and sage.*

Both dried oregano and thyme are popular herbs for flavouring the marinades prepared for olives, as they retain their flavour and texture in the olive oil, and they are also scattered over savoury breads.

Thyme comes from the same family as oregano, but is known as "mountain oregano", as it grows further up the hillsides. The fresh sprigs are used to flavour roasted meats and poultry, such as *ördek fırında*, roast duck with honey, thyme and almonds. In central and eastern Anatolia, fresh thyme is used to flavour dishes prepared with sheep's tail fat, as the herb is believed to cut the fat and aid digestion. The dried sprigs, on the other hand, are brewed in a herbal tea that is drunk as an aphrodisiac.

### SAGE *(ADI)*

The hillsides of the Mediterranean and Aegean regions of Turkey emit a delicious herby aroma as the sun-kissed wild sage bushes produce the most wonderfully perfumed and tasty leaves.

The fresh leaves are added to a variety of salads and vegetable dishes, and are good with grilled or lightly fried shellfish. The dried leaves are used in stews and soups, and are often added to melted butter that is drizzled over poached eggs, the Anatolian noodle dumplings, *mantı*, and the Circassian chicken and walnut dish, *çerkez tavüğü*. In the markets throughout Turkey, stalks of dried sage leaves are strung up at spice stalls, destined for an aromatic winter tea that is believed to be healing and cleansing.

*Above: Various
types of runny and set honey are
available in different regions of Turkey.*

## SUMAC *(SUMAK)*

A deep-red condiment, sumac is made
by crushing and grinding the dried
berries of a wild bush *(Rhus coriaria)*
that grows prolifically in Anatolia and
parts of the Middle East. The ground
spice has a fruity, sour taste and is
used sprinkled liberally over grilled
meats, fish and salads.

Long before the arrival of lemons in
Turkey and the Middle East, sumac was
used as one of the principal souring
agents, along with the juice of sour
pomegranates, to season, flavour and
preserve a variety of foods. When eating
in Turkey today, particularly in a kebab
house or a specialist *lokanta* (small
restaurant) for grilled chicken, fish,
pastries and *lahmacun* (Anatolian
pizza), small bowls of ground sumac
are often placed on the table as a
principal condiment, with dried oregano
and *kırmızı biber*.

## FLAVOURINGS

Many Turkish desserts are scented with
sweet flavourings – honey and rose,
perhaps, being the most well known.

## Honey *(bal)*

The hills and valleys of Turkey are
renowned, and much visited, for their
diverse fauna and flora, so it should
come as no surprise to discover that
the bees enjoy it, too, producing myriad
honeys that range in colour from black
coffee to muddy-river brown, sparkling
gold, amber yellow and frothy white.

The dark, fragrant honey from the pine
forests of the Aegean and Mediterranean
regions is much sought after in its
runny or comb form, as is the
pungent chestnut honey from
the Black Sea region.

Many villages sell honey
particular to that area
because of the type of
flowers that grow locally.
However, there is no type
more surprising than the
*deli bal* of the Kars region, where
opium poppies grow naturally and the
honey drives you wild as it momentarily
grips the back of your throat with a
fiery blast that brings with it mild
hallucinatory sensations. It is the most
bizarre honey I have ever had, and is
the most appropriately named one –
translating as "silly honey".

## Orange *(portakal)*

The perfumed blossoms of the bitter
orange tree are distilled to make a clear,
scented water which is used for
flavouring desserts and syrups in the
southern regions of Turkey.

## Rose *(gül)*

The origins and uses of rose petals can
be traced back to the bathing habits
of the ancient Egyptians and the wine
traditions of the Romans, but the
invention of a distilled rose water
*(gül suyu)* for culinary purposes is
attributed to the Persians.

Adopted by the Ottomans, this
tradition of scenting dishes with rose
water became popular in the Palace
kitchens, where it was used in many
syrupy pastries and milk desserts, such
as *güllaç* and *muhallebi*. Although the
roses petals used for culinary purposes,
such as the delicious syrupy jam, *gül
reçeli*, are generally in vibrant shades
of pink or red, the rose water is
distinctively scented but totally colourless.

## Saffron *(safron)*

The only spice in the world to be
measured by the carat, as it is worth its
weight in gold, genuine saffron is very
special indeed. Cultivated in Turkey and
neighbouring Iran, saffron is the dye

contained in the dried stigmas of the
purple crocus *(Crocus sativus)*, which
flowers for only two weeks in October. It
requires a staggering number of flowers
(roughly 10,000) to yield a mere 50g
(2oz) of saffron – hence the high price.

The dried stigmas are generally sold
in small quantities and resemble a
tangle of burnt-orangey-red threads –
the deeper the colour the better the
quality. Although only mildly perfumed
at this stage, the stigmas come into life
when soaked in water, as they impart a
magnificent yellow dye and a floral hint
to their flavour.

Used mainly in milk desserts and
ice cream, saffron is occasionally used
in savoury dishes in Turkey, but its key
role is in *zerde*, a special jelly-like rice
dessert that is often prepared for
wedding feasts.

## Vanilla *(vanilya)*

The only other traditional flavouring for
the Palace desserts is vanilla extract,
derived from moist, plump pods, which
arrive at the *Mısır Çarşısı*, the famous
Egyptian spice bazaar in Istanbul, from
places like Madagascar.

*Below: Vanilla and rose water are
traditional flavourings for desserts.*

# DRINKS

Coffee may be surrounded by tradition and ritual, but tea ranks as the king of drinks. Without a doubt, it is the national drink of Turkey, offered wherever you go. There are also a number of refreshing fruity sherbet drinks and some unusual beverages, such as the one made with bulgur wheat and the thick, nourishing orchid root drink.

## COFFEE *(KAHVE)*

For those who can afford it, the first small cup of *kahve* is enjoyed on rising, the second cup is drunk mid-morning, and a third may be drunk after a long meal. As it is more expensive, and more prestigious, than tea, coffee is not available to all on a daily basis. In some Anatolian communities, where it is reserved for special occasions, there still exists the tradition of selecting a suitable bride partially based on her ability to prepare and serve coffee, while the prospective mother-in-law and her son inspect the young girl's beauty and grace.

The traditional cooking vessel for Turkish coffee is a *cezve*, a slim, deep pot, often made from tin-lined copper,

*Below: Turkish coffee is traditionally made in a* cezve.

with a long handle. Generally, medium-roast arabica coffee beans are passed through a very fine grinder until almost powdery. A wide selection of suitable coffee beans are available in health food stores, supermarkets and delicatessens, but the Turkish setting on the grinding machines usually doesn't grind the beans fine enough for the desired effect, so make sure it is passed through the grinder twice.

Most Turks drink their coffee sweet, but you can drink it *sade* (black), *orta şekerli* (medium sweet), or *şekerli* (sweet). There is an art to making an acceptable cup of Turkish coffee.

### Making Turkish coffee

To make the coffee, measure the water by the coffee cup (a standard, small cylindrical cup) and the coffee by the teaspoon. The general rule allows for one coffee cup of water to 5ml/1 tsp coffee and 5ml/1 tsp sugar per person.

**1** Tip the water into the *cezve* and spoon the coffee and sugar on the top. Use a teaspoon to stir the sugar and coffee quickly into the surface of the water to give the desired froth a good kick-start.

**2** Put the pan over a medium heat and, using the teaspoon, gradually scrape the outer edges of the surface into the middle to create an island of froth. The key to achieving the perfect froth is always to work at the surface; never touch the bottom of the pot with the spoon.

**3** Once the coffee is hot, pour about one-third of it into the coffee cup to warm it and return the pan to the heat. Continue to gather the froth into the middle and, just as the coffee begins to bubble up, take it off the heat and pour it into the cup. Leave the coffee cup to stand for 1 minute to let the coffee grains settle and then drink it while it is hot.

## TEA *(ÇAY)*

The drinking of tea, *çay*, is such big business in Turkey that it could be regarded as the national drink. There

*Above: Tulip-shaped glasses of tea – the national drink of Turkey.*

are *çay* houses in every village, in every city street, at ports and stations, and near busy office buildings. The sight of young boys or men carrying trays of tea glasses through crowds or across busy roads is a common one, as tea is served throughout the day to passers-by, gatherings of friends and thirsty staff in the buildings. Tea is offered to you in banks while you wait, in shops and markets as you browse, in meetings of any description, and in houses when you are welcomed. It is a drink of friendship and hospitality and it is polite to accept.

Invariably, tea is served in tulip-shaped glasses, a legacy of Sultan Ahmet III (1703–30), who encouraged the design of tulips on tiles and other artefacts. Traditionally, it was made in a bulky copper samovar, but nowadays it is made in a modern tin or aluminium, version consisting of a small teapot, containing the tea, resting on a larger teapot, containing the water.

Generally, the tea leaves are home-grown, mainly from plantations at Rize on the Black Sea coast, and the tea is made strong. It is never drunk with milk and is served with lumps of sugar, which some people stir in, whereas others place them in their mouths and suck the tea through them.

*Above: Instant apple tea is available as granules or in bags.*

### Herbal and fruit teas

Alternative teas are often put in the category of "healing" teas, as most Turks would only abandon their regular tea for a herbal one if suffering from an ailment. There are numerous herbal and aromatic infusions, ranging from rose petals, camomile *(papatya)*, and lemon, to orange blossom, rosemary and mint. The dried leaves and blossom of the linden tree are sold as a medicinal tea, *ıhlamur çayı*, which is believed to aid the digestive system and clear up colds. An invigorating tea, *adı çayı*, is made from the steeped branches of wild, sun-dried sage.

Fruit, such as apples and oranges, are dried, too, and used to make tea, but there is also a commercial apple tea, *elma çayı*, which consists of sugar and apple-flavoured granules.

### TRADITIONAL DRINKS

There are a number of traditional drinks, apart from tea and coffee, including *salep*, a drink made from ground orchid root, and refreshing sherbets.

### Boza

In the winter, one of the traditional drinks is *boza*, a thick mixture made from fermented bulgur wheat and sprinkled with cinnamon. Glasses of the pale yellow liquid are lined up in pudding shop windows. The *boza* seller pulls his cart through the streets, laden with copper jugs filled with the beverage, and shouting *"bozacı"* to alert people to his presence so that they stop for a glass of the unusual, but popular, drink.

### Salep

A popular drink in the cold months of the winter is *salep*, made from ground orchid root. Thick, milky and sweet, dusted with a little cinnamon, it is warming and nourishing. Traditionally, it is made in large copper or brass urns, some of which are still in use in specialist pudding shops, but there are also sachets of instant *salep* available.

### Sherbet (şerbet)

The most common traditional cold drink in Turkey is *şerbet*, which is a cool, refreshing drink made from fruit syrups, such as lemon, cherry or pomegranate, as well as syrups made with rose petals, orange blossom, honey, almonds and tamarind. Preparing syrups with seasonal fruits or petals was part of traditional kitchen life and still is in some households.

### ALCOHOLIC DRINKS

Prior to the influence of Islam, the Turks enjoyed a variety of alcoholic drinks, such as crude beers and wines and the fermented milk of mares, *kımız*, all of which were collectively known as *çakır* (*çakırkeyif* means "tipsy"), and were usually accompanied by *meze* dishes. With the conversion to Islam, however, alcoholic drinks were prohibited.

In Turkey today, many devout Muslims still adhere to the strict Islamic rules but, with the influence of Europe, tourism and diverse religions within the country, there are some Turks who drink alcohol.

The best-known beer is called *Efes*, but there are a number of local beers, and Tuborg, the Danish company, makes beer under Turkish licence. Many Turkish wines are rather unpredictable and benefit from being decanted and aired. The two leading wine producers, Doluca and Kavaklıdere have quite a good range of wines, such as Dikmen (red) and Çankaya (white), but my favourite bottle of red is called Yakut.

### Rakı

The favourite alcoholic drink in Turkey is the aniseed-flavoured drink *rakı*, which turns cloudy when water is added and is often referred to as "lion's milk". It is traditionally a man's drink, although many women enjoy it, too, and it is the preferred drink to go with *meze* and fish.

*Rakı* can be drunk in three ways: neat as a shot; served in a tall glass with ice to which water is added; or served in two glasses, one containing a measure of *rakı*, the other filled with water; both glasses are drunk alternately with ice. A liquid form of *mastika* is sometimes added to the bottle to give it a chewy twang. Top-of-the-range *rakı* are Altınbaş and Yeni.

*Right: Beer, wine and, in particular, rakı are drunk by non-Muslims in Turkey.*

# MEZE AND SALADS

In Turkey meze and salads go hand in hand, as many salads
are served as meze and other dishes are called "salad", even
if they do not resemble one. The dishes are varied and
tantalizingly tempting. In these pages you will find famous
dips such as Hummus, and Sesame and Lemon Dip;
flavoursome and sustaining salads, such as Bulgur Salad,
and spicy Tomato, Pepper and Chilli Salad; and finger food,
such as Vine Leaves Stuffed with Aromatic Rice.

# HUMMUS

*THIS IS ONE OF THOSE DISHES THAT YOU SHOULD MAKE ACCORDING TO YOUR PERSONAL TASTE. SOME PEOPLE LIKE HUMMUS STRONGLY FLAVOURED WITH GARLIC, SOME LIKE IT THICKENED WITH SESAME PASTE, AND OTHERS PREFER IT LIGHT AND LEMONY. THIS CLASSIC TURKISH VERSION, HUMUS, IS LIGHT WITH A HINT OF CUMIN, AND IS DELICIOUS SERVED WITH WARM FLAT BREAD OR CRUDITÉS. IT IS NEARLY ALWAYS ACCOMPANIED BY A BOWL OF GREEN OLIVES OR PICKLED VEGETABLES AND CAN BE GARNISHED WITH CHOPPED PARSLEY OR SUMAC, OR WITH TOASTED PINE NUTS OR SESAME SEEDS.*

SERVES FOUR TO SIX

INGREDIENTS
   225g/8oz dried chickpeas, soaked
     in water for at least 6 hours
   45–60ml/3–4 tbsp olive oil
   juice of 1–2 lemons
   2 garlic cloves crushed
   5ml/1 tsp cumin seeds
   15–30ml/1–2 tbsp thick and
     creamy natural (plain) yogurt
   salt and ground black pepper
To garnish:
   15ml/1 tbsp olive oil
   *kırmızı biber*, or paprika

**1** Drain the chickpeas and place them in a pan with plenty of water. Bring to the boil, reduce the heat and simmer, covered, for about 1½ hours, or until they are very soft. Drain the chickpeas.

**2** Remove any loose skins by rubbing the chickpeas in a clean kitchen towel. Put the cooked chickpeas into a food processor or blender and process to a thick purée.

**3** Add the olive oil, lemon juice, garlic and cumin seeds, and blend thoroughly. Add the yogurt to lighten the mixture, and season to taste. Adjust the hummus to your taste by adding a little more lemon or olive oil.

**4** Transfer the hummus to a serving bowl and drizzle a little oil over the surface to keep it moist. Sprinkle a little *kırmızı biber* or paprika over the top of the hummus and serve with warm bread or carrot and celery sticks.

**Per portion** Energy 190kcal/798kJ; Protein 8.4g; Carbohydrate 19.3g, of which sugars 1.4g; Fat 9.4g, of which saturates 1.3g; Cholesterol 0mg; Calcium 70mg; Fibre 4.1g; Sodium 19mg.

# SESAME AND LEMON DIP

*THIS DELIGHTFUL LITTLE DIP, TAHIN TARAMA, IS FROM CENTRAL ANATOLIA, WHERE IT IS OFTEN SERVED IN OUTDOOR CAFÉS AND RESTAURANTS AS A MEZE DISH ON ITS OWN — A SORT OF WHETTING OF THE APPETITE WHILE YOU WAIT FOR THE ASSORTMENT OF EXCITING DISHES TO COME. SOMETIMES YOU WILL SEE GROUPS OF OLD MEN DRINKING RAKI OR REFRESHING TEA, SHARING A PLATE OF TAHIN TARAMA OR A BOWL OF ROASTED CHICKPEAS WHILE THEY PLAY CARDS OR BACKGAMMON. SWEET AND TANGY, IT IS GOOD MOPPED UP WITH CHUNKS OF CRUSTY BREAD OR TOASTED PITTA BREAD.*

SERVES TWO

INGREDIENTS

    45ml/3 tbsp light sesame paste *(tahin)*
    juice of 1 lemon
    15–30ml/1–2 tbsp clear honey or
      grape *pekmez*
    5–10ml/1–2 tsp dried mint
    lemon wedges, to serve

**VARIATION**
Popular for breakfast or as a sweet snack is *tahin pekmez*. Combine 30–45ml/ 2–3 tbsp light sesame paste with 30ml/ 2 tbsp grape *pekmez* to form a sweet paste, then scoop up with chunks of fresh bread. If you can't find *pekmez*, use date syrup from Middle Eastern and health food stores.

**1** Beat the sesame paste and lemon juice together in a bowl.

**2** Add the honey and mint and beat again until thick and creamy, then spoon into a small dish. Serve the dip at room temperature, with lemon wedges for squeezing.

**Per portion** Energy 160kcal/664kJ; Protein 4.3g; Carbohydrate 6.4g, of which sugars 6.2g; Fat 13.3g, of which saturates 1.9g; Cholesterol 0mg; Calcium 155mg; Fibre 1.8g; Sodium 6mg.

# SMOKED AUBERGINE AND YOGURT PURÉE

*ONE OF THE MOST POPULAR MEZE DISHES, THIS GARLIC-FLAVOURED PURÉE, PATLICAN EZMESI, VARIES FROM HOUSE TO HOUSE AND REGION TO REGION, SOMETIMES MADE WITH A ROBUST QUANTITY OF GARLIC OR A KICK OF CHILLI, OR WITH THE ADDITION OF FRESH-TASTING DILL, MINT OR PARSLEY. IT IS HEAVENLY WHEN FRESHLY MADE, SERVED WITH CHUNKS OF CRUSTY BREAD FOR SCOOPING.*

**3** Hold each aubergine by the stalk under cold running water and peel off the charred skin until you are left with just the flesh. Squeeze the flesh to get rid of any excess water and place it on a chopping board.

**4** Chop the aubergine flesh to a pulp, discarding the stalks. Put in a bowl with 30ml/2 tbsp oil, the lemon juice and garlic. Beat well to mix, then beat in the yogurt and season with salt and pepper.

**5** Transfer to a small bowl, drizzle with olive oil and garnish with dill. Serve at room temperature, with lemon wedges for squeezing.

## SERVES FOUR

### INGREDIENTS
2 large, plump aubergines (eggplants)
30ml/2 tbsp olive oil, plus extra for drizzling
juice of 1 lemon
2–3 garlic cloves, crushed
225g/8oz/1 cup thick and creamy natural (plain) yogurt
salt and ground black pepper
a few fresh dill fronds, to garnish
lemon wedges, to serve

### VARIATION
To make an aubergine (eggplant) salad *(patlican salatası)*, toss the smoked aubergine flesh with the oil and lemon juice, some sliced spring onions (scallions), chopped tomatoes, parsley and dill.

**1** Gripping them firmly between tongs, place the aubergines directly on the gas flame on top of the stove, or under a conventional grill (broiler), and turn them from time to time until the skin is charred on all sides and the flesh feels soft to the touch.

**2** Place the aubergines in a plastic bag and leave for a few minutes.

### COOK'S TIP
This is a great dish for a barbecue. Instead of charring the aubergines on the stove, lay them on the rack over hot charcoal and cook for 15–20 minutes, turning them from time to time until they are soft. Place them on a chopping board and slit open lengthways with a sharp knife. Scoop out the flesh and chop to a pulp, then continue as above.

**Per portion** Energy 103kcal/431kJ; Protein 4.4g; Carbohydrate 7.7g, of which sugars 6.4g; Fat 6.5g, of which saturates 1.2g; Cholesterol 1mg; Calcium 118mg; Fibre 2.3g; Sodium 49mg.

# CARROT AND CARAWAY PURÉE WITH YOGURT

*LONG, THIN CARROTS THAT ARE ORANGE, YELLOW, RED AND PURPLE ARE A COLOURFUL FEATURE IN THE VEGETABLE MARKETS THROUGHOUT TURKEY. USED MAINLY IN SALADS, LENTIL DISHES AND STEWS, THEY ARE ALSO STEAMED AND PURÉED, THEN SERVED WITH YOGURT IN THE MIDDLE, AS IN THIS RECIPE. TRY SERVING THE CARROT PURÉE WHILE IT IS STILL WARM, WITH CHUNKS OF CRUSTY BREAD.*

SERVES FOUR

INGREDIENTS

    6 large carrots, thickly sliced
    5ml/1 tsp caraway seeds
    30–45ml/2–3 tbsp olive oil
    juice of 1 lemon
    225g/8oz/1 cup thick and creamy
      natural (plain) yogurt
    1–2 garlic cloves, crushed
    salt and ground black pepper
    a few fresh mint leaves, to garnish

**COOK'S TIP**

It is always best to steam rather than boil vegetables, so they retain their taste, texture and goodness. This purée would not taste nearly as good if the carrots were boiled and watery.

**1** Steam the carrots for 25 minutes, until they are very soft. While they are still warm, mash them to a smooth purée, or blend them in a processor.

**2** Beat the caraway seeds into the carrot purée, followed by the oil and lemon juice. Season with salt and pepper.

**3** Beat the yogurt and garlic in a separate bowl, and season to taste.

**4** Spoon the warm carrot purée around the edge of a serving dish, or pile into a mound and make a well in the middle. Spoon the yogurt into the middle, and garnish with mint.

**Per portion** Energy 157kcal/651kJ; Protein 4.2g; Carbohydrate 15.3g, of which sugars 13.6g; Fat 9.2g, of which saturates 1.6g; Cholesterol 1mg; Calcium 140mg; Fibre 3.3g; Sodium 78mg.

# BAKED CHICKPEA PURÉE <u>WITH</u> LEMON <u>AND</u> PINE NUTS

*THIS RECIPE FOR BAKED HUMUS IS AN EASTERN ANATOLIAN SPECIALITY, AND MAKES A WELCOME CHANGE FROM THE STANDARD, COLD HUMUS THAT IS FOUND THROUGHOUT THE MIDDLE EAST. THICK AND GARLIC-FLAVOURED, IT VARIES SLIGHTLY IN TASTE, DEPENDING ON WHETHER YOU CHOOSE TO ADD SESAME PASTE AND CUMIN TO IT. ADDING YOGURT WILL MAKE IT LIGHTER IN TEXTURE. SERVE IT HOT AS PART OF A MEZE SPREAD OR AS A COMFORTING, SUSTAINING SNACK WITH GENEROUS HUNKS OF WARM, CRUSTY BREAD, TOASTED PITTA BREAD OR CHUNKS OF TURKISH PIDE. IT IS ALSO DELICIOUS SERVED AS A LIGHT LUNCH WITH A TOMATO AND HERB SALAD.*

SERVES FOUR

INGREDIENTS

225g/8oz/1¼ cups dried chickpeas, soaked in cold water for at least 6 hours or overnight
about 50ml/2fl oz/¼ cup olive oil
juice of 2 lemons
3–4 garlic cloves, crushed
10ml/2 tsp cumin seeds, crushed
30–45ml/2–3 tbsp light sesame paste *(tahin)*
45–60ml/3–4 heaped tbsp thick and creamy natural (plain) yogurt
30–45ml/2–3 tbsp pine nuts
40g/1½oz/3 tbsp butter or ghee
5–10ml/1–2 tsp oiled or roasted Turkish red pepper or paprika
salt and ground black pepper

**1** Drain the chickpeas, transfer them to a pan and fill the pan with plenty of cold water. Bring to the boil and boil for 1 minute, then lower the heat and partially cover the pan.

**2** Simmer the chickpeas for 1 hour, until they are soft and easy to mash.

**3** Drain the chickpeas, then rinse them well under cold running water. Remove any loose skins by rubbing the chickpeas in a clean kitchen towel. Preheat the oven to 200°C/400°F/Gas 6.

**4** Using a large mortar and pestle, pound the chickpeas with the oil, lemon juice, garlic and cumin.

**5** Beat in the sesame paste, then beat in the yogurt until the purée is light and smooth. Season to taste.

**6** Transfer the purée to an ovenproof dish – preferably an earthenware one – and smooth the top with the back of a spoon.

**7** Dry-roast the pine nuts in a small, heavy pan over a medium heat until golden brown. Lower the heat, add the butter and let it melt, then stir in the red pepper or paprika.

**8** Pour the mixture over the *humus* and bake for about 25 minutes, until it has risen slightly and the butter has been absorbed. Serve straight from the oven.

**Per portion** Energy 433kcal/1803kJ; Protein 15g; Carbohydrate 29.5g, of which sugars 3g; Fat 29.2g, of which saturates 7.7g; Cholesterol 21mg; Calcium 160mg; Fibre 6.8g; Sodium 91mg.

# FIERY CHEESE AND PARSLEY DIP

*THIS MEZE DISH, PAŞA EZMESI, IS FIT FOR A PAŞA (A TURKISH NOBLEMAN). A REGULAR FEATURE ON THE MEZE TABLE OF CENTRAL ANATOLIA, IT IS SPIKED WITH KIRMIZI BIBER AND USED TO WHET THE APPETITE FOR THE DISHES TO FOLLOW. AS IT CAN BE VERY HOT, IT IS OFTEN SERVED WITH TAHINLI TARAMA, A SWEET MEZE DISH OF SESAME PASTE, GRAPE SYRUP AND MINT, OR KAYMAK BAL, CLOTTED BUFFALO CREAM DRIZZLED IN HONEY, TO CUT THE SPICE. SERVE WITH WARM FLAT BREAD.*

SERVES THREE TO FOUR

INGREDIENTS
  250g/9oz *beyaz peynir*,
    or feta cheese
  15–30ml/1–2 tbsp *süzme*,
    or strained yogurt
  5–10ml/1–2 tsp *kırmızı biber*,
    or hot paprika or chilli powder
  1 small bunch flat leaf parsley,
    leaves finely chopped
  salt, to taste
  1 lemon, cut into wedges and
    1 small bunch flat leaf parsley,
    trimmed, to serve

**1** In a bowl, mash the cheese with a fork, or process it in a food processor or blender. Beat in the yogurt, again using the fork or the blender, until the mixture is fairly smooth and creamy.

**2** Add the *kırmızı biber* and the parsley. Taste the dip to see if you need to add any salt – often the cheese is sufficiently salty.

**3** Spoon the cheese dip into a dish and serve as part of a *meze* spread with warm flat bread, such as pitta pouches or Turkish *pide*, wedges of lemon to squeeze over each mouthful and leafy stalks of flat leaf parsley to chew on, to cut the spice.

**VARIATIONS**
• Crushed walnuts can be mixed in to the dip in step 2, or sprinkled over the top, to add some texture to the dip.
• Finely chopped fresh mint can be added to the parsley to give a refreshing lift to the dish.

**Per portion** Energy 170kcal/705kJ; Protein 10.7g; Carbohydrate 2.4g, of which sugars 1.5g; Fat 13.2g, of which saturates 8.6g; Cholesterol 44mg; Calcium 262mg; Fibre 0.6g; Sodium 908mg.

# SMOKED COD'S ROE DIP

*TRADITIONALLY, THIS DISH IS MADE WITH THE SMOKED ROE (TARAMA) OF GREY MULLET, A POPULAR FISH IN TURKEY. HOWEVER, THE ROE OF OTHER FISH CAN BE USED, AND THE MOST EASILY AVAILABLE IS SMOKED COD'S ROE. LIKE HUMUS, THE WELL-KNOWN CHICKPEA PURÉE, TARAMA NEEDS TO BE MADE ACCORDING TO TASTE, ADJUSTING THE OIL AND LEMON AND THE DENSITY OF THE PURÉE. WARM BREAD AND STRIPS OF CUCUMBER SPRINKLED WITH SALT ARE IDEAL ACCOMPANIMENTS.*

### SERVES FOUR TO SIX

INGREDIENTS
  2 slices white bread, with the
    crusts removed
  about 105ml/7 tbsp milk or water
  225g/8oz smoked cod's roe,
    skin removed
  2–3 garlic cloves, crushed
  45–60ml/3–4 tbsp olive oil, or a
    mixture of olive and sunflower oil
  juice of 2 lemons
  salt and ground black pepper
  finely chopped flat leaf parsley,
    to garnish

**1** First soak the bread in a little milk or water (the quantity will vary according to the size and type of bread). Squeeze the bread to remove the excess liquid.

**2** Using a mortar and pestle, or an electric blender, pound the cod's roe to a smooth paste. Add the bread and garlic, and gradually pour in the olive oil and lemon juice, until the purée is light and creamy – adjust the quantity of oil and lemon juice to your taste.

**3** Season the purée with salt and a generous grinding of black pepper, and transfer it to a serving bowl.

**4** Garnish the dip with a little chopped parsley and serve the *tarama* with warm bread and strips of cucumber sprinkled with salt.

**VARIATION**
Some cooks in Turkey prefer to make a delicious warm version of *tarama* by using mashed potato instead of the soaked bread. Simply mix the smoked roe with freshly made hot mashed potato and garnish it with chopped parsley. Using this method makes the purée a little heavier when left to stand.

**Per portion** Energy 118kcal/495kJ; Protein 9.6g; Carbohydrate 5.1g, of which sugars 1.2g; Fat 6.8g, of which saturates 1.1g; Cholesterol 125mg; Calcium 48mg; Fibre 0.5g; Sodium 94mg.

# SMOKED AUBERGINE AND PEPPER DIP

*This is a lovely Anatolian meze dish of smoked aubergine and peppers with a refreshing lemony tang. Arabic in origin, acvar is traditionally served warm with lemon wedges to squeeze over it. Alternatively, you can increase the quantities and serve it as a main dish with yogurt and bread, or serve it as an accompaniment to a barbecue spread.*

**2** One at a time, hold the charred vegetables under cold running water and peel off the skins.

**3** Place them on a chopping board and remove the stalks. Halve the peppers lengthways and scoop out the seeds, then chop the flesh to a pulp. Chop the aubergine flesh to a pulp.

**4** Pour the oil into a wide, heavy pan and toss in the onion, chilli, garlic and sugar. Cook over a medium heat for 2–3 minutes, until they begin to colour.

**5** Toss in the pulped peppers and aubergine, stir in the lemon juice and vinegar and season to taste with salt and pepper. Toss in the parsley and serve with lemon wedges and toasted pitta bread.

SERVES FOUR

INGREDIENTS
  2 red (bell) peppers
  1 fat aubergine (eggplant)
  30–45ml/2–3 tbsp olive oil
  1 red onion, cut in half lengthways
    and finely sliced along the grain
  1 fresh red chilli, seeded and
    finely sliced
  2 garlic cloves, chopped
  5–10ml/1–2 tsp sugar
  juice of 1 lemon
  dash of white wine vinegar
  a big handful of fresh flat leaf
    parsley, roughly chopped
  salt and ground black pepper
  lemon wedges and toasted pitta
    bread, to serve

**1** Place the peppers and aubergine directly on the gas flame on top of the stove, under a conventional grill (broiler), or on a rack over the hot coals of a barbecue. Turn from time to time until the skin is charred on all sides and the flesh feels soft. Place in a plastic bag and leave for a few minutes.

**Per portion** Energy 102kcal/425kJ; Protein 1.8g; Carbohydrate 10.5g, of which sugars 9.8g; Fat 6.2g, of which saturates 1g; Cholesterol 0mg; Calcium 19mg; Fibre 3.1g; Sodium 6mg.

# SPICY WALNUT DIP

*MADE PRIMARILY OF WALNUTS, THIS POPULAR, SPICY DIP IS USUALLY SERVED WITH TOASTED FLAT BREAD OR CHUNKS OF CRUSTY BREAD. IT CAN ALSO BE SERVED AS AN ACCOMPANIMENT TO GRILLED, BROILED OR BARBECUED MEATS. ARABIC IN ORIGIN, MUHAMMARA IS TRADITIONALLY MADE WITH POMEGRANATE SYRUP, BUT CONTEMPORARY RECIPES OFTEN USE LEMON JUICE INSTEAD.*

SERVES FOUR TO SIX

INGREDIENTS

    175g/6oz/1 cup broken
      shelled walnuts
    5ml/1 tsp cumin seeds,
      dry-roasted and ground
    5–10ml/1–2 tsp *kırmızı biber*, or
      1–2 fresh red chillies, seeded
      and finely chopped, or 5ml/1 tsp
      chilli powder
    1–2 garlic cloves (optional)
    1 slice of day-old bread, sprinkled
      with water and left for a few
      minutes, then squeezed dry
    15–30ml/1–2 tbsp tomato
      purée (paste)
    5–10ml/1–2 tsp granulated sugar
    30ml/2 tbsp pomegranate syrup
      or juice of 1 lemon
    120ml/4fl oz/½ cup olive or
      sunflower oil, plus extra for serving
    salt and ground black pepper
    a few sprigs of fresh flat leaf parsley,
      to garnish
    strips of pitta bread, to serve

**1** Using a mortar and pestle, pound the walnuts with the cumin seeds, *kırmızı biber* or chilli and garlic (if using).

**COOK'S TIP**
If you have an electric blender you can whiz all the ingredients together if you like, although many cooks prefer the traditional mortar and pestle method as the pounding releases the natural oils and flavour of the nuts, and this contributes considerably to the finished taste.

**2** Add the soaked bread and pound to a paste, then beat in the tomato purée, sugar and pomegranate syrup.

**3** Now slowly drizzle in 120ml/4fl oz/ ½ cup oil, beating all the time until the paste is thick and light. Season with salt and pepper, and spoon into a bowl.

**4** Splash a little olive oil over the top to keep it moist, and garnish with parsley leaves. Serve at room temperature.

**Per portion** Energy 339kcal/1399kJ; Protein 4.8g; Carbohydrate 5.1g, of which sugars 2.8g; Fat 33.4g, of which saturates 3.5g; Cholesterol 0mg; Calcium 34mg; Fibre 1.2g; Sodium 32mg.

# VINE LEAVES STUFFED WITH AROMATIC RICE

*DEVISED BY THE OTTOMANS, THESE STUFFED VINE LEAVES, YALANCI YAPRAK DOLMASI, ARE A POPULAR MEZE DISH THROUGHOUT THE MIDDLE EAST. THEY ARE CALLED YALANCI, WHICH MEANS "FALSE", BECAUSE THEY CONTAIN NO MEAT. THIS TERM APPLIES TO ALL VEGETABLES THAT ARE STUFFED SOLELY WITH AROMATIC RICE AND THEN COOKED IN OLIVE OIL AND SERVED COLD ON THEIR OWN OR AS PART OF A MEZE SPREAD. FRESH VINE LEAVES ARE READILY AVAILABLE IN SOME MIDDLE EASTERN AND GREEK MARKETS AND STORES; OTHERWISE, USE THE PACKS OR JARS OF VINE LEAVES PRESERVED IN BRINE THAT CAN BE FOUND IN MANY LARGE SUPERMARKETS.*

## SERVES SIX

### INGREDIENTS
24–30 fresh or preserved vine leaves, plus extra for lining the pan
45ml/3 tbsp olive oil
2 onions, finely chopped
2–3 garlic cloves, finely chopped
30ml/2 tbsp pine nuts
5ml/1 tsp ground allspice
5ml/1 tsp ground cinnamon
10–15ml/2–3 tsp sugar
225g/8oz/generous 1 cup short grain rice, well rinsed and drained
1 small bunch each of fresh parsley, mint and dill, leaves finely chopped
150ml/¼ pint/⅔ cup olive oil
150ml/¼ pint/⅔ cup water
juice of 1 lemon
salt and ground black pepper
2 lemons, thickly sliced, to serve

**1** Prepare the vine leaves (*see* Cook's Tip) and drain thoroughly. Stack them on a plate, cover with a clean dish towel to keep them moist, and set aside.

**2** Heat the oil in a heavy pan and stir in the onions and garlic. Cook until they begin to colour. Stir in the pine nuts, spices and 10ml/2 tsp sugar. Cook, stirring, for 1 minute.

**3** Add the rice, mix well, and season with salt and pepper.

**4** Pour in enough water (about 450ml/¾ pint/scant 2 cups) to just cover the rice and bring it to the boil. Reduce the heat and simmer for 10 minutes, or until all the water has been absorbed. The rice should have a bite to it. Toss in the herbs and leave the rice to cool.

**5** Place a vine leaf on a board and put a heaped teaspoon of rice at the base. Fold the stem edge over the filling, then bring both of the side edges in towards the middle of the leaf, so that the filling is sealed in. Now roll the leaf up like a small, fat cigar. Place in the palm of your hand and squeeze it lightly. Repeat with the remaining leaves and rice.

**6** In a small bowl, mix together the olive oil, water, lemon juice and remaining sugar. Line the base of a shallow pan with the extra vine leaves, then place the stuffed vine leaves on top, tightly packed side by side.

**7** Pour the olive oil mixture over the stuffed vine leaves and place a plate on top of them to prevent them from unravelling during cooking.

**8** Cover the pan and simmer gently for about 1 hour, topping up the cooking liquid if necessary. Leave the stuffed vine leaves to cool in the pan, then lift them out and arrange on a plate with slices of lemon to squeeze over them.

### COOK'S TIPS
• **Fresh leaves** Bring a pan of water to the boil and plunge the fresh leaves into it for 1–2 minutes. Drain and refresh under cold running water, then drain thoroughly. Trim off the stems, and keep covered in the refrigerator for 2–3 days.
• **Preserved leaves** Place the preserved leaves in a bowl and cover with boiling water. Soak for 15–20 minutes, using a fork to separate the leaves. Drain and return to the bowl with cold water. Soak for 2–3 minutes, then drain thoroughly.

**Per portion** Energy 411kcal/1702kJ; Protein 5g; Carbohydrate 39g, of which sugars 7.5g; Fat 26.1g, of which saturates 3.4g; Cholesterol 0mg; Calcium 58mg; Fibre 2.2g; Sodium 7mg.

# TOMATO, PEPPER AND CHILLI SALAD

*THE TURKISH WORD TAZE MEANS FRESH, WHICH IS EXACTLY WHAT THIS MEZE DISH IS — A MIXTURE OF CHOPPED FRESH VEGETABLES. ALONG WITH CUBES OF HONEY-SWEET MELON AND FETA, OR PLUMP, JUICY OLIVES SPIKED WITH RED PEPPER AND OREGANO, THIS IS MEZE AT ITS SIMPLEST AND BEST. POPULAR IN KEBAB HOUSES, TAZE EZMESI MAKES A TASTY SNACK OR APPETIZER, AND IS GOOD SERVED WITH CHUNKS OF WARM, CRUSTY BREAD OR TOASTED PITTA.*

### SERVES FOUR

INGREDIENTS

2 large tomatoes, skinned, seeded and finely chopped

2 Turkish green peppers or 1 green (bell) pepper, seeded and finely chopped

1 onion, finely chopped

1 green chilli, seeded and finely chopped

1 small bunch of fresh flat leaf parsley, finely chopped

a few fresh mint leaves, finely chopped

15–30ml/1–2 tbsp olive oil

salt and ground black pepper

pitta bread, toasted, to serve

**1** Put the finely chopped tomatoes, peppers, onion, green chilli, flat leaf parsley and mint in a medium bowl and mix well together.

**2** Bind the mixture with oil and season with salt and pepper.

**3** To toast the pitta bread, first split it in half using a sharp knife, then place on a hot griddle for 1–2 minutes, turn, and toast for a further 1 minute.

**4** Serve the salad at room temperature with the toasted pitta.

**VARIATION**

To turn this salad into a paste, add 15–30ml/1–2 tbsp tomato purée (paste) with a little extra chilli and 5–10ml/ 1–2 tsp sugar when you bind the chopped vegetables with the olive oil. The mixture will become a tangy paste to spread on fresh, crusty bread or toasted pitta, and it can also be used as a sauce for grilled, broiled or barbecued meats.

**Per portion** Energy 101kcal/420kJ; Protein 2.3g; Carbohydrate 9.3g, of which sugars 8g; Fat 6.3g, of which saturates 0.9g; Cholesterol 0mg; Calcium 66mg; Fibre 2.7g; Sodium 15mg.

# BULGUR SALAD

*COMBINING BULGUR WHEAT, CHOPPED VEGETABLES AND FRESH MINT AND PARSLEY, KISIR IS BOTH SUSTAINING AND REFRESHING. IT TASTES FABULOUS SERVED AT ROOM TEMPERATURE AS PART OF A BUFFET OR BARBECUE SPREAD, WITH LEMON WEDGES FOR SQUEEZING OVER IT. IN SOME TURKISH HOUSEHOLDS, IT IS OFFERED TO GUESTS BEFORE TEA IS SERVED. ON THESE OCCASIONS, THE KISIR IS SPOONED ON TO VINE LEAVES AND IS ACCOMPANIED BY SLICES OF TOMATO AND SOME PICKLES.*

### SERVES FOUR TO SIX

INGREDIENTS

175g/6oz/1 cup bulgur wheat, rinsed and drained
45–60ml/3–4 tbsp olive oil
juice of 1–2 lemons
30ml/2 tbsp tomato purée (paste)
10ml/2 tsp sugar
1 large or 2 small red onions, cut in half lengthways, in half again crossways, and sliced along the grain
10ml/2 tsp *kırmızı biber*, or 1–2 fresh red chillies, seeded and finely chopped
1 bunch each of fresh mint and flat leaf parsley, finely chopped
salt and ground black pepper
a few fresh mint and parsley leaves, to garnish

**1** Put the bulgur wheat into a wide bowl, pour over enough boiling water to cover it by about 2.5cm/1in, and give it a quick stir. Cover the bowl with a plate or a pan lid and leave the bulgur wheat to steam for about 25 minutes, until it has soaked up the water and doubled in quantity.

**VARIATION**
In the south-east of Turkey, where the juice of sour pomegranates is often used instead of lemons and hot red pepper is added liberally to food, a fiery *kısır* is moulded into small balls and served in lettuce-leaf wrappings.

**2** Pour the olive oil and squeeze the lemon juice over the bulgur and toss to mix.

**3** Add the tomato purée and toss the mixture again until everything is combined and the bulgur is well coated.

**4** Add the sugar, onion, *kırmızı biber* or chillies, and the chopped fresh herbs. Season with salt and pepper and mix well to combine.

**5** Serve at room temperature, garnished with a little mint and parsley.

**Per portion** Energy 149kcal/620kJ; Protein 3g; Carbohydrate 21.6g, of which sugars 5.4g; Fat 6.1g, of which saturates 0.8g; Cholesterol 0mg; Calcium 54mg; Fibre 1.7g; Sodium 19mg.

# FRIED AUBERGINE, COURGETTE AND PEPPER WITH YOGURT AND POMEGRANATE

*THIS VERY SIMPLE, TASTY DISH, CALLED ŞAKŞUKA, SEEMS TO CAUSE A CERTAIN AMOUNT OF DEBATE IN TURKEY, AS IT VARIES HUGELY ACROSS THE COUNTRY. HOWEVER, THE ONE COMMON DENOMINATOR IS THAT ALL VERSIONS INCLUDE COOKED VEGETABLES SERVED WITH YOGURT. THIS COLOURFUL VERSION IS FROM THE MEDITERRANEAN REGION AND IS DELICIOUS SERVED ON ITS OWN WITH BREAD.*

### SERVES FOUR

INGREDIENTS
    1 large aubergine (eggplant)
    1 courgette (zucchini)
    1 red (bell) pepper
    sunflower oil, for deep-frying
    4 Turkish çarliston peppers,
      kept whole with stalk
    200ml/7fl oz/scant 1 cup thick
      and creamy natural (plain) yogurt
    2–3 garlic cloves, crushed
    30–45ml/2–3 tbsp pomegranate
      seeds
    salt and ground black pepper

**1** Using a vegetable peeler, partially peel the aubergine in stripes.

**2** Cut the aubergine in half lengthways and then cut each half into thick slices. Drop the slices into a bowl of salted water to prevent them discolouring. Drain and squeeze them dry before frying, otherwise the excess water will cause the hot oil to spatter everywhere.

**3** Cut the courgette in half lengthways and then cut it widthways into thick slices. Deseed the pepper and cut it into bitesize pieces.

**4** Heat enough oil for deep-frying in a wide pan. Fry the vegetables in batches, until they are golden brown. Lift them out of the oil with tongs or a slotted spoon and drain on kitchen paper.

**5** In a bowl, beat the yogurt with the garlic, and season to taste with salt and pepper. Pile the hot vegetables on to a serving dish and spoon the yogurt over the top, reserving 15–30ml/1–2 tbsp in the base of the bowl.

**6** Fold half the pomegranate seeds into the remaining yogurt and spoon the mixture over the top of the prepared dish. Garnish with the remainder of the pomegranate seeds.

**7** Serve immediately, while the vegetables are still warm, to contrast with the cool yogurt. Accompany with chunks of fresh, crusty bread to scoop and mop up the tasty sauce.

### COOK'S TIPS
• A fruit from antiquity, the pomegranate has symbolized beauty, fertility and prosperity and, according to the medieval Islamic mystics, it purged the soul of anger and envy. Cultivated in the Middle East, it has long been used in the cooking of this region, and is also thought by some to have magical properties. The ruby-red grains of sweet pomegranates are eaten fresh, whereas the sour fruits are used in soups, marinades, dressings and syrups, and to make a cooling sherbet drink.
• To extract the seeds from a pomegranate, cut the fruit into quarters and invert each quarter by pushing the skin with your thumbs. Some seeds will fall out; the rest you will have to pick out individually.

**Per portion** Energy 225kcal/933kJ; Protein 6.5g; Carbohydrate 13.3g, of which sugars 11.6g; Fat 17.1g, of which saturates 4.2g; Cholesterol 0mg; Calcium 104mg; Fibre 4g; Sodium 43mg.

# WARM AUBERGINE SALAD <u>WITH</u> PEPPER <u>AND</u> TOMATOES

*IN TURKEY, AUBERGINES ARE OFTEN GRILLED OR BAKED TO BE USED IN A VARIETY OF MEZE DISHES, INCLUDING THIS SALAD. ALTHOUGH PATLICAN SALATASI CAN VARY, THE RESULT IS ALWAYS FRESH-TASTING. IT IS BEST SERVED WHILE THE FLESH IS STILL WARM, BUT IT CAN ALSO BE MADE IN ADVANCE AND SERVED AT ROOM TEMPERATURE. SERVE ON ITS OWN WITH BREAD OR AS PART OF A MEZE SPREAD.*

**2** Smoke the aubergines and the red pepper directly over the gas flame, over hot charcoal or under the grill (broiler).

**3** When the skin of the pepper has buckled and browned, plunge it immediately under cold running water and peel off the skin. Remove the stalk and seeds, chop the softened flesh, and set aside.

**4** When the aubergines are soft, place them on a board and slit them open. Scoop out the warm flesh, taking care to leave the skin behind (this is easier if the aubergines have been grilled over charcoal as the skin toughens up).

SERVES FOUR TO SIX

INGREDIENTS
  2 tomatoes
  2 large aubergines (eggplants),
    or 4 small thin ones
  1 red (bell) pepper
  4–6 spring onions (scallions),
    trimmed and finely chopped
  2 hot green peppers, or 1 green
    chilli, seeded and finely sliced
  1 good-sized bunch flat leaf parsley,
    leaves chopped
  1 small bunch dill fronds, chopped
  45–60ml/3–4 tbsp olive oil
  juice of 1–2 lemons
  2–4 garlic cloves, crushed
  salt and ground black pepper

**1** Plunge the tomatoes into boiling water for 30 seconds, then refresh in cold water. Peel away the skins. Remove the seeds and chop the flesh.

**5** Place the flesh in a wide bowl (some cooks like to chop it; others keep it in clumps). Add the pepper, spring onions, tomatoes, hot green pepper, parsley and dill. Add the olive oil, lemon juice and garlic, and toss well. Season to taste, and serve while still deliciously warm, with fresh crusty bread to scoop it up.

**Per portion** Energy 102kcal/424kJ; Protein 3.2g; Carbohydrate 8.2g, of which sugars 7.5g; Fat 6.5g, of which saturates 1g; Cholesterol 0mg; Calcium 59mg; Fibre 4g; Sodium 14mg.

# STIR-FRIED SPINACH WITH CURRANTS, PINE NUTS AND YOGURT

*THERE ARE ENDLESS VERSIONS OF TRADITIONAL SPINACH AND YOGURT MEZE DISHES, RANGING FROM PLAIN STEAMED SPINACH SERVED WITH YOGURT, TO THIS SWEET AND TANGY ANATOLIAN CREATION, WHICH IS TAMED WITH GARLIC-FLAVOURED YOGURT. SERVE THIS DISH WHILE IT IS STILL WARM, WITH WARM FLAT BREAD OR CHUNKS OF A CRUSTY LOAF TO ACCOMPANY IT.*

### SERVES THREE TO FOUR

INGREDIENTS
- 350g/12oz fresh spinach leaves, thoroughly washed and drained
- about 200g/7oz/scant 1 cup thick and creamy natural (plain) yogurt
- 2 garlic cloves, crushed
- 30–45ml/2–3 tbsp olive oil
- 1 red onion, cut in half lengthways, in half again crossways, and sliced along the grain
- 5ml/1 tsp sugar
- 15–30ml/1–2 tbsp currants, soaked in warm water for 5–10 minutes and drained
- 30ml/2 tbsp pine nuts
- 5–10ml/1–2 tsp *kırmızı biber*, or 1 fresh red chilli, seeded and finely chopped
- juice of 1 lemon
- salt and ground black pepper
- a pinch of paprika, to garnish

**1** Steam the spinach for 3–4 minutes, until wilted and soft. Drain off any excess water and chop the spinach.

**2** In a bowl, beat the yogurt with the garlic. Season and set aside.

**VARIATION**
To make a simple spinach and yogurt dish, steam the spinach until soft, then chop it to a pulp. Mix the yogurt with a finely chopped clove of garlic and beat in the spinach. Season and serve.

**3** Heat the olive oil in a heavy pan and gently fry the onion and sugar, stirring, until the onion begins to colour. Add the currants, pine nuts and *kırmızı biber* or chilli and fry until the nuts just begin to colour.

**4** Add the spinach, tossing it around the pan until everything is well mixed, then pour in the lemon juice and season with salt and pepper.

**5** Serve the spinach straight from the pan with the yogurt spooned on top, or tip into a serving dish and make a well in the middle, then spoon the yogurt into the well, drizzling some of it over the spinach. Serve hot, sprinkled with a little paprika.

Per portion Energy 145kcal/603kJ; Protein 5.8g; Carbohydrate 10.2g, of which sugars 9.8g; Fat 9.3g, of which saturates 1.3g; Cholesterol 1mg; Calcium 252mg; Fibre 2.2g; Sodium 165mg.

# BEAN SALAD

*Salads made with haricot, soya, borlotti or black-eyed beans are popular as meze dishes, or as accompaniments to grilled, broiled or barbecued meats. Often, the salads are simply made from beans, onions and flat leaf parsley tossed in olive oil. Others, such as this, are more elaborate, and make a tasty, healthy, and delicious lunch dish.*

### SERVES FOUR

INGREDIENTS

225g/8oz/1¼ cups dried haricot
   (navy), soya or black-eyed beans
   (peas), soaked in cold water for at
   least 6 hours or overnight
1 red onion, cut in half lengthways,
   in half again crossways, and sliced
   along the grain
45–60ml/3–4 tbsp black olives,
   drained
1 bunch of fresh flat leaf parsley,
   roughly chopped
60ml/4 tbsp olive oil
juice of 1 lemon
3–4 eggs, boiled until just firm,
   shelled and quartered
12 canned or bottled anchovy fillets,
   rinsed and drained
salt and ground black pepper
lemon wedges, to serve

**1** Drain the beans, transfer them to a pan and fill the pan with plenty of cold water. Bring the water to the boil and boil the beans for 1 minute, then lower the heat and partially cover the pan. Simmer for about 45 minutes, until the beans are cooked but still firm – they should have a bite to them, and not be soft and mushy.

**2** Drain the beans, rinse well under cold running water and remove any skins.

**3** Mix the beans in a wide, shallow bowl with the onion, olives and most of the parsley. Toss in the oil and lemon juice, and season with salt and pepper.

**4** Place the eggs and anchovy fillets on top of the salad and add the remaining parsley. Serve with lemon wedges.

**Per portion** Energy 402kcal/1674kJ; Protein 28g; Carbohydrate 10.4g, of which sugars 4.2g; Fat 28g, of which saturates 4.4g; Cholesterol 149mg; Calcium 221mg; Fibre 10g; Sodium 696mg.

# ORANGE AND ONION SALAD WITH OLIVES

*THIS REFRESHING SALAD, CALLED* PORTAKAL SALATASI, *IS POPULAR IN THE SOUTH OF TURKEY, NEAR THE SYRIAN BORDER, WHERE THE REGIONAL* GÜNEY *CUISINE IS PARTICULARLY FIERY. FROM MERSIN AND ADANA TO ANTAKYA AND GAZIANTEP, THERE ARE VARIATIONS OF THIS SALAD, SOME OF WHICH INCLUDE CHILLIES. SERVE WITH SPICY STEWS AND KEBABS.*

SERVES FOUR

INGREDIENTS
   3 sweet, juicy oranges
   1 red onion, finely sliced in rings
   10–12 plump black olives,
      such as Kalamata
   5ml/1 tsp cumin seeds, crushed
   5ml/1 tsp ground sumac
   5ml/1 tsp dried thyme
   30–45ml/2–3 tbsp olive oil
   salt
   1 small bunch fresh mint leaves,
      torn or roughly chopped, to garnish

**VARIATIONS**
• Occasionally, finely sliced beetroot (beet) is added to this salad, which lends a pinkish-purple hue to the orange slices.
• Use pink grapefruit instead of orange.

**1** Place each orange on a board and, using a small, sharp knife, carefully cut away the peel and pith, making sure that no pith remains.

**2** Thinly slice the orange into rings and then either keep the rings whole or cut them into half-moon shapes. Do the same with the onion rings.

**3** Arrange the oranges and onions in a shallow bowl or a serving dish and add the olives. Sprinkle the cumin, sumac and thyme over the sliced oranges and onions and pour over the oil.

**4** Toss the salad gently, season with salt to taste, and sprinkle the mint leaves over the top to garnish.

**Per portion** Energy 150kcal/629kJ; Protein 3g; Carbohydrate 18.9g, of which sugars 16.4g; Fat 7.6g, of which saturates 1.1g; Cholesterol 0mg; Calcium 102mg; Fibre 3.8g; Sodium 292mg.

# SALAD OF FETA, CHILLIES AND PARSLEY

*THERE ARE TWO COMMON SALADS EATEN AS MEZE, OR SERVED AS ACCOMPANIMENTS TO MEAT AND FISH DISHES. ONE, KNOWN AS ÇOBAN SALATASI, OR "SHEPHERD'S SALAD", IS MADE OF CHOPPED CUCUMBER, TOMATOES, PEPPERS, ONION AND FLAT LEAF PARSLEY; THE OTHER IS THIS GYPSY SALAD, ÇINGENE PILAVI, MEANING "GYPSY RICE". THE MIX IS SIMILAR TO SHEPHERD'S SALAD, ONLY A CHILLI IS INCLUDED TO GIVE A FIERY KICK, AND CRUMBLED FETA IS ADDED TO REPRESENT THE RICE.*

SERVES THREE TO FOUR

INGREDIENTS
    2 red onions, cut in half lengthways
      and finely sliced along the grain
    1 green (bell) pepper, seeded
      and finely sliced
    1 fresh green chilli, seeded
      and chopped
    2–3 garlic cloves, chopped
    1 bunch of fresh flat leaf parsley,
      roughly chopped
    225g/8oz firm feta cheese,
      rinsed and grated
    2 large tomatoes, skinned,
      seeded and finely chopped
    30–45ml/2–3 tbsp olive oil
    salt and ground black pepper
To serve
    scant 5ml/1 tsp *kırmızı biber*,
      or paprika
    scant 5ml/1 tsp ground sumac

**1** Place the sliced red onions in a small bowl and sprinkle with a little salt. Leave for 10 minutes to draw out the onion juices, then transfer the onions to a sieve (strainer) and rinse under cold running water. Pat the onions dry with kitchen paper.

**VARIATION**
Omit the green chilli if you do not like spicy food.

**2** Mix the onions and green pepper in a bowl with the chilli, garlic, parsley, feta and tomatoes.

**3** Add the olive oil and salt and pepper to taste and toss well to combine everything thoroughly.

**4** Transfer the salad to a large serving dish and sprinkle with the *kırmızı biber* or paprika and sumac.

**Per portion** Energy 253kcal/1049kJ; Protein 11.1g; Carbohydrate 13.4g, of which sugars 11g; Fat 17.6g, of which saturates 8.6g; Cholesterol 39mg; Calcium 260mg; Fibre 3.2g; Sodium 824mg.

# MELON AND CHEESE SALAD WITH *PASTIRMA*

*ONE OF THE MOST TRADITIONAL MEZE DISHES IS A PLATE OF SWEET MELON CUT INTO CUBES, WHICH IS OFTEN COMBINED WITH CUBES OF WHITE CHEESE (BEYAZ PEYNIR) TO MAKE A VERY REFRESHING SNACK OR NIBBLE. A MODERN VERSION, CALLED KAVUN VE PEYNIR SALATASI, INCLUDES FINE STRIPS OF CURED BEEF, PASTIRMA, AND HERBS. DELICIOUS AS A FIRST COURSE, AN ACCOMPANIMENT TO GRILLED FOOD, OR AS PART OF A BUFFET SPREAD, THIS SIMPLE SALAD IS A DELIGHT TO THE SENSES.*

SERVES FOUR TO SIX

INGREDIENTS

   1 ripe juicy melon, such as Galia
     or honeydew
   200g/7oz *beyaz peynir*, or plain feta
     cheese, cut into bitesize cubes
   115g/4oz *pastırma*, very finely sliced
     with the coating *(çemen)* removed,
     and cut into thin strips
   1 small bunch fresh green or purple
     basil leaves
   30ml/2 tbsp olive oil
   juice of 1 lemon

**1** Cut the melon in half and scoop out the seeds with a spoon. Cut each half in half again and, using a sharp knife, remove the flesh from the skin and cut it into bitesize cubes.

**2** Put the melon and feta cubes into a shallow bowl, or in serving dish, and add the strips of *pastırma* and most of the basil leaves. Add the olive oil and lemon juice, and toss the salad gently.

**3** Garnish with the remaining basil and serve on its own, or with grilled (broiled) food or other *meze* dishes.

**COOK'S TIP**
Don't dress the salad too far in advance as the melon will emit a lot of juice and the basil leaves will wilt.

**Per portion** Energy 172kcal/716kJ; Protein 10.2g; Carbohydrate 5.4g, of which sugars 5.3g; Fat 12.4g, of which saturates 5.8g; Cholesterol 34mg; Calcium 145mg; Fibre 0.7g; Sodium 520mg.

# LAMB'S LETTUCE SALAD

*THE LAMB'S LETTUCE IN TURKEY IS A SLIGHTLY THICKER VERSION OF THE PLANT THAN IS GENERALLY AVAILABLE ELSEWHERE. USUALLY, THE FRESH LEAVES ARE PICKED FOR THIS SUMMER SALAD, CALLED SEMIZ OTU SALATASI, WHICH IS SERVED AS PART OF A MEZE SPREAD, OR THEY ARE COOKED WITH MINCED MEAT AS PART OF A MORE SUBSTANTIAL DISH. EXTREMELY QUICK AND EASY, THIS SIMPLE SALAD IS ALSO DELICIOUS WITH GRILLED AND ROASTED MEATS AND POULTRY.*

**COOK'S TIP**
There is no rule regarding the ratio of yogurt to lamb's lettuce, as some households enjoy this salad packed with leaves, whereas others like it with double the amount of yogurt. Experiment with different ratios and make it according to your personal preference. If you do not like garlic, you could use just ¼ clove or omit it altogether.

SERVES FOUR

INGREDIENTS
about 500g/1¼lb thick and creamy
   natural (plain) yogurt
juice of 1 lemon
1–2 garlic cloves, crushed
225g/8oz fresh lamb's lettuce,
   well rinsed and drained
salt and ground black pepper

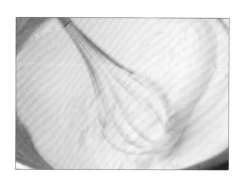

**1** In a wide bowl, beat the yogurt with the lemon juice and garlic. Season to taste with salt and pepper.

**2** Toss the lamb's lettuce into the dressing, making sure it is thoroughly coated with the yogurt.

**3** Transfer the salad to a serving bowl and serve immediately while the leaves are still fresh as a *meze* dish or as a salad with savoury pastries, or with grilled (broiled) and roasted meats.

**Per portion** Energy 78kcal/328kJ; Protein 6.8g; Carbohydrate 10.3g, of which sugars 10.3g; Fat 1.5g, of which saturates 0.7g; Cholesterol 2mg; Calcium 253mg; Fibre 0.5g; Sodium 106mg.

# CUCUMBER AND MINT SALAD

*REFRESHING AND VERSATILE, CACIK CAN BE SERVED AS A SALAD OR AS AN ACCOMPANIMENT. SOME FASHIONABLE RESTAURANTS IN ISTANBUL ALSO SERVE IT AS A COLD SOUP WITH CUBES OF ICE IN IT, TO BE EATEN THROUGHOUT THE MEAL. FOR THE SALAD, THE YOGURT IS KEPT THICK, WHEREAS IF SERVED AS A SOUP IT NEEDS TO BE DILUTED WITH WATER. IT CAN BE FLAVOURED WITH FRESH OR DRIED MINT, OR WITH FRESH DILL, AND THE SALAD IS OFTEN SERVED WITH OLIVE OIL ON THE TOP.*

SERVES FOUR

INGREDIENTS

1 large cucumber or 2 small ones
500g/1¼lb thick and creamy
  natural (plain) yogurt
2 garlic cloves, crushed
1 bunch fresh mint, leaves chopped
olive oil, for drizzling
salt and ground black pepper

**1** Using a vegetable peeler, partially peel the cucumber skin in stripes. Cut the cucumber in half lengthways and slice it finely.

**2** Place the slices in a colander and sprinkle with salt. Leave to weep for 5–10 minutes. Rinse the sliced cucumber and drain well.

**COOK'S TIP**
In kebab houses, *cakic* is often served as a cooling accompaniment to spicy kebabs. As a *meze* dish, you can slice, dice or grate the cucumber, depending on your personal preference.

**3** In a wide bowl, beat the yogurt with the garlic and most of the mint. Add the sliced cucumber and season to taste.

**4** Transfer to a serving bowl, drizzle a little olive oil over the top and garnish with the remaining chopped mint.

**5** Serve with chunks of fresh bread and other *meze* dishes.

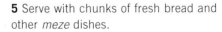

**Per portion** Energy 83kcal/348kJ; Protein 7.4g; Carbohydrate 11.2g, of which sugars 10.1g; Fat 1.4g, of which saturates 0.6g; Cholesterol 2mg; Calcium 273mg; Fibre 0.4g; Sodium 107mg.

# CELERY AND COCONUT SALAD WITH LIME

*THIS SALAD IS UNUSUAL FOR TURKEY IN ITS USE OF GRATED COCONUT, WHICH IS MAINLY RESERVED AS A GARNISH FOR SWEET DISHES, OR SERVED WITH SHELLED POMEGRANATE SEEDS AS A MEDIEVAL MEZE. JUICY AND REFRESHING, THIS SALAD IS WELCOME ON A HOT SUNNY DAY AS PART OF A BUFFET SPREAD OUTDOORS, OR AS AN ACCOMPANIMENT TO GRILLED, BROILED OR BARBECUED MEATS AND SPICY DISHES. IT LOOKS ESPECIALLY APPEALING SERVED IN COCONUT SHELL HALVES.*

SERVES THREE TO FOUR

INGREDIENTS

45–60ml/3–4 tbsp thick and creamy
   natural (plain) yogurt
2 garlic cloves, crushed
5ml/1 tsp grated lime zest
juice of 1 lime
8 long celery sticks, grated (leaves
   reserved for the garnish)
flesh of ½ fresh coconut, grated
salt and ground black pepper
a few sprigs of fresh flat leaf parsley,
   to garnish

**1** Mix the yogurt and garlic in a bowl, add the lime rind and juice and season with salt and pepper.

**2** Fold in the celery and coconut. Set aside for 20 minutes, then spoon into a bowl and garnish with celery and parsley.

**Per portion** Energy 126kcal/521kJ; Protein 2.1g; Carbohydrate 2.9g, of which sugars 2.9g; Fat 11.9g, of which saturates 10.1g; Cholesterol 0mg; Calcium 63mg; Fibre 3.6g; Sodium 69mg.

# GRATED BEETROOT AND YOGURT SALAD

*WITH ITS BENEFICIAL NUTRITIONAL PROPERTIES, YOGURT IS USED FREQUENTLY IN MEZE DISHES.*
*IT IS EVEN SERVED ON ITS OWN, DRIZZLED WITH A LITTLE HONEY, OR SPRINKLED WITH ICING SUGAR.*
*THE MOST FAMOUS OF THE YOGURT DIPS IS SMOKED AUBERGINE AND YOGURT PURÉE, BUT THERE ARE*
*A FEW OTHER GEMS THAT GET LITTLE MENTION, SUCH AS THIS ONE MADE WITH GRATED BEETROOT.*
*SPIKED WITH GARLIC AND A PRETTY SHADE OF PINK, IT IS DELICIOUS SCOOPED ON TO FLAT BREAD.*

SERVES FOUR

INGREDIENTS
   4 raw beetroot (beets), washed
     and trimmed
   500g/1¼lb/2¼ cups thick and
     creamy natural (plain) yogurt
   2 garlic cloves, crushed
   salt and ground black pepper
   a few fresh mint leaves, shredded,
     to garnish

**1** Boil the beetroot in plenty of water for
35–40 minutes until tender, but not soft
or mushy. Drain and refresh under cold
running water,

**VARIATIONS**
• To make a carrot version of this salad,
cut four carrots into chunks and steam
them for about 15 minutes, until they
are tender but still retain some bite.
Leave the carrot chunks until they are
cool enough to handle, then grate and
mix with the yogurt and garlic. Season to
taste with salt and pepper and garnish
with mint or dill.
• In some households, the beetroot
(beet) is diced and stir-fried with
coriander seeds, sugar and a splash of
apple vinegar. Then it is served warm
with the cooling garlic-flavoured yogurt
and garnished with dill.

**2** Peel off the skins and grate the
beetroot on to a plate. Squeeze it with
your fingers to drain off excess water.

**3** In a bowl, beat the yogurt with the
garlic and season with salt and pepper.

**4** Add the beetroot, reserving a little to
garnish the top, and mix well. Garnish
with mint leaves.

**Per portion** Energy 95kcal/403kJ; Protein 7.8g; Carbohydrate 14.4g, of which sugars 13g; Fat 1.4g, of which saturates 0.6g; Cholesterol 2mg; Calcium 249mg; Fibre 1.3g; Sodium 137mg.

# SOUPS AND HOT SNACKS

In every village, town and city, soup stalls and soup houses do brisk business, serving at all hours of the day. In rural Anatolia dishes such as Meadow Yogurt Soup with Rice and Mint are often eaten for breakfast, whereas in Istanbul late-night revellers head to the nearest işkembici, to tuck into Classic Tripe Soup. When not snacking on one of their favourite soups, Turks may well be eating a hot snack, such as Deep-fried Mussels in Beer Batter or Flatbreads with Spicy Lamb and Tomato.

# POMEGRANATE BROTH

*WITH ITS ORIGINS IN PERSIA AND AZERBAIJAN, THIS FRESH-TASTING, DELICATE BROTH, NARLI ÇORBA, IS PERHAPS THE BEST WAY OF APPRECIATING THE COLOUR AND FLAVOUR OF SOUR POMEGRANATES, AS IT IS PLEASING TO BOTH THE EYE AND THE TASTE BUDS. CLEAR AND REFRESHING, IT IS USUALLY SERVED AS A SOPHISTICATED PALATE CLEANSER BETWEEN COURSES, OR AS A LIGHT APPETIZER AT THE START OF A MEAL. SOUR POMEGRANATES ARE OFTEN AVAILABLE IN MIDDLE EASTERN STORES, BUT IF YOU CAN ONLY FIND SWEET POMEGRANATES, USE THEM IN THE SAME WAY, BUT STIR IN THE JUICE OF ONE LEMON TO ADD THE DESIRED ACIDITY AND TARTNESS.*

## SERVES FOUR

### INGREDIENTS
    5–6 sour or sweet pomegrantes
    1.2 litres/2 pints/5 cups clear
      chicken stock
    juice of 1 lemon, if using
      sweet pomegranates
    seeds of 1 sweet pomegranate
    salt and ground black pepper
    fresh mint leaves, to garnish

### COOK'S TIP
Do not use any metal other than stainless steel for squeezing or it will cause the juice to discolour and taste unpleasant.

**1** For 150ml/¼ pint/⅔ cup juice, you will need 5–6 sour pomegranates. Cut the pomegranates in half and extract the juice with a stainless-steel, glass or wooden lemon squeezer.

**2** Pour the stock into a pan and bring to the boil. Lower the heat, stir in the pomegranate juice, and lemon juice if using sweet pomegranates, then bring the stock back to the boil.

**3** Lower the heat again and stir in half the pomegranate seeds, then season and turn off the heat.

**4** Ladle into wamed bowls. Sprinkle the remaining pomegranate seeds over the top and garnish with mint leaves.

**Per portion** Energy 62kcal/260kJ; Protein 2g; Carbohydrate 3.9g, of which sugars 2.3g; Fat 4.4g, of which saturates 0.4g; Cholesterol 0mg; Calcium 14mg; Fibre 0.6g; Sodium 205mg.

# FISH BROTH WITH CELERIAC

*WITH SUCH AN EXTENSIVE COASTLINE, THERE IS A WIDE CHOICE OF FISH AVAILABLE IN TURKEY FOR MAKING THIS CLASSIC FISH SOUP — BALIK ÇORBASI — RANGING FROM SEA BASS, BLUE FISH, SCORPION FISH, MACKEREL, BONITO, TURBOT AND RED MULLET. ALONG THE BLACK SEA, THE LOCAL SOUP INVARIABLY INCLUDES SOME SALTY ANCHOVIES; IN CENTRAL ANATOLIA THE FRESHWATER FISH, SUCH AS CARP, ARE OCCASIONALLY USED IN THE SOUP, ALTHOUGH IN PARTS OF EASTERN ANATOLIA FISH SOUP IS UNHEARD OF. HOWEVER, WHATEVER THE VARIETY OF FISH AVAILABLE FOR USE, THE METHOD OF MAKING THE SOUP VARIES LITTLE FROM REGION TO REGION.*

SERVES FOUR TO SIX

INGREDIENTS

500g/1¼lb fresh fish, such as trout,
   cod or sea bass
250g/9oz prawns (shrimp)
2 onions, quartered with their
   skins on
4–6 peppercorns
1 whole celeriac
2 potatoes, peeled and diced
2 carrots, peeled and diced
1 small bunch celery leaves,
   coarsely chopped
1 small bunch flat leaf parsley,
   leaves coarsely chopped
2 garlic cloves, crushed
15ml/1 tbsp vinegar
salt and ground black pepper
1 lemon, cut into wedges, to serve

**1** First prepare the stock. Skin and fillet the fish and shell the prawns. Cut the fillets into bitesize pieces and set them aside with the prawns.

**2** Put the fish head and bones with the prawn shells into a large, heavy pan. Add the onions and peppercorns and about 2.5 litres/4 pints/10¼ cups water.

**3** Bring the water to the boil, reduce the heat and simmer for 25–30 minutes, skimming the top to remove any scum. Strain the stock into another pan.

**4** Peel and dice the celeriac, and cover with water until ready to use. Bring the stock to the boil and stir in the diced vegetables. Reduce the heat and simmer for about 15 minutes, or until the vegetables are tender.

**5** Stir in the celery leaves and parsley, and add the fish fillets and prawns. Simmer for about 5 minutes or until the fish and prawns are cooked.

**6** Season with salt and pepper to taste, and stir in the garlic and vinegar to sharpen the flavours.

**7** Ladle the broth into heated serving bowls and serve with wedges of lemon to squeeze into it to give both sweet and sour notes in every mouthful.

**Per portion** Energy 169kcal/712kJ; Protein 24.9g; Carbohydrate 14.9g, of which sugars 7.1g; Fat 1.5g, of which saturates 0.2g; Cholesterol 120mg; Calcium 117mg; Fibre 3.3g; Sodium 195mg.

# MEADOW YOGURT SOUP WITH RICE AND MINT

*IN EVERY SOUP HOUSE, BUS STATION AND ROADSIDE CAFÉ THROUGHOUT TURKEY, YOU WILL COME ACROSS YOGURT SOUP. BASED ON WELL-FLAVOURED STOCK AND YOGURT, IT USUALLY CONTAINS A LITTLE RICE, BULGUR, CHICKPEAS OR BARLEY, DEPENDING ON WHICH REGION YOU ARE IN, AND OCCASIONALLY IT IS COLOURED WITH SAFFRON OR SPRINKLED WITH PAPRIKA. WHEN IT IS FLAVOURED WITH DRIED MINT, IT IS CALLED YAYLA ÇORBASI, OR MEADOW SOUP.*

**3** Stir in the rice and most of the mint, reserving a little for the garnish. Lower the heat, cover the pan and simmer for about 20 minutes, until the rice is cooked. Season with salt and pepper.

**4** Beat the yogurt until smooth, then spoon almost all of it into the soup. Keep the heat low and stir vigorously to make sure the yogurt remains smooth and creamy and becomes well blended.

**5** Ladle the soup into serving bowls, swirl in the remaining yogurt, and garnish with the remaining mint.

SERVES FOUR

INGREDIENTS
    15ml/1 tbsp butter or sunflower oil
    1 large onion, finely chopped
    scant 15ml/1 tbsp plain
      (all-purpose) flour
    1.2 litres/2 pints/5 cups lamb or
      chicken stock
    75g/3oz/scant ½ cup long grain rice
      (wild or plain), well rinsed
    15–30ml/1–2 tbsp dried mint
    400ml/14fl oz/1⅔ cups thick and
      creamy natural (plain) yogurt,
      strained (*see* Cook's Tip)
    salt and ground black pepper

**1** Melt the butter or oil in a heavy pan, add the onion and cook until soft.

**2** Take the pan off the heat and stir in the flour, then pour in the stock, stirring constantly. Return to the heat and bring the stock to the boil, stirring often.

**COOK'S TIP**
If you can't get strained yogurt you can make it yourself. Line a sieve (strainer) with a piece of muslin (cheesecloth) and spoon thick and creamy natural (plain) yogurt into it. Allow the excess liquid to drip through the muslin, then transfer the yogurt from the sieve to a bowl.

**Per portion** Energy 187kcal/781kJ; Protein 7.6g; Carbohydrate 30.3g, of which sugars 11.1g; Fat 4.4g, of which saturates 2.5g; Cholesterol 9mg; Calcium 215mg; Fibre 1g; Sodium 108mg.

# LEEK SOUP WITH FETA, DILL AND PAPRIKA

*CREAMY LEEK SOUP IS A POPULAR HOME-COOKED DISH IN TURKEY. FLAVOURED WITH DILL AND TOPPED WITH CRUMBLED WHITE CHEESE, THIS ONE IS WARMING AND SATISFYING. THE SALTINESS OF FETA IS GOOD IN THIS SOUP, BUT YOU COULD JUST AS WELL USE ROQUEFORT OR PARMESAN, BOTH OF WHICH ARE EQUALLY SALTY, AND YOU COULD SUBSTITUTE CROÛTONS FOR THE CHEESE. SERVE WITH CHUNKS OF FRESH, CRUSTY BREAD AS AN APPETIZER, OR AS A LIGHT MEAL ON ITS OWN.*

SERVES THREE TO FOUR

INGREDIENTS

    30ml/2 tbsp olive or sunflower oil
    3 leeks, trimmed, roughly chopped
      and washed
    1 onion, chopped
    5ml/1 tsp sugar
    1 bunch of fresh dill, chopped, with
      a few fronds reserved for the garnish
    300ml/½ pint/1¼ cups milk
    15ml/1 tbsp butter (optional)
    115g/4oz feta cheese, crumbled
    salt and ground black pepper
    paprika, to garnish

**1** Heat the oil in a heavy pan and stir in the chopped leeks and onion. Cook for about 10 minutes, or until the vegetables are soft.

**2** Add the sugar and chopped dill, and pour in 600ml/1 pint/2½ cups water. Bring to the boil, lower the heat and simmer for about 15 minutes. Leave the liquid to cool a little, then process in a blender until smooth.

**3** Return the puréed soup to the pan, pour in the milk and stir over a gentle heat until it is hot (don't let it come to the boil).

**4** Season with a little salt and plenty of freshly ground black pepper, bearing in mind that the feta is salty. If using the butter, drop it on to the surface of the soup and let it melt.

**5** Ladle the soup into bowls and top with the crumbled feta. Serve immediately, garnished with a little paprika and the dill fronds.

**Per portion** Energy 203kcal/844kJ; Protein 10g; Carbohydrate 10.9g, of which sugars 9.4g; Fat 13.5g, of which saturates 5.7g; Cholesterol 25mg; Calcium 259mg; Fibre 4.1g; Sodium 454mg.

# PUMPKIN SOUP <u>WITH</u> YOGURT

*THIS SIMPLE PURÉED SOUP — BAL KABAĞI ÇORBASI — IS A GREAT WINTER TREAT. PUMPKIN SELLERS SET UP THEIR STALLS IN THE STREETS AND DEFTLY PEEL AND SEED HUGE WEDGES OF PUMPKIN FOR PASSERS-BY, SO ALL THEY HAVE TO DO IS GO HOME AND POACH IT IN SYRUP FOR THE SWEET-SCENTED DESSERT, BAL KABAĞI TATLISI, OR TRANSFORM IT INTO THIS NOURISHING SOUP OF SWEET PUMPKIN FLESH AND TART, CREAMY YOGURT. TRADITIONALLY, A MELTED BUTTER IS DRIZZLED OVER THE TOP.*

SERVES THREE TO FOUR

INGREDIENTS
    1kg/2¼lb prepared pumpkin flesh,
      cut into cubes
    1 litre/1¾ pints/4 cups
      chicken stock
    10ml/2 tsp sugar
    25g/1oz/2 tbsp butter, or ghee
    60–75ml/4–5 tbsp thick and
      creamy natural (plain) yogurt
    salt and ground black pepper

**COOK'S TIP**
If pumpkins are not in season, you can use butternut squash instead.

**1** Put the pumpkin cubes into a pan with the stock, and bring the liquid to the boil. Reduce the heat, cover the pan, and simmer for about 20 minutes, or until the pumpkin is tender.

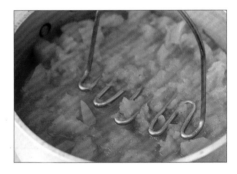

**2** Liquidize (blend) the soup in a blender, or use a potato masher to mash the flesh. Return the soup to the pan and bring it to the boil again.

**3** Add the sugar to the pan and season to taste with salt and pepper. Keep the pan over a low heat while you gently melt the butter or ghee in a small pan over a low heat.

**4** Pour the soup into a tureen, or ladle it into individual serving bowls. Swirl a little yogurt on to the surface of the soup and drizzle the melted butter over the top.

**5** Serve immediately, offering extra yogurt so that you can enjoy the contrasting burst of sweet and tart in each mouthful.

**Per portion** Energy 97kcal/406kJ; Protein 2.6g; Carbohydrate 9.3g, of which sugars 8g; Fat 5.8g, of which saturates 3.6g; Cholesterol 14mg; Calcium 104mg; Fibre 2.5g; Sodium 51mg.

# SPICY RED LENTIL SOUP <u>WITH</u> ONION

*IN ISTANBUL AND IZMIR, LENTIL SOUPS ARE LIGHT AND SUBTLY SPICED, AND SERVED AS AN APPETIZER OR AS A SNACK. IN ANATOLIA, LENTIL AND BEAN SOUPS ARE MADE WITH CHUNKS OF MUTTON AND FLAVOURED WITH TOMATO AND SPICES, AND ARE USUALLY SERVED AS A MEAL ON THEIR OWN. THIS RECIPE IS FOR A MEATLESS SOUP IN WHICH THE GARNISHINGS PLAY AN IMPORTANT ROLE. OFTEN, THE ONION, PARSLEY AND LEMON WILL BE PLACED IN A SEPARATE BOWL SO YOU CAN HELP YOURSELF.*

SERVES FOUR

INGREDIENTS
- 30–45ml/2–3 tbsp olive or vegetable oil
- 1 large onion, finely chopped
- 2 garlic cloves, finely chopped
- 1 fresh red chilli, seeded and chopped
- 5–10ml/1–2 tsp cumin seeds
- 5–10ml/1–2 tsp coriander seeds
- 1 carrot, finely chopped
- scant 5ml/1 tsp ground fenugreek
- 5ml/1 tsp sugar
- 15ml/1 tbsp tomato purée (paste)
- 250g/9oz/generous 1 cup split red lentils
- 1.75 litres/3 pints/7½ cups chicken stock
- salt and ground black pepper

To serve
- 1 small red onion, finely chopped
- 1 large bunch of fresh flat leaf parsley, finely chopped
- 4–6 lemon wedges

**1** Heat the oil in a heavy pan and stir in the onion, garlic, chilli, cumin and coriander seeds.

**2** When the onion begins to colour slightly, toss in the carrot and cook for 2–3 minutes.

**3** Add the fenugreek, sugar and tomato purée and stir in the lentils.

**4** Pour in the stock, stir well and bring to the boil. Lower the heat, partially cover the pan with a lid and simmer for 30–40 minutes, until the lentils have broken up.

**5** If the soup is too thick for your preference, thin it down to the desired consistency with a little water. Season with salt and pepper to taste.

**6** Serve the soup as it is or, if you prefer a smooth texture, leave it to cool slightly, then whiz it in a blender and reheat if necessary.

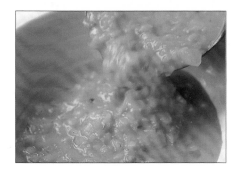

**7** Ladle the soup into bowls and sprinkle liberally with the chopped onion and parsley. Serve with a wedge of lemon to squeeze over the soup.

**Per portion** Energy 203kcal/856kJ; Protein 11.1g; Carbohydrate 31.8g, of which sugars 7.3g; Fat 4.4g, of which saturates 0.6g; Cholesterol 0mg; Calcium 45mg; Fibre 3.5g; Sodium 26mg.

# LAMB AND YOGURT SOUP

*DÜĞÜN ÇORBASI IS THE SOUP OF TURKISH WEDDINGS. STEEPED IN TRADITION, IT VARIES LITTLE THROUGHOUT THE COUNTRY, THE ONLY DIFFERENCE BEING THE INCLUSION OF CINNAMON TO FLAVOUR THE STOCK. MADE WITH LAMB STOCK AND CONTAINING CHUNKS OF COOKED LAMB, IT IS SLIGHTLY SOUR FROM THE CLASSIC LIAISON OF LEMON, EGG AND YOGURT.*

SERVES FOUR TO SIX

INGREDIENTS

   500g/1¼lb lamb on the bone
     – neck, leg or shoulder
   2 carrots, roughly chopped
   2 potatoes, roughly chopped
   1 cinnamon stick
   45ml/3 tbsp thick and creamy
     (natural) plain yogurt
   45ml/3 tbsp plain (all-purpose) flour
   1 egg yolk
   juice of ½ lemon
   30ml/2 tbsp butter
   5ml/1 tsp *kırmızı biber*, or paprika
   salt and ground black pepper

**1** Place the lamb in a deep pan with the carrots, potatoes and cinnamon.

**2** Pour in 2 litres/3½ pints/8 cups water and bring to the boil over a high heat, then skim any scum off the surface and lower the heat.

**3** Cover the pan and simmer the mixture gently for about 1½ hours, or until the meat is so tender that it almost falls off the bone.

**4** Lift the lamb out of the pan using a slotted spoon, drain, and place it on a chopping board.

**5** Remove the meat from the bone and chop it into small pieces.

**6** Strain the stock and discard the carrots and potatoes. Pour the stock back into the pan, season and bring to the boil.

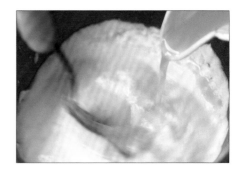

**7** In a deep bowl, beat the yogurt with the flour. Add the egg yolk and lemon juice and beat well again, then pour in about 250ml/8fl oz/1 cup of the hot stock, beating all the time so that the hot liquid doesn't cook the yolk.

**8** Lower the heat under the pan and pour the yogurt mixture into the stock, beating constantly.

**9** Add the meat to the pan and warm gently, ensuring the meat heats through but the mixture doesn't boil.

**10** Melt the butter in a small pan and stir in the *kırmızı biber* or paprika.

**11** Ladle the soup into bowls and drizzle the pepper butter over the top.

**Per portion** Energy 226kcal/943kJ; Protein 15g; Carbohydrate 14.4g, of which sugars 3.6g; Fat 12.4g, of which saturates 6.2g; Cholesterol 88mg; Calcium 54mg; Fibre 1.4g; Sodium 87mg.

# CLASSIC TRIPE SOUP

*REGARDED AS A FAITHFUL PICK-ME-UP,* TERBIYELI İŞKEMBE ÇORBASI *IS SOUGHT AFTER AT A REPUTED* IŞKEMBECI *(A CAFÉ THAT SPECIALISES IN TRIPE DISHES) LATE AT NIGHT. IT IS ALSO ONE OF THE CLASSIC DISHES PREPARED FOR THE RELIGIOUS FEAST,* KURBAN BAYRAMI, *WHEN EVERY PART OF THE SACRIFICED SHEEP IS USED TO MARK THE NEAR SACRIFICE OF* ISAAC.

SERVES FOUR TO SIX

INGREDIENTS
225g/8oz lamb tripe, washed
1.2 litres/2 pints/5 cups water
15ml/1 tbsp butter or ghee
25ml/1½ tbsp plain (all-purpose) flour
1 egg yolk
15ml/1 tbsp lemon juice
salt and ground black pepper
To serve
90ml/6 tbsp white wine vinegar
1–3 garlic cloves, crushed
25g/1oz/2 tbsp butter
5ml/1 tsp *kırmızı biber*, or paprika

**1** Put the tripe into a large, heavy pan and cover with the water. Bring it to the boil and skim off any froth. Continue to boil for 20–25 minutes, until the tripe is tender. Drain and reserve the cooking liquid. Cut the tripe into fine strips.

**2** Melt the butter or ghee in a heavy pan and stir in the flour to make a roux. Pour in the cooking liquid, stirring until it thickens. Stir in the tripe, increase the heat, and simmer for 15–20 minutes.

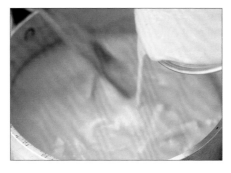

**3** In a small bowl, beat the egg yolk with the lemon juice. Beat in two spoonfuls of the hot soup, then pour it back into the pan, stirring constantly to ensure the egg doesn't curdle. Season the soup with salt and pepper to taste.

**4** Pour the vinegar into a small bowl and beat in the crushed garlic to taste and a little salt.

**5** In a small pan, gently melt the butter and stir in the *kırmızı biber* or paprika.

**6** Ladle the soup into individual serving bowls and pour a little of the melted butter mixture over each one.

**7** Serve the soup immediately, passing around the spiked vinegar to drizzle over the top.

**Per portion** Energy 101kcal/421kJ; Protein 4.8g; Carbohydrate 4g, of which sugars 0.2g; Fat 7.5g, of which saturates 4.2g; Cholesterol 83mg; Calcium 41mg; Fibre 0.2g; Sodium 60mg.

# TOMATO AND PEPPER RAGOÛT WITH EGGS

*MENEMEN IS TURKISH STREET FOOD. COOKED ON MAKESHIFT STOVES AT BUS AND TRAIN STATIONS, PORTS AND REST HOUSES, IT IS A SATISFYING SNACK OR MEAL. DEPENDING ON THE COOK, THE EGGS ARE EITHER STIRRED INTO THE RAGOÛT TO SCRAMBLE THEM, OR THEY ARE CRACKED ON TOP AND COOKED IN THE STEAM OF A DOMED LID UNTIL JUST SET.*

**4** Crack the eggs over the top of the tomato mixture, cover the pan and cook until the eggs are just done.

**5** Meanwhile, beat the yogurt with the garlic in a bowl and season with salt and pepper.

**6** Ladle the soup into bowls and serve hot, topped with parsley and dollops of garlic-flavoured yogurt.

**COOK'S TIPS**
• If you like, you can divide the tomato mixture between four small pans and crack an egg into each one, so that each person has their own serving.
• For breakfast, you will often be served the scrambled version of this dish that generally omits the (bell) pepper. It is fabulous served on toasted bread.

## SERVES FOUR

### INGREDIENTS
15ml/1 tbsp olive oil
15ml/1 tbsp butter
2 red onions, cut in half lengthways and sliced along the grain
1 red or green (bell) pepper, halved lengthways, seeded and sliced
2 garlic cloves, roughly chopped
5–10ml/1–2 tsp *kırmızı biber*, or 1 fresh red chilli, seeded and sliced
400g/14oz can chopped tomatoes
5–10ml/1–2 tsp sugar
4 eggs
salt and ground black pepper
To serve
90ml/6 tbsp thick and creamy natural (plain) yogurt
1–2 garlic cloves, crushed
a handful of fresh flat leaf parsley, roughly chopped

**1** Heat the oil and butter in a frying pan. Stir in the onions, pepper, garlic and *kırmızı biber* or chilli and cook until they begin to soften but not brown.

**2** Add the tomatoes and sugar to the pan and mix them in well.

**3** Cook for about 10 minutes, or until the liquid has reduced and the mixture is quite thick, then season with salt and pepper to taste.

**Per portion** Energy 190kcal/790kJ; Protein 8.6g; Carbohydrate 14.9g, of which sugars 12.4g; Fat 11.2g, of which saturates 3.5g; Cholesterol 196mg; Calcium 65mg; Fibre 3.1g; Sodium 101mg.

# POACHED EGGS WITH GARLIC YOGURT

*THIS DISH, ÇILBIR, IS SERVED AS A HOT MEZE DISH OR SNACK IN TURKEY, BUT IT WORKS EQUALLY WELL AS A SUPPER DISH WITH A GREEN SALAD. HEN'S EGGS OR DUCK'S EGGS CAN BE USED, AND YOU CAN EITHER POACH OR FRY THEM. SPIKED WITH TURKISH RED PEPPER OR PAPRIKA, AND SERVED WITH TOASTED FLAT BREAD OR CHUNKS OF A WARM, CRISPY LOAF, IT IS SIMPLE AND SATISFYING.*

SERVES TWO

INGREDIENTS

   500g/1¼ lb/2¼ cups thick and
     creamy natural (plain) yogurt
   2 garlic cloves, crushed
   30–45ml/2–3 tbsp white
     wine vinegar
   4 large (US extra large) eggs
   15–30ml/1–2 tbsp butter
   5ml/1 tsp *kırmızı biber*, or paprika
   a few dried sage leaves, crumbled
   salt and ground black pepper

**1** Beat the yogurt with the garlic and seasoning. Spoon into a serving dish or on to individual plates, spreading it flat to create a thick mattress for the eggs. Serve at room temperature as a contrast to the hot eggs, or heat it by placing the dish in a cooling oven, or by sitting it in a covered pan of hot water.

**2** Fill a pan with water, add the vinegar to seal the egg whites, and bring to a rolling boil. Stir the water to create a whirlpool and crack in the first egg.

**3** As the egg spins and the white sets around the yolk, stir the water ready for the next one. Poach each egg for 2–3 minutes so the yolk is still soft.

**COOK'S TIP**
Popular egg recipes include *yumurtali ispanak kavurmasi*, a dish of sautéed spinach and onions with an egg cooked in the middle, and a classic Palace dish of eggs cooked with *pastırma*.

**4** Lift the eggs out of the water with a slotted spoon and place them on the yogurt mattress.

**5** Quickly melt the butter in a small pan. Stir in the *kırmızı biber* or paprika and sage leaves, then spoon over the eggs. Serve immediately.

**Per portion** Energy 345kcal/1438kJ; Protein 25.4g; Carbohydrate 19.1g, of which sugars 19.1g; Fat 19.8g, of which saturates 8.3g; Cholesterol 400mg; Calcium 534mg; Fibre 0.1g; Sodium 393mg.

# CHICKPEA PARCELS

*FALLING BETWEEN A CHINESE DUMPLING AND ITALIAN PASTA, BAKED MANTI IS A POPULAR SNACK IN EASTERN ANATOLIA. THE CHICKPEA FILLING IS WARMING AND SATISFYING, MAKING IT PARTICULARLY GOOD FOR VEGETARIANS. SERVE AS A HOT SNACK, OR AS A MEAL ON ITS OWN.*

SERVES FOUR TO SIX

INGREDIENTS

   450g/1lb/4 cups plain
    (all-purpose) flour
   2.5ml/½ tsp salt
   1 whole egg, beaten with 1 egg yolk
   salt and ground black pepper
For the filling
   400g/14oz can chickpeas, drained
    and thoroughly rinsed
   5ml/1 tsp cumin seeds, crushed
   5ml/1 tsp Turkish red pepper
    or paprika
For the yogurt
   about 90ml/6 tbsp thick and creamy
    natural (plain) yogurt
   2–3 garlic cloves, crushed
For the sauce
   15ml/1 tbsp olive oil
   15ml/1 tbsp butter
   1 onion, finely chopped
   2 garlic cloves, finely chopped
   5ml/1 tsp *kırmızı biber*, or
   1 fresh red chilli, seeded and
    finely chopped
   5–10ml/1–2 tsp sugar
   5–10ml/1–2 tsp dried mint
   400g/14oz can chopped tomatoes,
    drained of juice
   600ml/1 pint/2½ cups vegetable
    or chicken stock
   1 small bunch each of fresh flat leaf
    parsley and coriander (cilantro),
    roughly chopped

**1** Make the dough. Sift the flour and salt into a wide bowl and make a well in the middle. Pour in the beaten egg and 50ml/2fl oz/¼ cup water. Using your fingers, draw the flour into the liquid and mix to a dough.

**2** Knead the dough for 10 minutes, cover the bowl with a damp dish towel and leave the dough to rest for 1 hour.

**COOK'S TIP**
*Mantı* can be baked or boiled, and the fillings range from spicy minced (ground) meat to chopped nuts or steamed spinach.

**3** Meanwhile, prepare the filling and yogurt. In a bowl, mash the chickpeas with a fork. Beat in the cumin, *kırmızı biber* or paprika and seasoning.

**4** In a separate bowl, beat the yogurt with the garlic and season with salt and pepper to taste.

**5** Make the sauce. Heat the oil and butter in a pan and gently fry the onion and garlic until softened. Add the red pepper or chilli, sugar and mint.

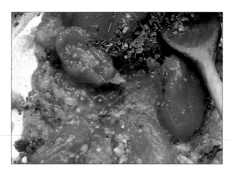

**6** Stir in the tomatoes and cook gently over a low heat for about 15 minutes, until the sauce is thick. Season and remove from the heat.

**7** Preheat the oven to 200°C/400°F/ Gas 6. Roll out the dough as thinly as possible on a lightly floured surface. Using a sharp knife, cut the dough into small squares (roughly 2.5cm/1in).

**8** Spoon a little chickpea mixture into the middle of each square and bunch together the corners to form a little pouch. Place the filled pasta parcels in a greased ovenproof dish, stacking them next to each other. Bake, uncovered, for 15–20 minutes, until golden brown.

**9** Pour the stock into a pan and bring to the boil. Take the parcels out of the oven and pour the stock over them.

**10** Return the dish to the oven and bake for a further 15–20 minutes, until almost all the stock has been absorbed. Meanwhile, reheat the tomato sauce.

**11** Transfer the pasta parcels to a serving dish and spoon the yogurt over them. Top the cool yogurt with the hot tomato sauce and sprinkle with the chopped herbs.

**Per portion** Energy 416kcal/1760kJ; Protein 14.8g; Carbohydrate 73.7g, of which sugars 5.9g; Fat 9g, of which saturates 2.6g; Cholesterol 71mg; Calcium 179mg; Fibre 5.9g; Sodium 360mg.

# FILO CIGARS FILLED <u>WITH</u> FETA, PARSLEY, MINT <u>AND</u> DILL

*THESE CLASSIC CIGAR-SHAPED PASTRIES, SIGARA BÖREĞI, ARE A POPULAR SNACK AND MEZE FOOD, AND THEY ARE ALSO GOOD AS NIBBLES WITH DRINKS. HERE THEY ARE FILLED WITH A MIXTURE OF CHEESE AND HERBS, BUT OTHER POPULAR FILLINGS INCLUDE AROMATIC MINCED MEAT, BAKED AUBERGINE AND CHEESE, OR MASHED PUMPKIN, CHEESE AND DILL. THE FILO PASTRY CAN BE FOLDED INTO TRIANGLES, BUT CIGARS ARE THE MOST TRADITIONAL SHAPE. THEY CAN BE PREPARED IN ADVANCE AND KEPT UNDER A DAMP DISH TOWEL IN THE REFRIGERATOR UNTIL YOU ARE READY TO FRY THEM.*

## SERVES THREE TO FOUR

### INGREDIENTS
225g/8oz feta cheese
1 large (US extra large) egg, lightly beaten
1 small bunch each of fresh flat leaf parsley, mint and dill, finely chopped
4–5 sheets of filo pastry
sunflower oil, for deep-frying
dill fronds, to garnish (optional)

**1** In a bowl, mash the feta with a fork. Beat in the egg and fold in the herbs.

**2** Place the sheets of filo on a flat surface and cover with a damp dish towel to keep them moist. Working with one sheet at a time, cut the filo into strips about 10–13cm/4–5in wide, and pile them on top of each other. Keep the strips covered with another damp dish towel.

**3** Lay one filo strip on the surface in front of you, making sure you recover the other strips with the dish towel. Place a heaped teaspoon of the cheese filling along one of the short ends.

**4** Roll the end of the pastry over the filling, quite tightly to keep it in place, then tuck in the sides to seal in the filling and continue to roll until you get to the other end of the pastry.

**5** As you reach the end, load the tip of the brush with a little water and brush it over the end of the pastry – this will help seal the filo and prevent it unravelling during cooking.

**6** Place the filled filo pastry cigar, join-side down, on a plate and cover with another damp dish towel to keep it moist. Continue with the remaining sheets of filo and filling until all the filling has been used.

**7** Heat enough oil for deep-frying in a wok or other deep-sided pan, and deep-fry the filo cigars in batches for 5–6 minutes until crisp and golden brown. Lift out of the oil with a slotted spoon and drain on kitchen paper.

**8** Serve immediately, garnished with dill fronds if you like.

### VARIATION
To make a puff pastry log, use the same filling as here. Roll out a 400g/14oz packet puff pastry and spoon on the filling. Roll into a log, tucking in the ends as you go, and place on an oiled baking tray. Cut diagonally into portions, keeping it intact at the base. Brush with a mixture of egg yolk and sunflower oil and bake in a preheated oven at 180°C/350°F/Gas 4 for 30 minutes, until crisp.

**Per portion** Energy 311kcal/1291kJ; Protein 12.4g; Carbohydrate 11.2g, of which sugars 1.6g; Fat 24.4g, of which saturates 9.5g; Cholesterol 92mg; Calcium 278mg; Fibre 1.6g; Sodium 838mg.

# ANATOLIAN FLAT BREADS WITH SPINACH

*THESE TRADITIONAL FLAT BREADS FROM CENTRAL ANATOLIA, CALLED GÖZLEME, ARE COOKED QUICKLY ON A HOT GRIDDLE AND CAN BE FILLED WITH VARIOUS COMBINATIONS OF INGREDIENTS, INCLUDING CHEESE AND HERBS, EGGS AND PASTIRMA, MINCED BEEF WITH PINE NUTS, OR WITH THIS CREAMY SPINACH AND ONION MIXTURE. FOR BREAKFAST, THEY ARE OFTEN COOKED PLAIN AND DRIZZLED WITH JUST A LITTLE HONEY. GREAT AS A SNACK, OR AS A LIGHT LUNCH, THIS IS A TRADITIONAL VILLAGE DISH THAT IS PREPARED IN THE HOME AND IN SMALL CAFÉS AND RESTAURANTS.*

SERVES TWO TO FOUR

INGREDIENTS
- 115g/4oz/1 cup strong unbleached white bread flour, plus extra for dusting
- 2.5ml/½ tsp salt
- 15ml/1 tbsp olive oil, melted butter or ghee
- 50ml/2fl oz/¼ cup water

For the filling
- 250g/9oz fresh spinach
- 15g/½oz/1 tbsp butter
- 1 onion, chopped
- pinch of freshly grated nutmeg
- 5ml/1 tsp *kırmızı biber*, or paprika
- 7.5ml/1½ tsp plain (all-purpose) flour
- 120ml/4fl oz/½ cup milk
- 45ml/3 tbsp *kaşar peynir* or Parmesan cheese, grated
- salt and ground black pepper

**1** Sift the flour with the salt into a bowl. Make a well in the centre and pour in the oil, or melted butter or ghee, and the water. Using your hand, draw in the flour from the sides and work the mixture into a dough. Knead thoroughly.

**2** Divide the dough into four pieces, knead them and roll into balls. Place the balls on a floured surface, cover with a damp cloth, and leave them to rest for 30 minutes.

**3** Meanwhile, prepare the filling. Place the spinach in a steamer, or in a colander set in a large pan with a lid, and steam the spinach until it wilts.

**4** Refresh the spinach under running cold water and drain well. Place the cooked spinach on a wooden board and chop it roughly.

**5** Melt the butter in a heavy pan and soften the onion. Stir in the chopped spinach and add the nutmeg and *kırmızı biber* or paprika.

**6** Stir in the flour and pour in the milk, stirring constantly until thickened. Beat in the cheese and season with salt and pepper. Cover the pan to keep the filling warm.

**7** On a lightly floured surface, roll out each of the balls of dough with a rolling pin into thin, flat rounds, about 15–20cm/6–8in in diameter.

**8** Heat a griddle, wipe it with a little oil, and place one of the rounds of dough on to it (if you have a wide griddle, as they do in Turkey, you can cook several at a time). Cook the dough for about 1 minute on one side, then flip it over and spread a thin layer of the spinach filling over the cooked side.

**9** Cook the second side for 1–2 minutes, allowing it to buckle and brown, then lift it off the griddle and place it on a piece of baking parchment.

**10** Roll up the *gözleme*, wrap the paper around it to make it easier to hold, and hand it to the first person waiting to try one before repeating with the others.

**VARIATION**
An alternative method is to spread the filling on one half of the cooking *gözleme* and fold the other half over to resemble a half moon. Make sure the edges are sealed and serve immediately.

**Per portion** Energy 246kcal/1033kJ; Protein 10.5g; Carbohydrate 27.9g, of which sugars 3.7g; Fat 11.1g, of which saturates 5.1g; Cholesterol 21mg; Calcium 327mg; Fibre 2.5g; Sodium 493mg.

# COURGETTE FRITTERS

*OFTEN SERVED AS A HOT MEZE DISH, KABAK KIZARTMASI ARE DELICIOUS SERVED WITH YOGURT, WHICH CAN BE PLAIN OR FLAVOURED WITH GARLIC, AS HERE. THEY ARE ALSO TASTY SERVED WITH LEMON WEDGES TO SQUEEZE OVER THEM, AND ARE EQUALLY GOOD AS A QUICK SNACK OR AS A LIGHT LUNCH WITH A SALAD. VARIATIONS OF THESE FRITTERS ARE COOKED ALL OVER TURKEY.*

### SERVES FOUR

INGREDIENTS

3–4 firm, fat courgettes
(zucchini)
2 eggs
30ml/2 tbsp plain
(all-purpose) flour
sunflower oil, for deep-frying
salt and ground black pepper

To serve

60ml/4 tbsp thick and creamy
natural (plain) yogurt
1 garlic clove, crushed
juice of ½ lemon

**1** Cut the courgettes on the diagonal, crossways, into thin slices. If moist, pat them dry with a piece of kitchen paper, so that the batter will stick to them.

**2** Beat the eggs in a bowl and add the flour. Beat until smooth and season with salt and pepper.

**3** Heat enough oil for deep-frying in a wide, shallow pan. Dip the courgette slices into the batter and then drop them into the oil. Fry them in batches for 3–4 minutes, or until golden brown all over. Drain the fritters on kitchen paper and keep warm.

**4** In a small bowl, quickly beat the yogurt with the garlic and lemon juice. Season to taste.

**5** Arrange the warm fritters on a serving dish with the yogurt. Enjoy the juicy fritters dipped in the garlic yogurt as a snack or as a hot *meze* dish.

**Per portion** Energy 207kcal/857kJ; Protein 8.3g; Carbohydrate 10.8g, of which sugars 4.7g; Fat 14.8g, of which saturates 2.4g; Cholesterol 95mg; Calcium 104mg; Fibre 2.1g; Sodium 50mg.

# DEEP-FRIED MUSSELS IN BEER BATTER

*FRIED IN HUGE, CURVED PANS, MIDYE TAVASI ARE SKEWERED ON STICKS AND SOLD IN BATCHES, WITH A GARLIC-FLAVOURED TARATOR SAUCE THAT CAN BE MADE WITH POUNDED WALNUTS, ALMONDS OR PINE NUTS, OR SIMPLY WITH DAY-OLD BREAD. A SPECIALITY FROM ISTANBUL AND IZMIR, THEY ARE PART OF THE STREET-FOOD SCENE, AS WELL AS BEING POPULAR IN FISH RESTAURANTS.*

SERVES FOUR TO FIVE

INGREDIENTS
    sunflower oil, for deep-frying
    about 50 fresh mussels, cleaned,
       shelled and patted dry (*see* below)
For the batter
    115g/4oz/1 cup plain (all-purpose)
       flour
    5ml/1 tsp salt
    2.5ml/½ tsp bicarbonate of soda
       (baking soda)
    2 egg yolks
    175–250ml/6–8fl oz/¾–1 cup beer
       or lager
For the sauce
    75g/3oz/½ cup broken
       shelled walnuts
    2 slices of day-old bread, sprinkled
       with water and left for a few
       minutes, then squeezed dry
    2–3 garlic cloves, crushed
    45–60ml/3–4 tbsp olive oil
    juice of 1 lemon
    dash of white wine vinegar
    salt and ground black pepper

**1** Make the batter. Sift the flour, salt and soda into a bowl. Make a well in the middle and drop in the egg yolks. Using a wooden spoon, slowly beat in the beer and draw in the flour from the sides until a smooth, thick batter is formed. Set aside for 30 minutes.

**2** Meanwhile, make the sauce. Pound the walnuts to a paste using a mortar and pestle, or blend them in a processor. Add the bread and garlic, and pound again to a paste.

**COOK'S TIP**
Raw mussels are prised from their shells with ease by the street vendors, but you may find the job too fiddly. An easier option is to steam them open for 3–4 minutes, then remove them from their shells, or use the ready-shelled mussels sold frozen in bags. They should be defrosted before use.

**3** Drizzle in the olive oil, stirring all the time, and beat in the lemon juice and vinegar. The sauce should be smooth, with the consistency of thick double (heavy) cream – if it is too dry, stir in a little water. Season with salt and pepper and set aside.

**4** Heat enough sunflower oil for deep-frying in a large wok or other large, heavy pan.

**5** Using your fingers, dip each mussel into the batter and drop into the hot oil. Fry in batches for a minute or two until golden brown. Lift out the mussels with a slotted spoon and drain well on kitchen paper.

**6** Thread the mussels on to wooden skewers, or spear them individually, and serve hot, accompanied by the garlic-flavoured dipping sauce.

**Per portion** Energy 439kcal/1827kJ; Protein 10.6g; Carbohydrate 24.6g, of which sugars 1.9g; Fat 33g, of which saturates 4g; Cholesterol 89mg; Calcium 115mg; Fibre 1.5g; Sodium 502mg.

# DEEP-FRIED SQUID <u>WITH</u> GARLIC BREAD SAUCE

*KALAMAR — DEEP-FRIED SQUID — IS OFTEN SERVED AS A HOT MEZE DISH IN FISH RESTAURANTS, AND IN SOME COASTAL AREAS IT WILL BE OFFERED TO YOU AS A SNACK TO ACCOMPANY A CHILLED GLASS OF BEER OR RAKI. CUT INTO RINGS OR STRIPS, THE SQUID IS GENERALLY SERVED WITH LEMON TO SQUEEZE OVER IT, A DILL-FLAVOURED MAYONNAISE, OR A GARLIC AND NUT OR BREAD SAUCE. THE MOST TRADITIONAL VERSION, WHICH IS MOST FREQUENTLY SERVED IN THE MAKESHIFT STALLS AND FISH LOKANTAS, IS THIS SIMPLE ONE MADE WITH BREAD. THE SQUID CAN BE SIMPLY TOSSED IN FLOUR BEFORE FRYING, OR DIPPED INTO A YEAST AND BEER BATTER, AS HERE.*

SERVES TWO TO FOUR

INGREDIENTS
   4 good-sized fresh squid, prepared
     (*see* Cook's Tip)
   sunflower oil, for deep-frying
   1 lemon, cut into wedges,
     to serve
For the batter
   15g/½oz fresh yeast
   300ml/½ pint/1¼ cups beer
   225g/8oz plain (all-purpose) flour
   5ml/1 tsp salt
For the sauce
   3 slices day-old white bread,
     with crusts removed
   100ml/3½ fl oz/scant ½ cup
     olive oil
   juice of 1 lemon
   2–3 garlic cloves, crushed
   salt and ground black pepper

**1** Cut the prepared squid into strips or rings and set aside.

**2** To make the batter, cream the yeast with 30ml/2 tbsp of the beer in a small bowl. Gradually stir in the remainder of the beer. Sift the flour with the salt into a bowl.

**3** Make a well in the centre of the flour and pour in the beer and yeast mixture, beating constantly. Use a whisk to produce a smooth batter, then cover it and leave to stand for 1 hour.

**4** To make the sauce, soak the bread in water for 10 minutes. Squeeze it dry and put it in a bowl.

**5** Using a fork, or a wooden spoon, beat the oil and lemon juice with the bread until it resembles a thick sauce.

**6** Beat in the garlic and season with salt and pepper. Transfer to a serving bowl and set aside.

**7** Heat enough oil for deep-frying in a pan. Dip the squid in the batter and fry it in batches. When the batter turns crisp and golden brown, lift the squid out of the oil and place the fried pieces on a trivet in the pan to keep them warm while you fry the remaining squid. When all of the squid has been cooked, drain on kitchen paper.

**8** Serve hot with the garlic sauce and lemon to squeeze over it.

**COOK'S TIPS**
• **Preparing the squid** First, hold the body sac in one hand and pull the head off with the other. Most of the innards should come out with the head, but reach inside the sac with your fingers to remove any that remain. Remove the transparent backbone and rinse the body sac inside and out. Pat the body sac dry and put it aside for stuffing. Sever the tentacles just above the eyes, so that you have the top of the head and the tentacles joined together. Put them aside with the sacs and discard everything else.
• **Tenderizing tip** To soften the squid and draw out its taste, some Turkish cooks rub it in lemon juice, sprinkle a little sugar over it with a teaspoon of bicarbonate of soda and chill it in the refrigerator for an hour. The squid is then rinsed and patted dry before cooking.

**Per portion** Energy 636kcal/2668kJ; Protein 34g; Carbohydrate 56.2g, of which sugars 2.5g; Fat 31g, of which saturates 4.5g; Cholesterol 394mg; Calcium 126mg; Fibre 2g; Sodium 296mg.

# FLATBREADS WITH SPICY LAMB AND TOMATO

*THIS ANATOLIAN SNACK, LAHMACUN, IS A GREAT CULINARY CREATION. THE THIN CRISPY BASE IS SMEARED WITH A LAYER OF LIGHTLY SPICED LAMB AND ROLLED INTO A CONE WITH FRESH PARSLEY, SUMAC AND A SQUEEZE OF LEMON. IT IS THE MOST PERFECT FORM OF STREET FOOD – HOT, PORTABLE AND DELICIOUS. IN RESTAURANTS, MINIATURE VERSIONS ARE OFTEN SERVED AS A HOT MEZE DISH.*

### SERVES TWO TO FOUR

INGREDIENTS
scant 5ml/1 tsp active dried yeast
2.5ml/½ tsp sugar
150ml/¼ pint/⅔ cup lukewarm water
350g/12oz/3 cups strong white
    bread flour
2.5ml/½ tsp salt
a few drops of sunflower oil
For the topping
15ml/1 tbsp olive oil
15ml/1 tbsp butter
1 onion, finely chopped
2 garlic cloves, finely chopped
225g/8oz/1 cup finely minced
    (ground) lean lamb
30ml/2 tbsp tomato purée (paste)
15ml/1 tbsp sugar
5–10ml/1–2 tsp *kırmızı biber*, or
    1 fresh red chilli, finely chopped
5ml/1 tsp dried mint
5–10ml/1–2 tsp ground sumac
1 bunch of fresh flat leaf parsley,
    roughly chopped
1 lemon, halved
salt and ground black pepper

**1** Make the dough. Put the yeast and sugar into a small bowl with half the lukewarm water. Set aside for about 15 minutes until frothy.

**2** Sift the flour and salt into a large bowl, make a well in the middle and add the creamed yeast and the rest of the lukewarm water. Using your hand, draw in the flour and work the mixture to a dough, adding more water if necessary.

**3** Turn the dough on to a lightly floured surface and knead until it is smooth and elastic. Drip a few drops of sunflower oil into the base of the bowl and roll the dough in it. Cover the bowl with a damp dish towel and leave in a warm place for about 1 hour or until the dough has doubled in size.

**4** Meanwhile, prepare the topping. Heat the oil and butter in a heavy pan and gently fry the onion and garlic until they soften. Leave to cool in the pan.

**5** Put the lamb in a bowl, add the tomato purée, sugar, *kırmızı biber* or chilli and mint, then the softened onion and garlic. Season with salt and pepper, and knead with your hands. Cover and keep in the refrigerator until you are ready to use.

**6** Place two baking sheets in the oven. Preheat the oven to 220°C/425°F/Gas 7. Punch down the risen dough, knead it on a lightly floured surface, then divide into two or four equal pieces. Roll each piece into a thin flat round, stretching the dough with your hands as you roll.

**7** Oil the hot baking sheets and place the dough rounds on them, then cover with a thin layer of the meat mixture, spreading it right to the edges. Bake in the oven for 15–20 minutes, until the meat is nicely cooked.

**8** As soon as the *lahmacun* are ready, sprinkle them with the sumac and parsley. Squeeze a little lemon juice over the top and roll them up while the dough is still pliable. Eat like a pizza – with your hands, or on plates with a knife and fork.

**Per portion** Energy 496kcal/2092kJ; Protein 20g; Carbohydrate 75.2g, of which sugars 8.1g; Fat 14.9g, of which saturates 6.1g; Cholesterol 51mg; Calcium 167mg; Fibre 3.8g; Sodium 333mg.

# LAYERED MINCED MEAT <u>AND</u> PINE NUT PIE

*A TEPSI IS A DEEP ROUND BAKING TRAY IN WHICH SAVOURY AND SWEET PASTRIES ARE BAKED. IN THIS DISH, TEPSI BÖREĞI, THE SHEETS OF TRADITIONAL FLAT BREAD, YUFKA, ARE LAYERED WITH A MINCED MEAT FILLING. ALTHOUGH NOT EXACTLY THE SAME, FILO PASTRY, WHICH IS MORE READILY AVAILABLE, WORKS AS A SUBSTITUTE FOR THE LARGE SHEETS OF TRADITIONAL YUFKA, BUT YOU MAY REQUIRE TWICE AS MANY SHEETS OF FILO, AS THEY ARE USUALLY SMALLER IN SIZE.*

### SERVES FOUR TO SIX

INGREDIENTS
  2 eggs
  300ml/½ pint/1¼ cups milk
  150ml/¼ pint/⅔ cup sunflower oil
    or olive oil, plus 15ml/1 tbsp extra
  5 sheets of *yufka* or 10–12 of filo
    pastry, thawed if frozen
For the filling
  15ml/1 tbsp olive oil
  15g/½oz/1 tbsp butter
  1 onion, finely chopped
  2–3 garlic cloves, crushed
  30–45ml/2–3 tbsp pine nuts
  250g/9oz lean veal or beef, finely
    minced (ground)
  10ml/2 tsp ground cinnamon
  10ml/2 tsp dried oregano
  1 small bunch fresh parsley, leaves
    finely chopped
  salt and ground black pepper
To serve
  7.5ml/1½ tsp olive oil or butter
  15ml/1 tbsp pine nuts

**1** Preheat the oven to 200°C/400°F/
Gas 6 and grease an ovenproof dish
(the size is not important – just vary the
number of layers according to the dish).

**2** For the filling, heat the olive oil and
butter in a heavy pan and stir in the
onion. Cook for 1–2 minutes until
softened. Add the garlic and pine nuts.
Once the pine nuts begin to turn golden,
add the meat.

**3** Cook the meat for 3–4 minutes, then
stir in the cinnamon and herbs. Season
with salt and pepper. Leave to cool.

**4** In a bowl, beat the eggs with the milk
and the oil. Lay a whole sheet of *yufka*
in the base of the dish, with the sides
overlapping the edge – this may require
two to three sheets of filo pastry,
overlapped in the base of the dish to
prevent seepage. (If using filo, keep the
unused pastry covered with a damp
dish towel to prevent drying.)

**5** Pour a little of the milk mixture into
the centre and spread it to the sides.

**6** Tear two sheets of *yufka* (or three to
four of filo) into wide strips and layer
them in the dish, brushing each layer
with the milk mixture. Leave the last
layer dry and spread the meat mixture
over it.

**7** Tear the remaining two sheets of *yufka*
(three to four of filo) and layer them up
in the same way with the milk mixture.
Reserve 15ml/1 tbsp of the mixture in
the bowl and beat in the 15ml/1 tbsp
of the oil.

**8** Pull up the dangling flaps of *yufka*
from the base sheet lining the dish
and fold them over the top of the pie,
sticking them down with the milk and
oil mixture, which you can apply with a
brush, but it is easier and more effective
to smear it on with your fingers.

**9** Make sure the very top pieces are
well oiled, and put the pie into the oven
for about 45 minutes. The pie should
puff up and turn golden brown.

**10** Remove the pie from the oven (it will
sink back down quite quickly) and cut it
into rectangular, square or triangular
wedges, according to your preference.

**11** To serve, heat the oil or butter in a
small pan, add the pine nuts and cook
until golden brown. Drain them on
kitchen paper and sprinkle a few over
each portion. Serve the pie hot or at
room temperature.

**Per portion** Energy 463kcal/1920kJ; Protein 15.1g; Carbohydrate 16.5g, of which sugars 3.6g; Fat 37.9g, of which saturates 8.1g; Cholesterol 97mg; Calcium 101mg; Fibre 0.9g; Sodium 94mg.

# VEGETABLE
# DISHES

*Turkish vegetable cuisine follows the cycle of natural seasonal*

*produce and everyone talks about the dishes they are going to*

*cook as each season brings its speciality. Summer vegetables in*

*particular are celebrated, with colourful, flavoursome dishes such*

*as Roasted Courgettes and Peaches with Pine Nuts, Artichokes*

*with Beans and Almonds, and Peppers Stuffed with Aromatic*

*Rice, and there are myriad ways of cooking the much-loved*

*aubergine, including stuffing, stewing, poaching and smoking.*

# SPINACH WITH EGGS AND PAPRIKA

*A MUCH-LOVED VEGETABLE IN TURKEY, SPINACH OFTEN FINDS ITS WAY INTO FILLINGS FOR SAVOURY PASTRIES AND FLAT BREADS, OR COMBINED WITH YOGURT IN A NUMBER OF DELICIOUS MEZE DISHES. THIS POPULAR EGG DISH, CALLED YUMURTALI ISPANAK KAVURMASI, IS OFTEN SERVED AS A SNACK IN CAFÉS, OR AS A LIGHT LUNCH IN THE HOME. FRESH, CRUSTY BREAD AND A LITTLE YOGURT GO WELL WITH THE DISH. A SIMILAR DISH IS MADE WITH STRIPS OF PASTIRMA, THE CURED BEEF, WHICH ARE FRIED WITH THE ONIONS BEFORE THE EGGS ARE CRACKED OVER THE TOP.*

**2** Refresh the spinach under running cold water and drain well. Place the cooked spinach on a wooden board and chop it roughly.

**3** Heat the oil and butter in a shallow pan until the butter has melted, then stir in the onion and garlic. Cook gently until softened.

**4** Toss in the spinach and mix well. Add the nutmeg, salt and pepper.

**5** Make two hollows in the spinach mixture and drop in the eggs. Cover the pan and leave the eggs to cook in the steam, until the whites are firm but the yolk remains soft.

**6** Sprinkle a little *kırmızı biber* or paprika, over the eggs.

**7** Serve immediately from the pan with chunks of fresh, crusty bread and a little yogurt.

SERVES TWO

INGREDIENTS
    750g/1lb 10oz fresh spinach
    15ml/1 tbsp olive oil
    15ml/1 tbsp butter
    1 onion, finely chopped
    1–2 garlic cloves, finely chopped
    2.5ml/½ tsp freshly grated nutmeg
    2 large eggs
    *kırmızı biber*, or paprika, to sprinkle
    salt and ground black pepper

**1** Place the spinach in a steamer, or in a colander set in a large pan with a lid, and steam the spinach until it wilts.

**Per portion** Energy 309kcal/1275kJ; Protein 18g; Carbohydrate 14g, of which sugars 11.3g; Fat 20.4g, of which saturates 6.6g; Cholesterol 206mg; Calcium 693mg; Fibre 9.3g; Sodium 644mg.

# SMOKED AUBERGINES IN CHEESE SAUCE

*THIS RECIPE IS ADAPTED FROM THE TRADITIONAL PALACE DISH, HÜNKAR BEĞENDI, WHICH WAS CREATED FOR ONE OF THE OTTOMAN SULTANS. INVARIABLY, THE DISH CONSISTS OF LAMB AND TOMATO STEW, OR MEATBALLS COOKED IN A TOMATO SAUCE, SERVED ON A BED OF AUBERGINE IN A CHEESE SAUCE. HERE, THE BEĞENDI IS BAKED IN THE OVEN AND SERVED ON ITS OWN — A WARMING AND NOURISHING DISH THAT IS POPULAR WITH CHILDREN. SERVE IT AS A MAIN DISH FOR LUNCH OR SUPPER WITH CHUNKS OF FRESH, CRUSTY BREAD AND A JUICY GREEN SALAD.*

## SERVES FOUR

### INGREDIENTS
2 large aubergines (eggplants)
50g/2oz/¼ cup butter
30ml/2 tbsp plain
    (all-purpose) flour
600ml/1 pint/2½ cups milk
    (you may need a little more)
115g/4oz Cheddar cheese, grated
salt and ground black pepper
finely grated Parmesan cheese,
    for the topping

**1** Preheat the oven to 200°C/400°F/ Gas 6. Put the aubergines directly on the gas flame on top of the stove, or under a conventional grill (broiler), and turn them until the skin is charred on all sides and the flesh is soft.

**2** Place the charred aubergines in a plastic bag and leave for a few minutes.

**3** Hold each aubergine by the stalk under cold running water and gently peel off the charred skin.

**4** Squeeze the flesh with your fingers to get rid of any excess water and place on a chopping board. Remove the stalks and chop the flesh to a pulp.

**5** Make the sauce. Melt the butter in a heavy pan, remove from the heat and stir in the flour.

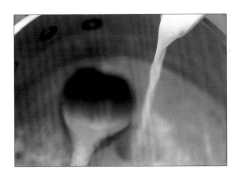

**6** Slowly beat in the milk, then return the pan to a medium heat and cook, stirring constantly, until the sauce is smooth and thick.

**7** Beat in the grated Cheddar cheese a little at a time, then beat in the aubergine pulp and season with salt and pepper.

**8** Transfer the cheese and aubergine mixture to a baking dish and sprinkle a generous layer of Parmesan over the top.

**9** Bake in the oven for about 25 minutes, until the top is browned.

**10** Serve immediately, with some warm bread and a green salad.

**Per portion** Energy 322kcal/1344kJ; Protein 14.1g; Carbohydrate 15.2g, of which sugars 9.3g; Fat 22.7g, of which saturates 14.5g; Cholesterol 63mg; Calcium 415mg; Fibre 2.2g; Sodium 350mg.

# STUFFED POACHED AUBERGINES

*WHETHER THE IMAM FAINTED FROM SHOCK OR PLEASURE AT THE QUANTITY OF OLIVE OIL USED IN THIS DISH, NO ONE KNOWS, BUT "THE IMAM FAINTED" IS THE TRANSLATION OF IMAM BAYILDI. THE AUBERGINES ARE SOMETIMES BAKED, BUT THE MORE TRADITIONAL METHOD IS GENTLE POACHING ON TOP OF THE STOVE — WHEN COOKED THIS WAY THEY MELT IN THE MOUTH. SERVE THESE COLOURFUL STUFFED VEGETABLES AS A MEZE DISH OR WITH A GREEN SALAD FOR LUNCH OR SUPPER.*

SERVES FOUR

### INGREDIENTS

2 large aubergines (eggplants)
sunflower oil, for shallow frying
1 bunch each of fresh flat leaf
  parsley and dill
1 large onion, halved and
  finely sliced
3 tomatoes, skinned and
  finely chopped
2–3 garlic cloves,
  finely chopped
5ml/1 tsp salt
150ml/¼ pint/⅔ cup olive oil
juice of ½ lemon
15ml/1 tbsp sugar
lemon wedges, to serve

**1** Using a vegetable peeler or a small, sharp knife, peel the aubergines lengthways in stripes like a zebra.

**2** Place the aubergines in a bowl of salted water and leave for 5 minutes, then drain and pat dry.

### VARIATION

Follow steps 1–6, then place the filled aubergines (eggplants) in an ovenproof dish. Drizzle the remaining olive oil and lemon juice over the top, cover with foil and bake in the oven for about 45 minutes at 180°C/350°F/Gas 4. Remove the foil, sprinkle a little grated Parmesan cheese over the top and return to the oven for about 15 minutes, until the aubergines are browned. Serve hot.

**3** Heat about 1cm/½in sunflower oil in a wok or deep-sided pan. Place the aubergines in the oil and fry quickly on all sides to soften them. This should take a total of 3–5 minutes.

**4** Lift the aubergines out on to a chopping board and slit them open lengthways to create pockets, keeping the bottoms and both ends intact so they look like canoes when stuffed.

**5** Reserve a few dill fronds and parsley leaves for the garnish, then chop the rest and mix them in a large bowl with the onion, tomatoes and garlic. Add the salt and a little of the olive oil.

**6** Spoon the mixture into the aubergine pockets, packing it in tightly so that all of it is used up.

### COOK'S TIP

Courgettes (zucchini) are often cooked in a similar way. First, they are cut in half and deseeded, then the filling is piled into the hollow and they are baked in the oven.

**7** Place the filled aubergines side by side in a deep, heavy pan. Mix the remaining olive oil with 50ml/2fl oz/¼ cup water and the lemon juice, pour it over the aubergines, and sprinkle the sugar over the top.

**8** Cover the pan with a lid and place over a medium heat to get the oil hot and create some steam. Once the oil is hot, lower the heat and cook the aubergines very gently for about 1 hour, basting from time to time. They should be soft and tender, with only a little oil left in the bottom of the pan.

**9** Leave the aubergines to cool in the pan, then carefully transfer them to a serving dish and spoon the oil from the bottom of the pan over them. Garnish with the reserved dill and parsley and serve at room temperature, with lemon wedges for squeezing.

**Per portion** Energy 407kcal/1680kJ; Protein 3g; Carbohydrate 16.7g, of which sugars 14.1g; Fat 37g, of which saturates 5.1g; Cholesterol 0mg; Calcium 67mg; Fibre 4.8g; Sodium 507mg.

# STUFFED LEEKS WITH A TANGY SAUCE

*TREMENDOUS CREATORS OF STUFFED DISHES, THE TURKS EVEN STUFF TUBES OF LEEKS AND SERVE THEM WITH THEIR CLASSIC EGG AND LEMON SAUCE – AN ELEGANT FINISH TO A HOUSEHOLD DISH, WHICH IS CALLED TERBIYELI PIRASI DOLMASI. ALTHOUGH A LITTLE FIDDLY TO PREPARE, THIS DISH IS WORTH THE EFFORT IN THE END. SERVED WITH A PLAIN, BUTTERY PILAF AND TOMATO AND CUCUMBER SALAD, IT MAKES A SATISFYING SUPPER DISH.*

SERVES FOUR

INGREDIENTS

2–3 fat leeks, trimmed at both ends
25ml/1½ tbsp long grain rice, rinsed
225g/8oz/1 cup finely minced (ground) beef
1 onion, finely chopped
1 small bunch flat leaf parsley, leaves finely chopped
5–10ml/1–2 tsp *kırmızı biber*, or paprika
15ml/1 tbsp long grain rice, rinsed and drained
15g/½oz/1 tbsp soft butter
15ml/3 tsp tomato purée (paste)
salt and ground black pepper
mint leaves, to garnish

For the sauce
2 egg yolks
30ml/2 tbsp plain (all-purpose) flour
juice of ½ lemon
15ml/1 tbsp natural (plain) yogurt
250ml/8fl oz/1 cup water
1 small bunch fresh mint, leaves finely chopped

**3** Meanwhile bring a pan of water to the boil. Pour in the rice and boil for about 10 minutes, or until the rice is cooked but still firm. Drain and refresh under cold water.

**4** In a large bowl, mix the meat with the onion, parsley and *kırmızı biber*. Add the rice, and salt and pepper. Using your hands, bind the mixture with the butter so that it becomes pasty.

**5** Take one of the prepared leek tubes in your hand, and gently push some of the meat filling into it, like stuffing a sausage. Don't pack it too tightly as the rice will expand more on cooking, and you want the tubes to remain intact. Leave a little room at either end of the tube to use as flaps that can be tucked underneath the filled leek, so that the stuffing doesn't ooze out during cooking.

**6** Stuff as many leeks as you can and place them, side by side, in a large, heavy pan.

**7** Put the tomato purée in a bowl and stir in about 300ml/½ pint/1¼ cups water (add more if necessary – it should be the consistency of pouring cream). Season with salt and pepper and pour over the stuffed leeks.

**8** Cover the pan and cook the leeks gently for about 30 minutes, or until the rice has expanded and the meat has cooked. Lift the stuffed leeks on to a serving dish and keep warm. Pour the cooking liquid into a small pan.

**9** Just before serving, prepare the sauce. Put all the sauce ingredients in a bowl and beat with a wire whisk. Add two spoonfuls of the cooking liquid to the bowl, beating thoroughly, then pour the whole lot into the pan with the remainder of the cooking liquid.

**10** Gently heat the sauce, beating constantly with a wooden spoon. Take it off the heat just as it is about to boil, stir in the chopped mint and check and adjust the seasoning.

**11** Spoon the sauce over the leeks, garnish with the fresh mint leaves, and serve while hot.

**1** Cut the leeks into equal lengths, about 15cm/6in long, and remove the green outer layers. Place in a steamer basket and steam for 10 minutes to soften them. Refresh the leeks under cold running water and drain.

**2** Carefully, using your fingers, push out the inner layers of each leek to create a collection of soft hollow tubes. Put the tubes aside.

**Per portion** Energy 289kcal/1205kJ; Protein 17.3g; Carbohydrate 18.7g, of which sugars 4.6g; Fat 16.5g, of which saturates 6.9g; Cholesterol 143mg; Calcium 122mg; Fibre 4g; Sodium 97mg.

# PEPPERS STUFFED <u>WITH</u> AROMATIC RICE

*GENERALLY SERVED COLD AS A MEZE DISH, STUFFED GREEN PEPPERS — ZEYTINYAĞLI BIBER DOLMASI — ARE A UBIQUITOUS SIGHT THROUGHOUT TURKEY. IN THE HOME THEY ARE SOMETIMES SERVED HOT AS AN ACCOMPANIMENT TO A MEAT OR PASTRY DISH. THE GREEN PEPPERS IN TURKEY ARE MUCH SMALLER, LESS FLESHY AND A BRIGHTER GREEN THAN THE BELL PEPPERS. HOWEVER, LARGE BELL PEPPERS WORK JUST AS WELL, AND YOU CAN MAKE AN ATTRACTIVE DISH BY USING THE WHOLE RANGE OF COLOURS — RED, YELLOW, ORANGE AND GREEN — IN ONE SERVING. A THICK, CREAMY, GARLIC-FLAVOURED YOGURT CONTRASTS VERY WELL WITH THE HOT PEPPERS, OR YOU CAN SERVE THEM COLD WITH JUST SOME WEDGES OF LEMON TO SQUEEZE OVER.*

## SERVES FOUR

INGREDIENTS
- 30ml/2 tbsp currants
- 30ml/2 tbsp olive oil
- 2 red onions, finely chopped
- 5ml/1 tsp sugar, plus extra
  for sprinkling
- 45ml/3 tbsp pine nuts
- 10ml/2 tsp ground cinnamon
- 5ml/1 tsp dried mint
- 2.5ml/½ tsp ground allspice
- 175g/6oz/scant 1 cup short grain
  rice, washed and drained
- 1 small bunch flat leaf parsley,
  leaves finely chopped
- 1 small bunch dill,
  finely chopped
- 1 small bunch mint, leaves
  finely chopped
- 3 tomatoes
- 4–6 colourful (bell) peppers,
  with stalks removed and seeded,
  but kept whole
- salt and ground black pepper

For the cooking liquid
- 50ml/2fl oz/¼ cup olive oil
- juice of 1 lemon

**1** Soak the currants in warm water for 15 minutes and then drain them thoroughly in sieve (strainer). This will rehydrate the raisins, making them plump and juicy.

**2** Heat the olive oil in a heavy pan and stir in the onions and sugar. When the onions begin to colour, stir in the pine nuts and currants. Cook, stirring, until the pine nuts turn golden brown in colour. Take care not to let them burn.

**3** Add the cinnamon, dried mint and allspice. Stir in the rice, making sure it is coated in the spices. Pour in just enough water to cover the rice and season with a little salt and pepper.

**4** Give the rice a stir and bring the water to the boil. Reduce the heat and let it simmer, uncovered, until all the water has been absorbed.

**5** Turn off the heat and cover the rice with a clean dish towel. Leave it to steam for 10 minutes, then toss in the fresh herbs.

**6** Slice off the ends of each tomato to use as lids for the peppers (you don't need the remainder of the tomatoes for this recipe, but they can be used in a salad to accompany the peppers).

**7** Spoon the rice mixture into each pepper and seal them with their tomato lids. Place them upright, packed tightly, in a heavy pan.

**8** To make the cooking liquid, mix together the olive and lemon juice in a bowl and pour in about 250ml/8fl oz/ 1 cup of water.

**9** Pour the mixture over and around the peppers and sprinkle a little sugar over the top.

**10** Bring the liquid to the boil, reduce the heat, cover the pan and cook gently for 25–30 minutes, or until the peppers are tender.

**11** Serve hot with thick, creamy yogurt spiked with a little garlic, or leave them to cool in the pan and eat cold with wedges of lemon to squeeze over them.

**Per portion** Energy 489kcal/2036kJ; Protein 9.1g; Carbohydrate 61.7g, of which sugars 23.6g; Fat 23.4g, of which saturates 2.8g; Cholesterol 0mg; Calcium 108mg; Fibre 6g; Sodium 24mg.

# BAKED STUFFED APPLES

*VEGETABLES AND FRUIT STUFFED WITH AN AROMATIC PILAFF ARE A GREAT FAVOURITE IN TURKEY. ANYTHING WITH A CAVITY CAN BE STUFFED – AND IF THERE IS NO CAVITY, IT IS EASY TO MAKE ONE. AUBERGINES, PUPKINS, COURGETTES, TOMATOES, APPLES AND PLUMS ARE ALL STUFFED WITH AROMATIC RICE, OR WITH A MIXTURE OF RICE AND MINCED MEAT. THIS RECIPE, ELMA DOLMASI, IS FOR STUFFED APPLES, BUT YOU CAN EASILY USE IT TO MAKE AN IMPRESSIVE MEDLEY OF DIFFERENT STUFFED FRUIT AND VEGETABLES FOR A BUFFET OR A SUMMER LUNCH.*

SERVES FOUR

INGREDIENTS
4 cooking apples, or any firm,
  sour apple of your choice
30ml/2 tbsp olive oil
juice of ½ lemon
10ml/2 tsp sugar
salt and ground black pepper
For the filling
30ml/2 tbsp olive oil
a little butter
1 onion, finely chopped
2 garlic cloves
30ml/2 tbsp pine nuts
30ml/2 tbsp currants, soaked in
  warm water for 5–10 minutes
  and drained
5–10ml/1–2 tsp ground cinnamon
5–10ml/1–2 tsp ground allspice
5ml/1 tsp sugar
175g/6oz/scant 1 cup short grain
  rice, thoroughly rinsed and drained
1 bunch each of fresh flat leaf
  parsley and dill, finely chopped
To serve
1 tomato
1 lemon
a few fresh mint or basil leaves

**1** Make the filling. Heat the oil and butter in a heavy pan, stir in the onion and garlic and cook until they soften. Add the pine nuts and currants and cook until the nuts turn golden.

**COOK'S TIP**

Long, slender aubergines (eggplants) are especially suitable for stuffing. Roll the whole aubergine on the work surface and pummel it with your hand to separate the flesh from the skin. Now, using a knife, cut round the stalk without severing it, and pull the stalk out. If the innards have been sufficiently separated from the skin, they should come out with the stalk. The cavity is now ready to stuff.

**2** Stir in the spices, sugar and rice, and stir to combine thoroughly. Pour in enough water to cover the rice – roughly 1–2cm/½–¾in above the grains – and bring to the boil.

**3** Taste, then season the mixture with salt and pepper to taste and stir to combine. Lower the heat and simmer for about 10–12 minutes, until almost all the water has been absorbed.

**4** Toss in the chopped herbs, stir to combine and turn off the heat. Cover the pan with a dry, clean dish towel and the lid, and leave the rice to steam for 5 minutes.

**5** Preheat the oven to 200°C/400°F/ Gas 6. Using a knife, cut the stalk ends off the apples and keep to use as lids.

**6** Carefully core each apple, removing some of the flesh to create a cavity that is large enough to stuff.

**7** Take spoonfuls of the rice and pack it into the apples. Replace the lids and stand the apples, upright and tightly packed, in a small baking dish.

**8** In a jug (pitcher), mix together 100ml/3½fl oz/scant ½ cup water with the oil, lemon juice and sugar. Pour over and around the apples, then bake for 30–40 minutes, until the apples are tender and the juices are caramelized.

**9** Serve with a tomato and lemon garnish and a sprinkling of mint or basil leaves.

**Per portion** Energy 382kcal/1595kJ; Protein 5g; Carbohydrate 54.1g, of which sugars 18.8g; Fat 16.5g, of which saturates 1.9g; Cholesterol 0mg; Calcium 26mg; Fibre 2.1g; Sodium 4mg.

# AUBERGINE STEW

*WITH OVER 200 DISHES MADE WITH AUBERGINES ALONE IN TURKEY, THERE ARE MANY TO CHOOSE FROM. THIS ONE — PATLICAN BASTISI — IS SIMPLE AND CAN BE SERVED HOT AS A STEW ON ITS OWN, OR AS A SIDE DISH TO ACCOMPANY MEAT, OR IT CAN BE ENJOYED COLD AS A MEZE DISH. SERVE WITH THICK, CREAMY YOGURT AND PLENTY OF CRUSTY BREAD TO MOP UP THE SAUCE.*

### SERVES FOUR TO SIX

INGREDIENTS

60ml/4 tbsp olive oil
2 potatoes, peeled and cut into
   small bitesize chunks
10ml/2 tsp coriander seeds, crushed
2–3 garlic cloves, chopped
400g/14oz can chopped tomatoes
10ml/2 tsp tomato purée (paste)
15ml/1 tbsp sugar
2 slim aubergines (eggplants),
   cut into small bitesize pieces
2 green Turkish *çarliston* peppers,
   or 2 (bell) peppers, seeded and
   cut into bitesize pieces
1 small bunch flat leaf parsley,
   leaves chopped
1 small bunch dill, chopped
salt and ground black pepper

**1** Heat the oil in a wide, heavy pan and stir in the potatoes. Fry them over a medium heat for about 5–6 minutes to soften them. Stir in the coriander seeds and garlic.

**COOK'S TIP**
In some parts of Anatolia, diced potato is added to make a more substantial stew.

**2** Add the tomatoes, tomato purée and the sugar, followed by the aubergines and peppers. Top up the liquid with enough water (about 150–175ml/ 5–6fl oz/¼–⅔ cup) to surround the vegetables. Bring the liquid to the boil, partially cover the pan, and cook gently for 15–20 minutes.

**3** Remove the lid and cook for a further 5–10 minutes. Season with salt and pepper to taste, and stir in half the parsley and dill. Transfer the stew to a serving dish and garnish with the remainder of the herbs.

**4** Serve it hot with a dollop of thick, creamy yogurt and plenty of crusty bread to mop up the sauce.

**Per portion** Energy 164kcal/685kJ; Protein 2.9g; Carbohydrate 20.7g, of which sugars 10.5g; Fat 8.3g, of which saturates 1.3g; Cholesterol 0mg; Calcium 34mg; Fibre 3.7g; Sodium 23mg.

# VEGETABLE STEW

*Türlü is a seasonal vegetable stew made with winter or summer vegetables. Some versions contain lamb or chicken, but this one is made solely with vegetables. It can be served on its own with yogurt and chunks of fresh bread, or it can be served as an accompaniment to grilled or roasted meats. Traditionally, türlü is cooked in an earthenware pot.*

SERVES SIX

INGREDIENTS
- 60ml/4 tbsp olive oil
- 15ml/1 tbsp coriander seeds
- 2 cinnamon sticks
- 3–4 garlic cloves, crushed
- 3 red onions, cut into quarters lengthways
- 3 fresh artichoke hearts, cut into quarters
- 150g/5oz green beans, trimmed and cut into bitesize pieces
- 1 aubergine (eggplant), halved lengthways and sliced, or cut into bitesize chunks
- 2 courgettes (zucchini), thickly sliced, or cut into bitesize chunks
- 6 red or green Turkish *çarliston* peppers, left whole, or 2 (bell) peppers, cut into bitesize chunks
- 400g/14oz can plum tomatoes
- 15ml/3 tsp sugar
- 15ml/1 tbsp tomato purée (paste)
- 15ml/1 tbsp white wine vinegar
- 300ml/½ pint/1¼ cups water
- 1 small bunch flat leaf parsley, leaves roughly chopped
- 1 small bunch dill, chopped
- salt and ground black pepper

**5** Cover the pan and cook gently for about 35 minutes, or until the vegetables are tender. Toss in the herbs and season with salt and pepper. Serve hot.

**1** Heat the oil in a heavy pan, or flameproof earthenware pot. Stir in the coriander seeds, cinnamon sticks and garlic to flavour the oil.

**COOK'S TIP**
A winter stew, *türlü*, is generally made with pumpkin, potato and dried beans.

**2** Add the red onions, artichoke hearts and green beans, and fry them gently for 2–3 minutes. Add the aubergine, courgettes, and peppers.

**3** Cover the pan or pot with a lid and let the vegetables cook in the steam for 2–3 minutes.

**4** Add the tomatoes, sugar, tomato purée, vinegar and water – add more water, if necessary.

**Per portion** Energy 166kcal/690kJ; Protein 4.4g; Carbohydrate 18.3g, of which sugars 17.3g; Fat 8.8g, of which saturates 1.4g; Cholesterol 0mg; Calcium 68mg; Fibre 5.5g; Sodium 41mg.

# CARROT <u>AND</u> APRICOT ROLLS <u>WITH</u> MINT YOGURT

*THESE SWEET, HERBY CARROT ROLLS ARE A GREAT TREAT IN ISTANBUL AND IZMIR, BUT RARELY FOUND ELSEWHERE. SERVED WITH A DOLLOP OF YOGURT FLAVOURED WITH MINT AND GARLIC, THEY MAKE A DELICIOUS LIGHT LUNCH OR SUPPER WITH A GREEN SALAD AND WARM CRUSTY BREAD. ALTERNATIVELY, YOU CAN MOULD THE MIXTURE INTO MINIATURE BALLS AND SERVE THEM ON STICKS AS A NIBBLE TO GO WITH DRINKS, USING THE YOGURT AS A DIP.*

<u>SERVES FOUR</u>

INGREDIENTS
   8–10 carrots, cut into thick slices
   2–3 slices of day-old bread, ground
     into crumbs
   4 spring onions (scallions),
     finely sliced
   150g/5oz/generous ½ cup dried
     apricots, finely chopped or sliced
   45ml/3 tbsp pine nuts
   1 egg
   5ml/1 tsp *kırmızı biber*, or
     1 fresh red chilli, seeded and
     finely chopped
   1 bunch of fresh dill, chopped
   1 bunch of fresh basil,
     finely shredded
   salt and ground black pepper
   plain (all-purpose) flour, for coating
   sunflower oil, for shallow-frying
   lemon wedges, to serve
For the mint yogurt
   about 225g/8oz/1 cup thick and
     creamy natural (plain) yogurt
   juice of ½ lemon
   1–2 garlic cloves, crushed
   1 bunch of fresh mint,
     finely chopped

**1** Steam the carrot slices for about 25 minutes, or until very soft. Do not boil them as they will will lose some of their flavour and natural sweetness.

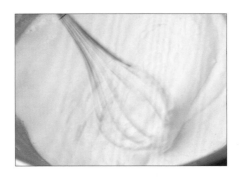

**2** Meanwhile, make the mint yogurt. Beat the yogurt in a bowl with the lemon juice and garlic, season with salt and pepper and stir in the mint. Set aside, or chill in the refrigerator.

**3** Mash the carrots to a paste while they are warm. Add the breadcrumbs, spring onions, apricots and pine nuts and mix well with a fork. Beat in the egg and stir in the *kırmızı biber* or chilli and herbs. Season with salt and pepper to taste.

**4** Put a small heap of flour on a flat surface. Take a plum-sized portion of the carrot mixture in your fingers and mould it into an oblong roll. If the mixture is very sticky, make it easier to deal with by adding more breadcrumbs or wetting your hands.

**5** Coat the carrot roll in the flour and put it on a plate. Repeat with rest of the mixture, to get 12–16 rolls altogether.

**6** Heat enough sunflower oil for shallow-frying in a heavy frying pan. Place the carrot rolls in the hot oil and fry over a medium heat for 8–10 minutes, turning them from time to time, until they are golden brown on all sides.

**7** Remove from the pan with a slotted spoon and drain on kitchen paper. Serve the rolls hot, with lemon wedges and the mint yogurt.

**VARIATIONS**
• You can make similar *köfte* (rolls) using the cooked flesh of sweet potatoes, combined with spices such as cinnamon, ground cumin or *kırmızı biber*.
• Alternatively, shape the rolls from a mixture of plain mashed potato and lots of fresh herbs, such as flat leaf parsley or dill.

**Per portion** Energy 401kcal/1673kJ; Protein 8.7g; Carbohydrate 46g, of which sugars 29.1g; Fat 21.5g, of which saturates 2.5g; Cholesterol 48mg; Calcium 144mg; Fibre 8.5g; Sodium 145mg.

# COURGETTE AND FETA PATTIES

*IDEAL FOR LUNCH, SUPPER, A SAVOURY SNACK OR APPETIZER, KABAK MUCVER ARE INCREDIBLY VERSATILE. YOU CAN EVEN MAKE MINIATURE ONES AND SERVE THEM AS A NIBBLE WITH DRINKS. IF YOU LIKE A LITTLE FIRE ON YOUR TONGUE, ADD MORE TURKISH RED PEPPER OR CHILLIES.*

**3** Transfer the flour to a bowl and beat in the eggs to form a smooth batter. Beat in the cooled courgette mixture. Add the feta, herbs and *kırmızı biber* or chilli, and season with black pepper. Add salt if you like, but usually the feta is quite salty. Mix well.

**4** Heat enough sunflower oil for shallow-frying in a heavy, non-stick pan. Drop four spoonfuls of the mixture into the hot oil, leaving space between each one, then fry over a medium heat for 6–8 minutes, or until firm to the touch and golden brown on both sides.

**5** Remove from the pan with a slotted spoon and drain on kitchen paper while you fry the remainder.

**6** Serve while still warm, garnished with mint leaves.

### SERVES FOUR TO SIX

INGREDIENTS
- 3 firm courgettes (zucchini), washed and ends trimmed
- 30–45ml/2–3 tbsp olive oil
- 1 large onion, cut in half lengthways, in half again crossways, and sliced along the grain
- 4 garlic cloves, chopped
- 45ml/3 tbsp plain (all-purpose) flour
- 3 eggs, beaten
- 225g/8oz feta cheese, crumbled
- 1 bunch each of fresh flat leaf parsley, mint and dill, chopped
- 5ml/1 tsp *kırmızı biber*, or 1 fresh red chilli, seeded and chopped
- sunflower oil, for shallow-frying
- salt and ground black pepper
- mint leaves, to garnish

**1** Hold the courgettes at an angle and grate them, then put them in a sieve (strainer) and sprinkle with a little salt. Leave them to weep for 5 minutes.

**2** Squeeze the grated courgettes in your hand to extract the juices. Heat the oil in a frying pan, stir in the courgettes, onion and garlic and fry until they begin to colour. Remove from the heat.

**Per portion** Energy 327kcal/1354kJ; Protein 12.3g; Carbohydrate 12.4g, of which sugars 5.4g; Fat 25.7g, of which saturates 7.9g; Cholesterol 121mg; Calcium 214mg; Fibre 2.3g; Sodium 581mg.

# POTATOES BAKED WITH TOMATOES AND FETA

*THIS TASTY POTATO DISH COMES FROM WESTERN ANATOLIA. TRADITIONALLY BAKED IN AN EARTHENWARE DISH, IT MAKES A FABULOUS ACCOMPANIMENT TO MEAT, POULTRY OR FISH, OR SERVE IT ON ITS OWN AS A MAIN COURSE WITH A SQUEEZE OF LEMON OR A DOLLOP OF YOGURT, AND A GREEN SALAD.*

SERVES FOUR TO SIX

INGREDIENTS

   675g/1½lb new potatoes
   15ml/1 tbsp butter
   45ml/3 tbsp olive oil
   2 red onions, cut in half lengthways,
     in half again crossways, and sliced
     along the grain
   3–4 garlic cloves, chopped
   5–10ml/1–2 tsp cumin seeds, crushed
   5–10ml/1–2 tsp *kırmızı biber*, or
     1 fresh red chilli, seeded
     and chopped
   10ml/2 tsp dried oregano
   10ml/2 tsp sugar
   15ml/1 tbsp white wine vinegar
   400g/14oz can chopped tomatoes,
     drained of juice
   12–16 black olives
   115g/4oz feta cheese, crumbled
   salt and ground black pepper
   olive oil, for drizzling
   1 lemon, cut into wedges

**1** Preheat the oven to 200°C/400°F/ Gas 6. Put the potatoes into a pan of cold water, bring to the boil and cook for 15–20 minutes, or until tender but not soft. Drain and refresh under cold running water, then peel off the skins and cut the potatoes into thick slices.

**2** Heat the butter and 30ml/2 tbsp of the oil in a heavy pan, stir in the onions and garlic and cook until soft. Add the cumin seeds, *kırmızı biber* or chilli and most of the oregano – reserve a little for the top – then stir in the sugar and vinegar, then the tomatoes. Season.

**3** Put the potatoes and olives into a baking dish – preferably an earthenware one – and spoon the tangy tomato mixture over them. Crumble the feta on top and sprinkle with the reserved oregano. Drizzle with the remaining oil, then bake for 25–30 minutes.

**4** Serve hot, with lemon wedges to squeeze over.

**Per portion** Energy 243kcal/1016kJ; Protein 6.3g; Carbohydrate 27.5g, of which sugars 9.3g; Fat 12.8g, of which saturates 5g; Cholesterol 19mg; Calcium 102mg; Fibre 2.9g; Sodium 447mg.

# ARTICHOKES WITH BEANS AND ALMONDS

*In the early summer, markets and street-sellers display crates of globe artichokes, which the Turks love to poach in olive oil. Often the seller will have them prepared ready for poaching, or will do it while you wait. The tender bottoms are traditionally filled with fresh broad beans and flavoured with dill, but sometimes diced carrots, potatoes, whole baby shallots and fresh peas are used as a filling, or the poached artichokes are simply served by themselves with a little dill. Ready-prepared artichoke bottoms are available frozen in some supermarkets and Middle Eastern stores, otherwise follow the preparation below. Serve as an appetizer or as a side dish.*

SERVES FOUR

INGREDIENTS
 4 large globe artichokes
 175g/6oz/2 cups broad (fava) beans
 120ml/4fl oz/½ cup olive oil
 juice of 1 lemon
 10ml/2 tsp granulated sugar
 75g/3oz/¾ cup blanched almonds
 1 small bunch of fresh dill, chopped
 2 tomatoes, skinned, seeded
  and diced
 salt

**1** To prepare the artichokes, cut off the stalks and pull off all the leaves. Dig out the hairy choke from the middle with a spoon, then cut away any hard bits with a sharp knife and trim into a neat cup shape. Rub the cups – called bottoms – with a mixture of lemon juice and salt to prevent them from discolouring.

**COOK'S TIPS**
• Until ready to use, fresh artichokes should be treated like flowers and put in a jug (pitcher) of water.
• Buy fresh-looking almonds in their skins. Put them in a bowl and cover with boiling water. Leave to soak for a few hours until the skins loosen, then rub the skins off with your fingers. If you leave them for as long as 24 hours, the nuts soften, too.

**2** To prepare the beans, split them down the seam at the side using your thumb nail, then push out the beans with the pad of your thumb.

**3** Put the beans in large pan of water and bring to the boil. Lower the heat and simmer for 10–15 minutes or until tender. Drain and refresh under cold running water, then peel off the skins.

**4** Place the artichokes in a heavy pan. Mix together the oil, lemon juice and 50ml/2fl oz/¼ cup water and pour over the artichokes.

**5** Cover the pan and poach the artichokes gently for about 20 minutes, then add the sugar, beans and almonds. Cover again and continue to poach gently for a further 10 minutes, or until the artichokes are tender.

**6** Toss in half the dill, season with salt, and turn off the heat. Leave the artichokes to cool in the pan.

**7** Lift the artichokes out of the pan and place them hollow-side up in a serving dish. Mix the tomatoes with the beans and almonds, spoon into the middle of the artichokes and around them, and garnish with the remaining dill. Serve at room temperature.

**Per portion** Energy 351kcal/1455kJ; Protein 8.2g; Carbohydrate 13.4g, of which sugars 8.3g; Fat 29.8g, of which saturates 3.6g; Cholesterol 0mg; Calcium 110mg; Fibre 5.5g; Sodium 29mg.

# GREEN BEANS WITH TOMATOES AND DILL

*THIS IS ONE OF THE DELICIOUS "OLIVE OIL" DISHES THAT HAVE SURVIVED FROM THE OTTOMAN EMPIRE, AND WHICH INCLUDE LEEKS, CELERIAC, GREEN BEANS, ARTICHOKES OR BORLOTTI BEANS COOKED IN OLIVE OIL. AS PART OF A MEZE SPREAD IT IS SERVED AT ROOM TEMPERATURE, BUT IN A TURKISH HOME IT MAY BE SERVED HOT AS A SIDE DISH TO ACCOMPANY GRILLED, BROILED OR BARBECUED POULTRY AND MEAT, OR AS A MAIN COURSE WITH YOGURT.*

SERVES FOUR (AS A MAIN DISH)

INGREDIENTS

1–2 onions, roughly chopped
2 garlic cloves, roughly chopped
30–45ml/2–3 tbsp olive oil
500g/1¼lb stringless runner
  (green) beans, trimmed and
  each cut into 3–4 pieces
15ml/1 tbsp sugar
juice of 1 lemon
2 x 400g/14oz cans
  chopped tomatoes
a handful of fresh dill,
  roughly chopped
salt and ground black pepper

**1** Put the onions, garlic and oil in a wide, heavy pan and stir over a low heat until they soften. Toss in the beans, coating them in the onions and oil, then stir in the sugar and lemon juice.

**2** Add the tomatoes to the pan and bring to the boil, then lower the heat and add the dill. Cook gently for 35–40 minutes, or until the beans are tender and the tomato sauce is fairly thick. Season with salt and pepper to taste before serving.

**Per portion** Energy 141kcal/588kJ; Protein 4.5g; Carbohydrate 16.5g, of which sugars 14g; Fat 6.8g, of which saturates 1.1g; Cholesterol 0mg; Calcium 75mg; Fibre 5.7g; Sodium 20mg.

# SWEET-AND-SOUR LADIES' FINGERS

*THIS IS A DELIGHTFUL WAY TO EAT OKRA, AS THEY ARE DELICIOUSLY TENDER AND CRUNCHY AS WELL AS BEING VERY EASY TO PREPARE. COOKED THIS WAY, THEY CAN BE SERVED AS A MEZE DISH, OR AS A SIDE DISH, EATEN HOT OR COLD. OTHER DISHES USING OKRA INCLUDE CHICKEN CASSEROLES, VEGETABLE STEWS AND AN ANATOLIAN SOUP MADE WITH SMALL, SOUR-TASTING OKRA, BUT THIS SIMPLE SWEET-AND-SOUR METHOD — BAMIA — IS PERHAPS THE FAVOURITE WAY OF USING THEM.*

### SERVES FOUR

INGREDIENTS
  350g/12oz fresh, springy okra,
    left whole
  juice of 2 lemons
  45ml/3 tbsp olive oil
  15ml/1 tbsp sugar
  salt and ground black pepper

**1** Put all the okra into a wide bowl and toss them in the lemon juice. Leave them to soak in the lemon juice for 5–10 minutes (this is a traditional trick to ensure the okra retains its vibrant green colour on cooking).

**2** Gather up the okra with your hands and place them in a colander, leaving most of the lemon juice behind. Pour the juice into a cup.

**3** Heat the olive oil in a wide, heavy pan. Toss in the okra for 2–3 minutes, then sprinkle them with the sugar. Toss them again and pour in the reserved lemon juice.

**4** Season the okra with salt and pepper to taste, and pour in a little water, just enough to cover the base of the pan. Keep tossing the okra over a high heat until the juices in the pan are almost caramelized.

**5** Lift the okra out of the pan and arrange them on a serving dish. Drizzle the pan juices over them and serve hot or cold.

**COOK'S TIP**
For this dish you must choose very fresh, vibrant green, firm okra and be careful not to overcook them.

**Per portion** Energy 116kcal/482kJ; Protein 2.5g; Carbohydrate 6.6g, of which sugars 6.1g; Fat 9.1g, of which saturates 1.5g; Cholesterol 0mg; Calcium 142mg; Fibre 3.5g; Sodium 7mg.

# CARAMELIZED MUSHROOMS <u>WITH</u> ALLSPICE <u>AND</u> HERBS

*BUTTON MUSHROOMS CARAMELIZE BEAUTIFULLY IN THEIR OWN JUICES WHILE STILL RETAINING THEIR MOISTNESS AND NUTTY FLAVOUR. THIS DISH IS USUALLY SERVED AS A SIDE DISH FOR GRILLED LAMB CHOPS OR LIVER, OR AS A HOT OR COLD MEZE DISH WITH CHUNKS OF BREAD TO MOP UP THE TASTY COOKING JUICES, BUT THE MUSHROOMS ARE ALSO GOOD SERVED ON TOASTED CRUSTY BREAD AS A LIGHT LUNCH WITH A FRESH SALAD. USE WHATEVER HERBS AND SPICES YOU HAVE AVAILABLE, JUST AS THEY WOULD IN THE DIFFERENT REGIONS OF TURKEY.*

**2** Cover and cook for about 10 minutes, shaking the pan from time to time, until the mushrooms start to caramelize.

**3** Remove the lid and toss in the mint with some of the sage and parsley. Cook for a further 5 minutes, until most of the liquid has evaporated, then season.

**4** Transfer to a serving dish and sprinkle the rest of the sage and parsley over the top. Serve hot or at room temperature, with lemon wedges for squeezing.

**COOK'S TIP**
Button (white) mushrooms are ideal as they don't release much liquid and caramelize well. Don't wash before cooking, just wipe with a clean dish towel.

SERVES FOUR

INGREDIENTS
  45ml/3 tbsp olive oil
  15ml/1 tbsp butter
  450g/1lb button (white) mushrooms,
    wiped clean
  3–4 garlic cloves, finely chopped
  10ml/2 tsp allspice berries, crushed
  10ml/2 tsp coriander seeds
  5ml/1 tsp dried mint
  1 bunch each of fresh sage and flat
    leaf parsley, chopped
  salt and ground black pepper
  lemon wedges, to serve

**1** Heat the oil and butter in wide, heavy pan, then stir in the mushrooms with the garlic, allspice and coriander. Mix everything gently to combine.

**Per portion** Energy 125kcal/517kJ; Protein 2.8g; Carbohydrate 1.2g, of which sugars 0.8g; Fat 12.2g, of which saturates 3.3g; Cholesterol 8mg; Calcium 58mg; Fibre 2.5g; Sodium 37mg.

# COURGETTE AND APPLE WITH A HAZELNUT AND LEMON SAUCE

*STEAMED, FRIED, GRILLED OR ROASTED VEGETABLES ARE OFTEN SERVED WITH A NUT SAUCE, TARATOR, IN TURKEY. IN THIS RECIPE — TARATORLU KABAK — THE COURGETTES AND APPLES ARE ROASTED, BUT THEY COULD BE COOKED BY ANY METHOD, SUCH AS GRILLING OR STEAMING. ALONG THE BLACK SEA COAST, THE NUT SAUCE IS OFTEN MADE WITH THE LOCAL HAZELNUTS, WHICH MAKES A LIGHTER SAUCE THAN A WALNUT VERSION AND IS NOT AS CREAMY AS ONE MADE WITH PINE NUTS OR ALMONDS. THIS DISH CAN BE SERVED AS A SIDE DISH TO GRILLED AND ROASTED MEATS, OR AS A HOT MEZE DISH.*

SERVES FOUR

INGREDIENTS

  2 firm, fat courgettes (zucchini)
  2 sweet, firm red, pink, or
    yellow apples
  30–45ml/2–3 tbsp olive oil
  15–30ml/1–2 tbsp chopped
    roasted hazelnuts, to garnish
For the nut sauce
  115g/4oz/²⁄₃ cup hazelnuts
  1–2 garlic cloves
  30ml/2 tbsp olive oil
  juice of 1 lemon
  15ml/1 tbsp grape *pekmez*, or
    molasses or clear honey
  salt and ground black pepper

**1** Preheat the oven to 180°C/350°F/ Gas 4. Using a vegetable peeler, partially peel the courgettes in stripes. Slice them on the diagonal. Quarter and core the apples then cut each quarter into 2 or 3 segments.

**2** Place the courgette and apple slices in an ovenproof dish and pour over the olive oil. Put into the oven and roast for 35–40 minutes, or until golden brown.

**COOK'S TIP**
Other vegetables served this way include whole Mediterranean (bell) peppers, sliced aubergine (eggplant), pumpkin and squash, and fruit, such as plums.

**3** Meanwhile, make the nut sauce. Using a mortar and pestle, or a food processor, pound the hazelnuts with the garlic to form a thick paste.

**4** Gradually beat in the oil and lemon juice, until the mixture is quite creamy. Sweeten with the *pekmez*, molasses or clear honey, and season to taste.

**5** Arrange the roasted courgette and apple on a serving dish and drizzle the nut sauce over them. Sprinkle the roasted hazelnuts over the top and serve while still warm.

**Per portion** Energy 365kcal/1513kJ; Protein 6.6g; Carbohydrate 13.3g, of which sugars 12.6g; Fat 32.1g, of which saturates 3.2g; Cholesterol 0mg; Calcium 74mg; Fibre 4.2g; Sodium 5mg.

# ROASTED COURGETTES AND PEACHES WITH PINE NUTS

*A FAVOURITE DISH IN TURKEY IS A MIXTURE OF DEEP-FRIED OR GRILLED VEGETABLES SERVED WITH A GARLIC-FLAVOURED SAUCE MADE WITH YOGURT, NUTS OR SESAME PASTE. COURGETTES, AUBERGINES AND CARROTS ARE THE MOST COMMON VEGETABLES USED, AND THEY ARE OFTEN DEEP-FRIED IN BATTER. THIS RECIPE, HOWEVER, COMBINES FRUIT AND VEGETABLES TO MAKE A COLOURFUL MEDLEY THAT IS BAKED RATHER THAN DEEP-FRIED OR GRILLED. YOU CAN SERVE IT ON ITS OWN WITH A YOGURT OR TARATOR SAUCE, OR A TAHINI DRESSING, AND WARM, CRUSTY BREAD, OR AS AN ACCOMPANIMENT TO GRILLED, BROILED OR BARBECUED MEAT OR POULTRY.*

SERVES FOUR

INGREDIENTS
  2 courgettes (zucchini)
  2 yellow or red (bell) peppers,
    seeded and cut into wedges
  100ml/3½ fl oz/scant ½ cup
    olive oil
  4–6 plum tomatoes
  2 firm peaches, peeled, halved and
    stoned (pitted), then cut into wedges
  30ml/2 tbsp pine nuts
  salt and ground black pepper
For the yogurt sauce
  500g/1¼ lb/2¼ cups thick and
    creamy natural (plain) yogurt
  2–3 garlic cloves, crushed
  juice of ½ lemon

**VARIATIONS**
This dish is also delicious served with tarator sauce or tahini dressing.
• To make the tarator sauce, sprinkle 1–2 slices of day-old bread with a little water, leave for a few minutes until the water is absorbed, then squeeze dry. Roughly pound 115g/4oz/⅔ cup shelled walnuts, hazelnuts, almonds or pine nuts to a paste with 1–2 garlic cloves and the bread. Beat in the juice of ½ lemon and drizzle in enough olive oil to form a thick, creamy sauce, beating all the time as when making mayonnaise. Season with salt and ground black pepper.
• To make tahini dressing, thin down about 30ml/2 tbsp sesame paste with a little water and lemon juice, beat in some crushed garlic and, if you like, a little roasted *kırmızı biber*. Season with salt and ground black pepper. This can be used as a dressing for roasted or steamed vegetables or for a salad of carrots, red onion and chickpeas tossed with chopped fresh mint, parsley and coriander (cilantro).

**1** Preheat the oven to 200°C/400°F/ Gas 6. Using a vegetable peeler, peel the courgettes lengthways in stripes like a zebra, then halve and slice them lengthways, or cut into wedges.

**2** Place the courgettes and peppers in a baking dish, preferably an earthenware one. Drizzle the oil over them and sprinkle with salt, then bake in the oven for 20 minutes.

**3** Take the dish out of the oven and turn the vegetables in the oil, then mix in the tomatoes and peaches. Bake for a further 20–25 minutes, until everything is nicely browned.

**4** Meanwhile, make the yogurt sauce. In a small bowl, beat the yogurt with the garlic and lemon juice. Season to taste with salt and pepper and set aside until required, or chill in the refrigerator.

**5** Dry-roast the pine nuts in a small, heavy pan, shaking them constantly, until they turn golden brown and give off a nutty aroma. Be careful not to let them burn. Remove from the heat.

**6** When the roasted vegetables are ready, remove the dish from the oven and sprinkle the pine nuts over the top. Serve immediately with the yogurt sauce and some warm bread.

**Per portion** Energy 362kcal/1507kJ; Protein 11.7g; Carbohydrate 26.7g, of which sugars 26.3g; Fat 24.1g, of which saturates 3.7g; Cholesterol 2mg; Calcium 284mg; Fibre 4.8g; Sodium 120mg.

# BEANS, PEAS, LENTILS AND PILAFFS

*Most Turks eat rice, bulgur wheat or pulses for at least one meal*

*every day. Generally, pilaffs are served as stand-alone dishes, such*

*as Rice with Lamb, Carrots, Onions and Spices, or as an*

*accompaniment to a meat or poultry dish, such as Sultan's Chickpea*

*Pilaff. Pulse dishes, on the other hand, might be prepared as part of*

*a meze spread, a snack on their own, such as Chickpea Patties*

*with Red Onion and Parsley, or as an accompaniment to meat.*

# LENTILS <u>WITH</u> CARROTS <u>AND</u> SAGE

*ADAPTED FROM ONE OF THE OTTOMAN ZEYTINYAĞLI DISHES, WHICH IS FLAVOURED WITH MINT AND DILL, THIS SIMPLE RECIPE USES SAGE INSTEAD. IN ANATOLIA, PUNGENT SAGE LEAVES ARE DRIED IN THE SUN, WHICH CAPTURES THEIR STRONG HERBY AROMA. THE SAME SAGE IS IDEAL FOR COOKING, AS ITS WARMING FLAVOUR SPREADS THROUGH THE DISH. SERVE WITH GRILLED, BROILED OR BARBECUED MEATS, OR ON THEIR OWN WITH A DOLLOP OF YOGURT SEASONED WITH GARLIC, SALT AND PEPPER, AND LEMON.*

SERVES FOUR TO SIX

INGREDIENTS
  175g/6oz/¾ cup green lentils,
    rinsed and picked over
  45–60ml/3–4 tbsp fruity olive oil
  1 onion, cut in half lengthways, in
    half again crossways, and sliced
    along the grain
  3–4 plump garlic cloves, roughly
    chopped and bruised with the flat
    side of a knife
  5ml/1 tsp coriander seeds
  a handful of dried sage leaves
  5–10ml/1–2 tsp sugar
  4 carrots, sliced
  15–30ml/1–2 tbsp tomato
    purée (paste)
  salt and ground black pepper
  1 bunch of fresh sage or flat leaf
    parsley, to garnish

**1** Bring a pan of water to the boil and add the lentils. Lower the heat, partially cover the pan and simmer gently for 10 minutes. Drain and rinse well under cold running water.

**2** Heat the oil in a heavy pan, stir in the onion, garlic, coriander, sage and sugar, and cook until the onion begins to colour.

**3** Add the carrots and cook for 3 minutes, then add the lentils and pour in 250ml/ 8fl oz/1 cup water, making sure the lentils and carrots are covered.

**4** Stir in the tomato purée and cover the pan, then cook the lentils and carrots gently for about 20 minutes, until most of the liquid has been absorbed. The lentils and carrots should both be tender, but still have some bite. Season with salt and pepper to taste.

**5** Garnish with the fresh sage or flat leaf parsley, and serve hot or warm.

**COOK'S TIP**
Cooked in olive oil and almost always served cold, *zeytinyağlı* dishes include leeks and carrots, celeriac, runner or green beans, and artichokes.

**Per portion** Energy 166kcal/696kJ; Protein 7.6g; Carbohydrate 21.1g, of which sugars 6.7g; Fat 6.2g, of which saturates 0.9g; Cholesterol 0mg; Calcium 38mg; Fibre 4g; Sodium 22mg.

# CHICKPEA STEW

*BEAN AND CHICKPEA STEWS ARE OFTEN PREPARED WITH CHUNKS OF LAMB, THE SPICY SAUSAGE, SUCUK, OR THE POPULAR CURED BEEF, PASTIRMA, BUT THIS IS A MEATLESS VERSION, CALLED NOHUTLU YAHNISI. IT CAN BE SERVED AS A MEAL ON ITS OWN WITH WEDGES OF LEMON TO SQUEEZE OVER IT AND A RICE OR BULGUR WHEAT PILAFF TO ACCOMPANY IT, OR IT CAN BE SERVED AS A SIDE DISH WITH ROASTED OR GRILLED MEATS OR FISH.*

SERVES THREE TO FOUR

INGREDIENTS

15–30ml/1–2 tbsp ghee, or 15ml/
   1 tbsp olive oil plus a knob (pat)
   of butter
2 red onions, halved and sliced
4 garlic cloves, chopped
10ml/2 tsp coriander seeds
5ml/1 tsp cumin seeds, crushed
5ml/1 tsp fennel seeds
5–10ml/1–2 tsp *kırmızı biber*,
   or paprika
10ml/2 tsp sugar
2 x 400g/14oz cans chickpeas,
   rinsed thoroughly and drained
400g/14oz can chopped tomatoes,
   drained of juice
1 small bunch parsley, leaves chopped
salt and ground black pepper
200g/7oz baby spinach leaves

To serve
1 lemon, cut into wedges
60–75ml/4–5 tbsp thick and creamy
   natural (plain) yogurt

**1** Heat the ghee, or oil and butter, in a heavy pan. Stir in the onion, garlic and spices, and cook until the onions begin to brown.

**VARIATIONS**
You can use *sucuk*, the spicy sausage, or *pastirma*, the cured beef, in this dish. Simply slice and add to the pan at stage 1 with the onion and garlic, so that they flavour the cooking juices. Continue as above, but omit the spinach leaves.

**2** Stir in the tomatoes and sugar, then toss in the chickpeas to brown them lightly. Add the parsley and season with salt and pepper.

**3** Toss in the spinach leaves, cover the pan, and let the leaves wilt in the steam. Transfer to a bowl and serve immediately. Squeeze the wedges of lemon over it and serve with a dollop of yogurt.

**Per portion** Energy 178kcal/741kJ; Protein 5.3g; Carbohydrate 17.4g, of which sugars 10.6g; Fat 10.2g, of which saturates 1.5g; Cholesterol 0mg; Calcium 136mg; Fibre 4.3g; Sodium 128mg.

# CHICKPEA PATTIES <u>WITH</u> RED ONION <u>AND</u> PARSLEY

*THESE TASTY CUMIN-FLAVOURED PATTIES, CALLED NOHUTLU MÜCVER, CAN BE SERVED AS A SNACK OR AS PART OF A LIGHT MEAL WITH A CRUNCHY GREEN SALAD. MINI VERSIONS OF THE PATTIES ARE DELICIOUS STUFFED INTO PITTA BREAD POCKETS WITH LOTS OF RED ONION, FLAT LEAF PARSLEY AND A DRIZZLE OF YOGURT. EASY TO PREPARE, THEY CAN BE FRIED OR GRILLED AND CAN ALSO BE PREPARED AHEAD OF TIME AND KEPT IN THE REFRIGERATOR UNTIL REQUIRED.*

SERVES FOUR

INGREDIENTS

    400g/14oz can chickpeas, drained
      and thoroughly rinsed
    45–60ml/3–4 tbsp olive oil
    1 red onion, finely chopped
    10ml/2 tsp cumin seeds, crushed
    10ml/2 tsp ground coriander
    5–10ml/1–2 tsp *kırmızı biber*,
      or paprika
    1 small bunch flat leaf parsley,
      leaves finely chopped
    1 small bunch dill, finely chopped
    rind of 1 lemon
    plain (all-purpose) flour, for dusting
    salt and ground black pepper
To serve
    45–60ml/3–4 tbsp thick and creamy
      natural (plain) yogurt
    1–2 garlic cloves, crushed
    1 red onion, halved and sliced
    1 small bunch flat leaf parsley,
      leaves roughly chopped
    1 lemon, sliced

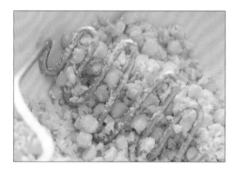

**1** In a bowl, pound the chickpeas with a potato masher, or process them to a paste in a food processor or blender.

**COOK'S TIP**
You could pound the chickpeas with the soaked bread, beans and the rest of the ingredients, then mould the mixture into balls to form *köfte* that are similar to the popular Middle Eastern *falafel*.

**2** Bind with 15ml/1 tbsp of the olive oil and beat in the onion, cumin, coriander, and *kırmızı biber* or paprika with a wooden spoon.

**3** Add the parsley, dill and lemon rind, and season the mixture with salt and pepper to taste.

**4** Mould portions of the chickpea mixture into small balls and flatten them in the palm of your hand to form thick patties (make these as big or as small as you like).

**5** Dust the patties in a little flour and fry them for 2 minutes on each side in the remaining olive oil in a non-stick pan. Drain them on kitchen paper.

**6** In a small bowl, beat the yogurt with the garlic, and season to taste.

**7** Arrange the patties on a large serving plate and serve them hot, or at room temperature, with the red onion, parsley, and lemon to squeeze over them, or a little garlic yogurt to drizzle over the top. Alternatively, you can tuck the patties into pitta pouches with the same ingredients.

**Per portion** Energy 246kcal/1032kJ; Protein 10.2g; Carbohydrate 24.7g, of which sugars 2.3g; Fat 12.8g, of which saturates 1.7g; Cholesterol 0mg; Calcium 118mg; Fibre 5.1g; Sodium 238mg.

# BEANS WITH PASTIRMA AND LAMB'S LETTUCE

*THE FLAVOURING OF THIS SIMPLE YET DELICIOUS DISH COMES FROM THE FENUGREEK AND CUMIN COATING ON THE DRIED FILLET OF BEEF, PASTIRMA. YOU CAN USE ANY BEANS, ALTHOUGH THIS DISH, CALLED BOSTANA, IS GENERALLY MADE WITH BORLOTTI, HARICOT OR BLACK-EYED BEANS. SERVE WITH LEMON WEDGES OR, TO MAKE A MORE SUSTAINING MAIN MEAL, PUSH ASIDE THE MIXTURE TO CREATE POCKETS INTO WHICH EGGS CAN BE DROPPED AND GENTLY COOKED.*

SERVES THREE TO FOUR

INGREDIENTS
   175g/6oz borlotti beans, black-eyed
     beans (peas), haricot (navy) or
     butter (lima) beans, soaked
     overnight and rinsed
   30ml/2 tbsp olive oil and a
     little butter
   1 onion, chopped
   2 garlic cloves, chopped
   175g/6oz *pastırma*, finely sliced
   400g/14oz can chopped tomatoes,
     drained of juice
   225g/8oz fresh lamb's lettuce,
     rinsed and drained
   1 small bunch parsley, leaves
     roughly chopped
   salt and ground black pepper
   1 lemon, cut into wedges, to serve

**1** Put the beans into a pan and cover with water. Bring to the boil and simmer until tender (this will take 45 minutes for black-eyed beans, 50 minutes for haricot beans and 1 hour for butter beans).

**2** Heat the oil and butter in a heavy pan and stir in the onion and garlic, until they begin to colour.

**3** Toss in the beans, followed by the *pastırma*, and sauté for 3–4 minutes to release the flavour. Add the tomatoes and cook for 2–3 minutes, then toss in the lamb's lettuce until it begins to wilt. Season and garnish with the parsley.

**4** Serve with wedges of lemon to squeeze over the top.

**Per portion** Energy 283kcal/1192kJ; Protein 21.4g; Carbohydrate 29.6g, of which sugars 9.6g; Fat 9.7g, of which saturates 2.3g; Cholesterol 27mg; Calcium 112mg; Fibre 10.1g; Sodium 44mg.

# BORLOTTI BEANS WITH TOMATO AND GARLIC

*THIS IS A GREAT FAVOURITE IN TURKEY — WHERE IN THE MARKETS THEY SELL MEATY, PINKISH BORLOTTI BEANS IN THEIR DAPPLED PODS FOR THE SOLE PURPOSE OF PREPARING THIS DISH. IN POOR HOMES, WHERE MEAT MAY BE SERVED INFREQUENTLY, DISHES MADE FROM BORLOTTI BEANS AND AUBERGINES MAKE A REGULAR APPEARANCE. COOKED IN LOTS OF OLIVE OIL, THIS IS ANOTHER ZEYTINYAĞLI DISH, WHICH YOU WILL ENCOUNTER ALL OVER THE WESTERN REGION OF TURKEY.*

### SERVES FOUR

### INGREDIENTS

175g/6oz/scant 1 cup dried borlotti beans, soaked in cold water overnight
45–60ml/3–4 tbsp olive oil
2 red onions, cut in half lengthways, in half again crossways, and sliced along the grain
4 garlic cloves, chopped
400g/14oz can tomatoes
10ml/2 tsp sugar
1 bunch each of fresh flat leaf parsley and dill, coarsely chopped
4 ripe plum tomatoes
salt and ground black pepper
1 lemon, cut into quarters

**1** Drain the beans, transfer them to a pan and fill the pan with plenty of cold water. Bring to the boil and boil for 1 minute, then lower the heat and partially cover the pan. Simmer the beans for about 30 minutes, or until they are tender but not soft or mushy. Drain, rinse well under cold running water and remove any loose skins.

**2** Heat the oil in a heavy pan and stir in the onions and garlic. When they begin to soften, add the canned tomatoes, sugar and half the herbs. Toss in the beans, pour in 300ml/½ pint/1¼ cups water and bring to the boil. Lower the heat, partially cover the pan, then simmer for about 20 minutes, until most of the liquid has gone.

**3** Meanwhile, bring a small pan of water to the boil, drop in the tomatoes for a few seconds, then plunge them into a bowl of cold water. Peel off the skins and coarsely chop the tomatoes.

**4** Add the tomatoes to the beans with the rest of the herbs – reserving a little for the garnish. Season and cook for a further 5–10 minutes. Serve hot or at room temperature, with lemon wedges for squeezing.

**Per portion** Energy 266kcal/1119kJ; Protein 12.4g; Carbohydrate 34.4g, of which sugars 14.4g; Fat 9.8g, of which saturates 1.5g; Cholesterol 0mg; Calcium 103mg; Fibre 10.6g; Sodium 33mg.

# BLACK-EYED BEAN STEW WITH SPICY SAUSAGE

*BEAN STEWS MADE WITH SPICY CURED SAUSAGE, OR CURED, DRIED BEEF, ARE POPULAR IN TURKEY. IN THE AEGEAN REGION, BLACK-EYED BEANS ARE USED, BUT ANY BEANS OR CHICKPEAS MAY BE SUBSTITUTED. ACCOMPANY WITH A SALAD OF HOT GREEN PEPPERS AND PARSLEY, OR PICKLED VEGETABLES.*

**1** Drain the beans, transfer them to a pan and fill the pan with plenty of cold water. Bring to the boil and boil for 1 minute, then lower the heat and partially cover the pan. Simmer the beans for about 25 minutes, or until they are *al dente*. Drain, rinse well under cold running water and remove any loose skins.

**2** Preheat the oven to 180°C/350°F/ Gas 4. Melt the ghee in a heavy pan or flameproof earthenware pot. Stir in the onion, garlic and spices and fry until the onion begins to colour.

**3** Stir in the sugar or honey, toss in the spicy sausage and cook until it begins to brown.

## VARIATIONS

• This dish can also be made with *pastırma* – a cured fillet of beef encased in *çemen*, which is a dark red paste made from ground fenugreek, cumin, red pepper and garlic.

• For this recipe use any Turkish, Greek or Italian spicy sausage. The Turkish *sucuk* is horseshoe-shaped and spiked with cumin, while the long *pastırma* fillets are coated in fenugreek. Both are sold in Middle Eastern shops.

SERVES FOUR TO SIX

INGREDIENTS
    175g/6oz/scant 1 cup dried
        black-eyed beans (peas), soaked
        in cold water overnight
    30ml/2 tbsp ghee or 15ml/1 tbsp
        each olive oil and butter
    1 large onion, cut in half lengthways
        and sliced along the grain
    2–3 garlic cloves, roughly chopped
        and bruised with the flat side of
        a knife
    5ml/1 tsp cumin seeds
    5–10ml/1–2 tsp coriander seeds
    5ml/1 tsp fennel seeds
    5–10ml/1–2 tsp sugar or clear honey
    1 spicy cured sausage, about
        25cm/10in long, sliced
    150ml/¼ pint/⅔ cup white wine
    400g/14oz can tomatoes
    1 bunch of fresh flat leaf parsley,
        roughly chopped
    salt and ground black pepper

**4** Add the beans, followed by the wine. Bubble up the wine, then lower the heat and add the tomatoes. Stir in half the parsley and season with salt and pepper.

**5** Cover and bake for about 40 minutes. Before serving, taste for seasoning and sprinkle with the remaining parsley.

**Per portion** Energy 382kcal/1594kJ; Protein 18g; Carbohydrate 20g, of which sugars 6.7g; Fat 24.4g, of which saturates 10g; Cholesterol 52mg; Calcium 55mg; Fibre 6g; Sodium 944mg.

# BROAD BEAN PURÉE

*THIS BROAD BEAN PURÉE IS A TRADITIONAL DISH THAT IS MADE WHEN THE BEANS ARE IN SEASON. AN ACQUIRED TASTE, FAVA IS PARTICULARLY SOUGHT AFTER IN ISTANBUL. IT IS MADE WITH LARGE QUANTITIES OF OLIVE OIL FOR TASTE AND FOR THE DESIRED SMOOTH AND SILKY CONSISTENCY.*

SERVES FOUR

INGREDIENTS
225g/8oz/1¼ cups dried broad
  (fava) beans, soaked overnight
175g/6oz fresh broad (fava)
  beans, shelled
550ml/18fl oz/2½ cups water
1 onion, chopped
1 potato, peeled and chopped
150ml/¼ pint/⅔ cup olive oil
5ml/1 tsp salt
10ml/2 tsp sugar
For the garnish
  1 tomato
  a few dill fronds, trimmed
    into feathers

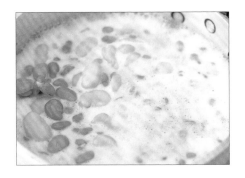

**1** Put the dried and fresh beans into a pan with the water and bring to the boil. Add the onion and potato and reduce the heat.

**2** Pour in the oil and sprinkle the salt and sugar over the top. Cover and simmer for 1 hour, stirring occasionally and topping up the water if necessary, until the purée has a pouring consistency.

**3** Press the purée through a sieve (strainer), or process it in food processor or blender. Pour it into a wet mould or bowl. Leave to cool and set.

**4** To make the garnish, plunge the tomato into a bowl of boiling water for 30 seconds, then refresh in cold water. Peel away the skin. Remove and discard the seeds and finely chop the flesh.

**5** Invert the mould or bowl on to a serving plate and garnish the purée with a cluster of chopped tomato on the very top with the dill feathers sprinkled about.

**6** Serve at room temperature with other *meze* dishes.

**Per portion** Energy 465kcal/1944kJ; Protein 17g; Carbohydrate 42.8g, of which sugars 6.2g; Fat 26.2g, of which saturates 3.8g; Cholesterol 0mg; Calcium 89mg; Fibre 12.5g; Sodium 21mg.

# Kurdish Bulgur Wheat with Yogurt

*In the east of Anatolia, bulgur wheat is eaten far more often than rice. Both the Turks and the Kurds of this region eat it with a wide range of dishes or on its own. Eaten from a communal pot and served with creamy yogurt, this dish — Kürt bulgur pilavi — is traditionally made with the strong-tasting fat from the sheep's tail, or with ghee. It can also be made with plain butter or olive oil, but ghee is the most authentic.*

**3** Turn off the heat, cover the pan with a clean dish towel, and press the lid on top. Leave to steam for a further 10–15 minutes, then fluff it up with a fork and form it into a mound on a serving dish. Make a well in the centre and spoon the yogurt into it.

**4** Melt the remaining ghee or butter in a small pan. Drizzle it over the yogurt and serve the bulgur wheat immediately.

### VARIATION

A similar dish, *kuskus*, can be made with couscous. Soak the couscous first, then rub with oil to separate the grains, and heat them in the oven with 45ml/3 tbsp ghee. Serve this simple couscous dish straight from the oven with a dollop of creamy natural (plain) yogurt.

SERVES FOUR TO SIX

INGREDIENTS
    45ml/3 tbsp ghee or butter
    2 onions, chopped
    350g/12oz bulgur wheat, thoroughly
      rinsed and drained
    600ml/1 pint/2½ cups water
      or lamb stock
    500g/1¼lb tub thick and creamy
      natural (plain) yogurt
    salt and ground black pepper

**1** Melt 30ml/2 tbsp of ghee or butter in a heavy pan and stir in the onions. Cook the onions to soften. Add the bulgur wheat, tossing it thoroughly.

**2** Pour in the water or stock, season with salt and pepper to taste and stir to combine thoroughly. Bring to the boil for 1–2 minutes, then reduce the heat and simmer until all the liquid has been completely absorbed.

**Per portion** Energy 394kcal/1640kJ; Protein 11.1g; Carbohydrate 57.8g, of which sugars 6.6g; Fat 15.7g, of which saturates 8.2g; Cholesterol 16mg; Calcium 154mg; Fibre 2.4g; Sodium 108mg.

# ANATOLIAN BULGUR WITH NUTS AND DATES

*THERE ARE SEVERAL HEARTY ANATOLIAN DISHES MADE WITH RICE OR BULGUR THAT INCLUDE VEGETABLES, DRIED FRUIT AND NUTS. THIS ONE IS OFTEN ATTRIBUTED TO THE BEDOUIN, NOMADIC HERDSMEN IN THE DESERTS OF ARABIA AND NORTH AFRICA WHO DEPENDED HEAVILY ON DATES. THIS DISH IS DELICIOUS SERVED WITH ROASTED MEAT OR CHICKEN AND, IN EASTERN ANATOLIA, IT IS OFTEN SERVED ON ITS OWN. YOU CAN ADD DRIED FIGS, PRUNES OR APRICOTS, IF YOU LIKE.*

SERVES FOUR TO SIX

INGREDIENTS

- 350g/12oz/2 cups coarse grain bulgur wheat, rinsed under running water and drained
- 30ml/2 tbsp ghee
- 2 medium carrots, cut into matchsticks
- 75g/3oz/¾ cup blanched almonds
- 30–45ml/2–3 tbsp pine nuts
- 30–45ml/2–3 tbsp shelled pistachio nuts, chopped
- 175g/6oz/1 cup soft dried dates, roughly chopped
- salt

To serve

- a handful of fresh coriander (cilantro), chopped
- about 25g/1oz/2 tbsp ghee or butter, melted (optional)
- thick and creamy natural (plain) yogurt

**1** Put the bulgur wheat into a bowl, pour over enough boiling water to cover it by 2.5cm/1in, and give it a quick stir.

**2** Cover the bowl and leave the bulgur wheat to steam for about 25 minutes, until it has soaked up the water and doubled in volume.

**COOK'S TIP**
In Bedouin camps in eastern Turkey, this dish is normally served piled in a mound with yogurt spooned into a hollow and eaten communally.

**3** Meanwhile, melt the ghee in a wide, heavy pan, add the carrots and fry for about 10 minutes, until tender and golden. Toss in the nuts and cook for a further minute, or until they give off a nutty aroma and begin to colour.

**4** Add the dates and, if they look dry, splash in 15–30ml/1–2 tbsp water. Transfer the bulgur wheat to the pan, add the salt and toss until everything is mixed well together. Turn off the heat, cover the pan with a dish towel and lid, and leave to steam for 5–10 minutes.

**5** To serve, stir the coriander through the bulgur, and pour over the melted ghee or butter, if you like. Hand round yogurt in a small bowl.

Per portion Energy 412kcal/1719kJ; Protein 9g; Carbohydrate 54g, of which sugars 23.4g; Fat 19.1g, of which saturates 3.9g; Cholesterol 11mg; Calcium 71mg; Fibre 3.4g; Sodium 74mg.

# TOMATO BULGUR WITH SPICY LAMB

*KUZULU BULGUR PILAVI IS A VERY TASTY DISH FROM THE AREA AROUND KAYSERI IN CENTRAL ANATOLIA, WHICH IS WELL KNOWN FOR ITS MEAT DISHES. TRADITIONALLY, SHEEP'S TAIL FAT IS USED, BUT GHEE CAN BE USED, TOO. THE DISH IS SERVED WITH PLAIN YOGURT, OR WITH CACIK, A CUCUMBER, MINT AND YOGURT SALAD. IT IS ALSO DELICIOUS SERVED WITH THE SHEPHERD'S SALAD, ÇOBAN SALATASI, MADE WITH TURKISH GREEN PEPPERS, ONIONS, TOMATOES, PARSLEY AND SUMAC.*

### SERVES FOUR

INGREDIENTS
  30ml/2 tbsp ghee, or butter
  2 onions, chopped
  10ml/2 tsp sugar
  350g/12oz bulgur wheat, rinsed
    and drained
  10ml/2 tsp tomato purée (paste)
  600ml/1 pint/2½ cups lamb or
    chicken stock, or water
  10ml/2 tsp *kırmızı biber*, or paprika
  5–10ml/1–2 tsp ground cumin
  5ml/1 tsp ground coriander
  250g/9oz shoulder of lamb,
    cut into bitesize pieces
  salt and ground black pepper
  flat leaf parsley sprigs, to garnish
  sliced lemon or yogurt, to serve

**1** Melt the ghee or butter in a heavy pan. Stir in the onion with the sugar and fry gently for 3–4 minutes, or until golden brown.

**2** Toss in the bulgur wheat, coating it in the onion and ghee, and stir in the tomato purée.

**3** Pour in the stock or water, season with salt and pepper, and bring it to the boil. Reduce the heat and simmer until all the water has been absorbed. Turn off the heat, cover the pan with a clean dish towel, place the lid on firmly, and leave to steam for 10–15 minutes.

**4** Put the spices and lamb pieces in a plastic bag and shake to coat. Heat a wide, heavy, non-stick frying pan. Toss the meat quickly on its own in the pan, frying it in its own juices, until it is lightly browned.

**5** Add the bulgur wheat to the pan with the meat, and toss both around the pan for 2–3 minutes, or until the flavours are thoroughly mixed.

**6** Transfer the bulgur wheat and lamb to a serving dish, garnish with the sprigs of parsley and serve hot with lemon slices or yogurt.

**Per portion** Energy 541kcal/2259kJ; Protein 21.1g; Carbohydrate 86.1g, of which sugars 9g; Fat 15g, of which saturates 7.2g; Cholesterol 64mg; Calcium 49mg; Fibre 3.3g; Sodium 110mg.

# ANCHOVY AND RICE DOME

*PACKED FULL OF ANCHOVIES, THIS FAMOUS RICE DISH IS FROM THE BLACK SEA COAST, WHERE ANCHOVIES ARE USED IN MANY DISHES AND WRITTEN ABOUT IN SONGS AND POETRY. THERE ARE SEVERAL WAYS OF MAKING IT: WHOLE ANCHOVIES CAN BE FRIED AND TOSSED THROUGH THE RICE; THE ANCHOVIES AND RICE CAN BE LAYERED AND BAKED IN A FLAT DISH; OR THE ANCHOVIES CAN BE BONED, AS HERE, AND USED TO LINE A BOWL, WHICH IS THEN INVERTED TO CREATE A DOME.*

SERVES FOUR TO SIX

INGREDIENTS
   600g/1lb 6oz fresh anchovies, gutted,
     with heads and backbones removed
   30ml/2 tbsp olive oil
   15ml/1 tbsp butter
   1 onion, finely chopped
   30ml/2 tbsp pine nuts
   15ml/1 tbsp dried mint
   5ml/1 tsp ground allspice
   450g/1lb/2¼ cups long grain rice,
     thoroughly rinsed and drained
   1 small bunch of fresh dill,
     finely chopped
   salt and ground black pepper
   fresh dill fronds and lemon wedges,
     to serve

**1** Rinse the anchovies and pat dry. Open them out like butterflies and sprinkle with salt. Lightly grease a dome-shaped ovenproof dish or bowl and line it with anchovies, skin side down. Reserve some anchovies for the top.

**2** Heat the oil and butter in a heavy pan, stir in the onion and cook until soft. Add the pine nuts and cook until golden, then stir in the mint, allspice and rice. Season, and pour in enough water to cover the rice by 2cm/¾in. Bring to the boil, lower the heat, partially cover and simmer for 10–12 minutes, until the water has been absorbed.

**3** While the rice is cooking, preheat the oven to 180°C/350°F/Gas 4.

**4** Turn off the heat under the pan and sprinkle the dill over the rice. Cover the pan with a dish towel, put the lid tightly on top and leave the rice to steam for 10 minutes.

**5** Fluff up the rice with a fork to mix in the dill, then tip it into the anchovy mould. Lay the remaining anchovies, skin side up this time, over the rice.

**6** Splash a little water over the top of the fish and place the dish in the oven for 25 minutes.

**7** To serve, invert a serving plate over the dish and turn out the anchovy mould encasing the rice. Garnish with dill fronds and lemon wedges and serve immediately, on its own or as an accompaniment to a fish dish.

**Per portion** Energy 481kcal/2004kJ; Protein 19.5g; Carbohydrate 64g, of which sugars 3g; Fat 16g, of which saturates 3.1g; Cholesterol 37mg; Calcium 178mg; Fibre 0.8g; Sodium 1982mg.

# Pumpkin Stuffed <u>with</u> Saffron <u>and</u> Apricot Pilaff

*In Cappadocia, where there is an extraordinary landscape of troglodyte cave dwellings, fairy chimneys and churches carved out of the rock, extensive use is made of pumpkins and apricots in cooking. Pumpkins make ideal cooking vessels, filled with aromatic pilaffs as in this recipe, or with meat and rice, vegetables or soup. This sumptuous fruit and nut pilaff would normally be reserved for special occasions, such as a wedding feast.*

<u>SERVES FOUR TO SIX</u>

INGREDIENTS
1 medium-sized pumpkin, weighing about 1.2kg/2½lb
225g/8oz/generous 1 cup long grain rice, well rinsed
30–45ml/2–3 tbsp olive oil
15ml/1 tbsp butter
a fingerful of saffron threads
5ml/1 tsp coriander seeds
2–3 strips of orange peel, pith removed and finely sliced
45–60ml/3–4 tbsp shelled pistachio nuts
30–45ml/2–3 tbsp dried cranberries, soaked in boiling water for 5 minutes and drained
175g/6oz/¾ cup dried apricots, sliced or chopped
1 bunch of fresh basil, leaves loosely torn
1 bunch each of fresh coriander (cilantro), mint and flat leaf parsley, coarsely chopped
salt and ground black pepper
lemon wedges and thick and creamy natural (plain) yogurt, to serve

**1** Preheat the oven to 200°C/400°F/ Gas 6. Wash the pumpkin and cut off the stalk end to use as a lid. Scoop all the seeds out of the middle with a spoon, and pull out the stringy bits.

**2** Replace the lid, put the pumpkin on a baking tray and bake for 1 hour.

**3** Meanwhile, put the rice in a pan and pour in just enough water to cover. Add a pinch of salt and bring to the boil, then lower the heat and partially cover the pan. Simmer for 10–12 minutes, until all the water has been absorbed and the grains of rice are cooked but still have a bite.

**4** Heat the oil and butter in a wide, heavy pan. Stir in the saffron, coriander seeds, orange peel, pistachios, cranberries and apricots, then toss in the cooked rice, making sure everything is thoroughly combined. Season with salt and pepper to taste.

**5** Turn off the heat, cover the pan with a clean, dry dish towel and press the lid tightly on top of the pan. Set to one side and leave the pilaff to steam for 10 minutes, then toss in the herbs.

**6** Take the pumpkin out of the oven. Lift off the lid and spoon the pilaff into the cavity. Put the lid back on and pop it back in the oven for about 20 minutes.

**7** To serve, remove the lid and slice a round off the top of the pumpkin. Place the ring on a plate and spoon some pilaff in the middle. Prepare the rest in the same way. Serve with lemon wedges and a bowl of yogurt.

**Per portion** Energy 345kcal/1443kJ; Protein 9.9g; Carbohydrate 50.1g, of which sugars 18.6g; Fat 12g, of which saturates 2.6g; Cholesterol 5mg; Calcium 299mg; Fibre 9.6g; Sodium 93mg.

# AUBERGINE PILAFF <u>WITH</u> CINNAMON <u>AND</u> MINT

*THIS RICE DISH VARIES FROM REGION TO REGION. IN ISTANBUL, WHERE IT IS KNOWN AS SULTAN REŞAT PILAVI, IT IS MADE WITH OLIVE OIL AND SERVED COLD. VARIATIONS MAY USE BULGUR, OR TINY PASTA "TEARS" COOKED WITH THE RICE, BUT ALL RECIPES INCLUDE MEATY CHUNKS OF AUBERGINE.*

### SERVES FOUR TO SIX

INGREDIENTS

2 large aubergines (eggplants)
30–45ml/2–3 tbsp olive oil
30–45ml/2–3 tbsp pine nuts
1 large onion, finely chopped
5ml/1 tsp coriander seeds
30ml/2 tbsp currants, soaked in
  warm water for 5–10 minutes
  and drained
10–15ml/2–3 tsp sugar
15–30ml/1–2 tbsp ground cinnamon
15–30ml/1–2 tbsp dried mint
1 small bunch of fresh dill,
  finely chopped
3 tomatoes, skinned, seeded and
  finely chopped
350g/12oz/generous 1¾ cups long
  or short grain rice, well rinsed
  and drained
sunflower oil, for deep-frying
juice of ½ lemon
salt and ground black pepper
fresh mint sprigs and lemon wedges,
  to serve

**1** Using a vegetable peeler or a small, sharp knife, peel the aubergines lengthways in stripes like a zebra. Quarter them lengthways, then slice each quarter into bitesize chunks and place in a bowl of salted water. Cover with a plate to keep them submerged, and leave to soak for at least 30 minutes.

**2** Meanwhile, heat the oil in a heavy pan, stir in the pine nuts and cook until they turn golden. Add the onion and soften it, then stir in the coriander seeds and currants. Add the sugar, cinnamon, mint and dill and stir in the tomatoes.

**3** Toss in the rice, coating it well in the tomato and spices, then pour in 900ml/ 1½ pints/3¾ cups water, season with salt and pepper and bring to the boil. Lower the heat and partially cover the pan, then simmer for 10–12 minutes, until almost all of the water has been absorbed. Turn off the heat, cover the pan with a dish towel and press the lid tightly on top. Leave the rice to steam for about 15 minutes.

**4** Heat enough sunflower oil for deep-frying in a wok or other deep-sided pan. Drain the aubergines and squeeze them dry, then toss them in batches in the oil, for a few minutes at a time. When they are golden brown, lift them out with a slotted spoon and drain on kitchen paper.

**5** Transfer the rice to a serving bowl and toss the aubergine chunks through it with the lemon juice. Garnish with fresh mint sprigs and serve warm or cold, with lemon wedges for squeezing.

**Per portion** Energy 369kcal/1539kJ; Protein 6.1g; Carbohydrate 52.2g, of which sugars 11g; Fat 15.2g, of which saturates 1.8g; Cholesterol 0mg; Calcium 38mg; Fibre 2.7g; Sodium 8mg.

# RICE <u>WITH</u> GREEN PEAS, MINT <u>AND</u> DILL

*THIS PLAIN BUTTERY PILAFF,* BEZELIYELI PILAV, *IS A POPULAR ONE TO SERVE WITH FRIED OR GRILLED CHICKEN AND FISH DISHES. DOTTED WITH FRESH GREEN PEAS, IT IS DELICIOUS SERVED HOT OR AT ROOM TEMPERATURE. IT MAKES AN ATTRACTIVE ADDITION TO A BUFFET SPREAD OR BARBECUE.*

## SERVES FOUR

### INGREDIENTS

- 15ml/1 tbsp olive oil
- 25g/1oz/2 tbsp butter
- 1 onion, finely chopped
- 350g/12oz/1¾ cups long grain rice, thoroughly rinsed and drained
- 750ml/1¼ pints/3 cups chicken stock or water
- 200g/7oz/1¾ cups fresh or frozen peas
- 1 small bunch dill, finely chopped
- 1 small bunch mint, leaves finely chopped
- salt and ground black pepper

### VARIATION

To make a more substantial rice dish, you can add diced carrot and diced artichoke bottoms with the peas in step 3.

**1** Heat the oil and butter in a heavy pan and stir in the onion. Cook until softened. Add the rice, coating it in the butter and onion, and pour in the stock or water.

**2** Season and bring the stock to the boil. Reduce the heat and simmer for 10 minutes, or until almost all the liquid has been absorbed.

**3** Toss the peas into the rice with half the fresh herbs. Cover the pan with a clean dish towel and a lid and leave the rice to steam with the peas for a further 10 minutes.

**4** Transfer the cooked rice mixture to a serving dish, garnish with the remaining fresh herbs, and serve the pilaff hot or at room temperature.

**Per portion** Energy 437kcal/1819kJ; Protein 10.5g; Carbohydrate 77g, of which sugars 2.3g; Fat 9.3g, of which saturates 3.8g; Cholesterol 13mg; Calcium 57mg; Fibre 3.2g; Sodium 43mg.

# SULTAN'S CHICKPEA PILAFF

*THERE IS A STORY THAT MAHMUT PASHA, THE GRAND VIZIER OF MEHMET THE CONQUEROR, USED TO INVITE HIS MINISTERS TO LUNCH EVERY FRIDAY, WHEN HE WOULD SERVE A SPECIAL MOUND OF RICE AND CHICKPEA PILAFF AT THE END OF THE MEAL. AS EACH MINISTER DIPPED INTO THE RICE WITH HIS SPOON, SOLID GOLD BALLS THE SAME SIZE AS THE CHICKPEAS WOULD BE REVEALED, BRINGING GOOD FORTUNE TO THOSE WHO MANAGED TO GET ONE ON THEIR SPOON. A CLASSIC BUTTERY PILAFF, FIT FOR A SULTAN, THIS DISH IS A PERFECT ACCOMPANIMENT TO ALMOST ANY MEAT OR FISH DISH.*

**4** Gently melt the butter with the oil in a heavy pan, stir in the onion and cook until it softens.

**5** Add the rice and chickpeas to the pan and cover with the water or stock. Season with salt and pepper and bring to the boil. Lower the heat, partially cover the pan and simmer for about 10 minutes, until almost all of the water has been absorbed.

**6** Turn off the heat, cover the pan with a clean, dry dish towel and put the lid tightly on top. Leave the rice to steam for 10 minutes, then fluff up with a fork before serving.

### SERVES FOUR

INGREDIENTS
  50g/2oz/⅓ cup dried chickpeas,
    soaked in cold water overnight
  30ml/2 tbsp butter
  15ml/1 tbsp olive or sunflower oil
  1 onion, chopped
  225g/8oz/generous 1 cup long grain
    rice, well rinsed and drained
  600ml/1 pint/2½ cups water or
    chicken stock
  salt and ground black pepper

**1** Drain the chickpeas, put them in a pan and fill the pan with plenty of cold water. Bring to the boil and boil for 1 minute, then lower the heat and partially cover the pan.

**2** Simmer the chickpeas for about 45 minutes, or until tender.

**3** Drain the chickpeas in a colander, rinse well under cold running water and remove any loose skins by rubbing them in a dry, clean dish towel.

**Per portion** Energy 328kcal/1368kJ; Protein 7.1g; Carbohydrate 52.3g, of which sugars 1.2g; Fat 9.9g, of which saturates 4.4g; Cholesterol 16mg; Calcium 36mg; Fibre 1.6g; Sodium 51mg.

# SOUR CHERRY PILAFF

*THIS POPULAR SUMMER PILAFF IS MADE WITH FRESH, SMALL, SOUR CHERRIES RATHER THAN THE MORE COMMON PLUMP, SWEET ONES. WITH ITS REFRESHING BURSTS OF FLAVOUR, IT MAKES A GOOD ACCOMPANIMENT TO MOST VEGETABLE, MEAT AND FISH DISHES. IF YOU ARE UNABLE TO OBTAIN FRESH SOUR CHERRIES, YOU CAN USE DRIED ONES OR DRIED CRANBERRIES INSTEAD. ALTERNATIVELY, YOU CAN SUBSTITUTE THEM WITH DRIED BARBERRIES, WHICH ARE TINY, SOUR, RED BERRIES THAT ARE USUALLY AVAILABLE IN MIDDLE EASTERN STORES AND SOME LARGER SUPERMARKETS.*

SERVES THREE TO FOUR

INGREDIENTS
 30ml/2 tbsp butter
 225g/8oz fresh or dried sour cherries, such as morello, pitted if fresh
 5–10ml/1–2 tsp sugar
 5ml/1 tsp caraway seeds
 225g/8oz/generous 1 cup long grain rice, well rinsed and drained
 salt and ground black pepper

**5** Fluff up the rice with a fork, transfer to a serving dish and garnish with the reserved cherries.

**1** Melt the butter in a heavy pan. Set a handful of the cherries aside, and toss the rest in the butter with the sugar and caraway seeds.

**2** Cook for a few minutes, then add the rice and 600ml/1 pint/2½ cups water. Season with salt and pepper to taste.

**3** Bring the mixture to the boil, lower the heat and partially cover the pan. Simmer for 10–12 minutes, until most of the water has been absorbed.

**4** Turn off the heat, cover with a dish towel, and put the lid tightly on top. Leave for 20 minutes.

**COOK'S TIP**
Due to their acidity, sour cherries are often consumed cooked or poached with sugar in sorbets, jam, bread pudding, cakes, and in a pretty compôte that is traditionally spooned over rice or yogurt.

Per portion Energy 295kcal/1231kJ; Protein 4.7g; Carbohydrate 54g, of which sugars 9.1g; Fat 6.5g, of which saturates 3.9g; Cholesterol 16mg; Calcium 21mg; Fibre 0.5g; Sodium 46mg.

# CHICKEN LIVER PILAFF <u>WITH</u> CURRANTS, PINE NUTS <u>AND</u> ALMONDS

*THIS DELICIOUS RICE PILAFF, IÇ PILAVI, IS MOST OFTEN ASSOCIATED WITH ISTANBUL, WHERE IT IS USUALLY SERVED ON ITS OWN. THE RURAL ANATOLIAN VERSION GENERALLY CONTAINS LAMB'S LIVER AS WELL. SOPHISTICATED AND TASTY, THIS DISH IS GOOD SERVED ON ITS OWN WITH LEMON OR NATURAL YOGURT, AND IT ALSO GOES WELL AS AN ACCOMPANIMENT TO KEBABS.*

SERVES FOUR TO SIX

INGREDIENTS
    30ml/2 tbsp currants
    45ml/3 tbsp ghee, butter or olive oil
    1 onion, chopped
    30–45ml/2–3 tbsp pine nuts
    45ml/3 tbsp blanched almonds
    5–10ml/1–2 tsp ground allspice
    5ml/1 tsp ground cinnamon
    350g/12oz/1¾ cups long grain rice,
      thoroughly rinsed and drained
    about 750ml/1¼ pints/3 cups
      chicken stock
    250g/9oz chicken livers, cut into
      small bitesize pieces
    1 bunch parsley, leaves finely chopped
    1 small bunch dill, finely chopped
    salt and ground black pepper
To garnish
    15ml/1 tbsp pine nuts
    a few dill fronds, with stalks removed
    1 lemon, cut into thick slices
      for squeezing

**1** Soak the currants in warm water for 15 minutes and then drain. Melt 30ml/2 tbsp of the ghee in a heavy pan and stir in the onion. Cook until softened.

**2** Add the pine nuts and almonds. When they begin to turn golden, stir in the currants, spices and rice and mix well.

**COOK'S TIP**
At *Kurban Bayrami*, the liver of the slaughtered lamb is used instead of chicken livers.

**3** Pour in the stock, season with salt and pepper, and bring to the boil. Reduce the heat and simmer until the liquid has been absorbed. Turn off the heat, cover the pan with a clean dish towel, and place the lid on tightly. Leave to steam for 10–15 minutes.

**4** Meanwhile, melt the remaining ghee in a heavy pan and sauté the chicken livers until nicely browned. Fluff up the rice with a fork and toss in the chicken livers and herbs.

**5** To make the garnish, dry-roast the pine nuts in a small frying pan until golden. Transfer the pilaff to a serving dish and garnish with the dill fronds and slices of lemon. Sprinkle the pine nuts over the top and serve.

Per portion Energy 430kcal/1790kJ; Protein 14.9g; Carbohydrate 54.8g, of which sugars 6.9g; Fat 16.6g, of which saturates 5.8g; Cholesterol 179mg; Calcium 67mg; Fibre 1.9g; Sodium 38mg.

# RICE <u>WITH</u> LAMB, CARROTS, ONIONS <u>AND</u> SPICES

*AN ANCIENT MONGOLIAN DISH AND A GREAT ANATOLIAN FAVOURITE, THIS PILAFF — KAŞGAR PILAV — IS COOKED IN A LARGE PAN AND EATEN COMMUNALLY WITH YOGURT AS A MEAL ON ITS OWN. AS YOU TRAVEL FURTHER EAST IN TURKEY, VARIATIONS OF THIS DISH APPEAR UNDER DIFFERENT NAMES, IDENTIFYING IT WITH UZBEKISTAN, TURKMENISTAN, AND AZERBAIJAN.*

SERVES FOUR

INGREDIENTS

 30ml/2 tbsp ghee, or olive oil with
  a knob (pat) butter
 2 onions, chopped
 4 garlic cloves, chopped
 about 450g/1lb cooked lamb, cubed
 2 medium carrots, peeled and
  coarsely grated
 350g/12oz/1¾ cups long grain rice,
  rinsed and thoroughly drained
 5ml/1 tsp ground cinnamon
 10ml/2 tsp ground allspice
 1 litre/1¾ pints/4 cups lamb or
  chicken stock
 salt and ground black pepper
 a few parsley sprigs, to garnish
 thick and creamy natural (plain)
  yogurt, to serve

**1** Heat the ghee, or olive oil and butter, in a heavy pan and stir in the onions and garlic. Cook until they begin to colour. Toss in the cubed lamb and cook for 1–2 minutes, then stir in the carrots.

**2** Toss in the rice with the spices and pour in the stock.

**3** Stir the rice and season with salt and pepper. Bring to the boil and boil for 1–2 minutes, then reduce the heat and simmer for 10–12 minutes, or until all the liquid has been absorbed.

**4** Turn off the heat, cover the pan with a clean dish towel and place the lid on top. Leave to steam for 10–15 minutes.

**5** Transfer to a serving dish, garnish with the parsley sprigs and serve with dollops of creamy natural yogurt.

**Per portion** Energy 621kcal/2590kJ; Protein 30g; Carbohydrate 77.1g, of which sugars 4.2g; Fat 21.2g, of which saturates 9.5g; Cholesterol 86mg; Calcium 51mg; Fibre 1.1g; Sodium 100mg.

# VEILED PILAFF

*LITERALLY TRANSLATED AS "VEILED" OR "CURTAINED" RICE, THIS TRADITIONAL ANATOLIAN WEDDING DISH, CALLED* PERDELI PILAV, *IS MADE WITH RICE BAKED WITHIN A SHEET OF PASTRY. ANCIENT RECIPES FOR THIS DISH INCLUDED PARTRIDGES, WHICH SYMBOLIZE PEACE, PISTACHIO NUTS AND ALMONDS, WHICH REPRESENT CHILDREN, AND RICE, WHICH IS A SYMBOL OF ABUNDANCE. TODAY, THE ALMONDS ARE STILL INCLUDED, BUT THE PARTRIDGE IS REPLACED BY CHICKEN AND THE "VEIL" IS MADE OUT OF YUFKA, THE TRADITIONAL FLAT BREAD, OR PUFF PASTRY. YOU CAN MAKE THIS STUNNING DISH WITH LEFTOVER ROAST CHICKEN, OR BY POACHING A WHOLE CHICKEN IN WATER AND USING THE COOKING LIQUID AS THE STOCK FOR THE RICE.*

### SERVES SIX TO EIGHT

INGREDIENTS
- 45ml/3 tbsp olive oil
- 25g/1oz/2 tbsp butter
- 175g/6oz/1 cup blanched almonds
- 115g/4oz/²⁄₃ cup blanched pistachio nuts
- 350g/12oz/1¾ cups medium grain rice, rinsed thoroughly
- 10ml/2 tsp sugar
- 900ml/1½ pints/3¾ cups chicken stock
- 225g/8oz puff pastry, thawed if frozen
- 500g/1¼ lb roasted or grilled (broiled) chicken meat, cut into small pieces or shredded
- 1 egg yolk
- 10ml/2 tsp nigella seeds
- salt and ground black pepper

To garnish
- 30ml/2 tbsp blanched pistachio nuts
- 15ml/1 tbsp butter

**1** Preheat the oven to 180°C/350°F/Gas 4 and lightly grease a round baking tin (pan).

**2** Heat 15ml/1 tbsp of the olive oil and butter in a large, heavy pan and stir in the blanched almonds and pistachio nuts for 3 minutes, until they begin to colour.

**3** Add the rice and the sugar, making sure the rice grains are completely coated in the butter. Pour in the stock and bring to the boil. Season to taste with salt and pepper, reduce the heat, and simmer for 10–12 minutes, or until the stock has been absorbed.

**4** On a floured surface roll out the puff pastry into a circle, about 2mm/¹⁄₁₀in thick (reserve a small, apricot-sized portion for the top). Press the pastry into the tin with the edges overlapping the sides.

**5** Form the rice into a dome in the middle and arrange the chicken over the top and around the edges.

**6** Pull up the sides of the pastry over the rice and chicken, overlapping the edges to seal in the rice. Roll out the reserved portion of pastry into a square. Trim off six thin strips (the width of matchsticks) and set aside for decorating. Brush the top of the dome with a little egg yolk and place the pastry square over the top to cover the sealed edges.

**7** Beat the remainder of the egg yolk with the remaining olive oil and brush it all over the pastry dome. Decorate the dome with the pastry strips, placing them on the pastry to create segments over the dome. Brush the strips with the egg and olive oil mixture.

**8** Sprinkle a few nigella seeds over the dome and place it in the oven. Bake the pastry for about 25–30 minutes, or until it is golden brown all over. Carefully remove the domed pastry from the tin and place it on a serving dish.

**9** For the garnish, melt the butter in a frying pan and toss in the pistachio nuts, until they begin to brown. Pour the nuts and the butter over the pastry dome and serve immediately.

**Per portion** Energy 617kcal/2567kJ; Protein 27.4g; Carbohydrate 48g, of which sugars 2.1g; Fat 35.3g, of which saturates 4.6g; Cholesterol 76mg; Calcium 100mg; Fibre 2.5g; Sodium 224mg.

# FISH AND SHELLFISH

Generally, fish is bought very fresh, straight off the boats or at the
market, although some is smoked before it is sold. It is not
unusual for the fish to be swimming around in buckets, or they
are laid out on ice, displaying their bright eyes and gleaming skins.
The fish sellers are often knowledgeable and willing to help you
select and prepare the fish for the chosen dish, such as a good-sized
mackerel for Mackerel Stuffed with Nuts and Spices, or for
Mackerel Pilâki, in which the fish is baked with diced vegetables.

# ANCHOVIES POACHED ᴵᴺ VINE LEAVES

*STREET VENDORS IN CITIES PREPARE LARGE PANS OF THESE POACHED ANCHOVIES — HAMSI SARMASI*
*— WHICH CAN BE EASILY EATEN WITH THE FINGERS, AS THE WRAPPED FISH IS SIMPLY POPPED INTO*
*THE MOUTH AND EATEN WHOLE. THIS IS A POPULAR DISH IN THE EARLY WEEKS OF SUMMER, WHEN*
*THE ANCHOVIES ARE SWEET AND JUICY AND THE VINE LEAVES TENDER.*

### SERVES FOUR TO SIX

INGREDIENTS
    about 24 fresh anchovies, gutted and
        cleaned, with the backbone removed
    about 24 fresh or preserved vine
        leaves, plus extra for lining the pan
    60ml/4 tbsp olive oil
    juice of 1 lemon
    1–2 garlic cloves, crushed (optional)
    salt and ground black pepper
To serve
    1 lemon, cut into thick slices
    5–10ml/1–2 tsp sumac

**1** Place the anchovies on a flat surface and wrap them in the vine leaves with their heads poking out.

**2** Line a shallow pan with a few of the extra vine leaves and place the wrapped anchovies on top, packing them together quite tightly.

**3** Mix the olive oil and lemon juice together, beat in the garlic, if using, and salt and pepper. Pour the mixture over the anchovies.

**4** Place a plate directly on top of the wrapped anchovies to keep them in place while cooking. Cover the pan and poach the anchovies gently for 10 minutes.

**5** Arrange the anchovies on a serving dish with the lemon slices. Sprinkle a little sumac over the top of the fish and eat them whole while still hot, or at room temperature.

**Per portion** Energy 190kcal/788kJ; Protein 14.4g; Carbohydrate 2.5g, of which sugars 2.5g; Fat 13.6g, of which saturates 2.9g; Cholesterol 0mg; Calcium 81mg; Fibre 1.1g; Sodium 84mg.

# JEWELLED MACKEREL SALAD IN A DOME

*THIS SALAD, USKUMRU SALATASI, CAN BE SERVED AS A MEZE DISH OR AS A LIGHT MEAL. GENERALLY, IT IS MADE WITH FRESH MACKEREL, BUT SOME COOKS LIKE TO MAKE IT WITH THE SMOKED FISH, WHICH MAKES THE OVERALL DISH HEAVIER. THE TURKS PRESENT THIS DISH ATTRACTIVELY, MAKING IT AN IDEAL SALAD FOR A BUFFET SPREAD, OR AN IMPRESSIVE FIRST COURSE AT A DINNER PARTY.*

SERVES TWO TO FOUR

INGREDIENTS
    15ml/1 tbsp currants
    3 tomatoes
    sunflower oil, for shallow-frying
    2 fresh mackerel, gutted and
      thoroughly cleaned
    45ml/3 tbsp pine nuts
    30ml/2 tbsp olive oil
    1 crisp cos or romaine lettuce,
      cut into thin strips
    a handful of fresh rocket
      (arugula) leaves
    1 bunch fresh dill fronds,
      stalks removed
    1 red onion, sliced into thin rings
For the dressing
    60–75ml/4–5 tbsp olive oil
    juice of 1 lemon
    15ml/1 tbsp apple or white
      wine vinegar
    5ml/1 tsp yellow mustard
    5–10ml/1–2 tsp clear honey
    salt and ground black pepper

**1** Soak the currants in warm water for 15 minutes then drain them.

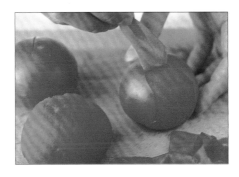

**2** Plunge the tomatoes into a large bowl of boiling water for 30 seconds, then refresh immediately in cold water. Peel away the tomato skins with your fingers, then remove the seeds and cut the flesh into thin strips (reserve one round slice for the top of the dome).

**3** Heat enough sunflower oil in a heavy pan for shallow-frying the mackerel.

**4** Fry the mackerel for 5–6 minutes on each side. Drain on kitchen paper and leave to cool. Alternatively, you can grill (broil) the mackerel.

**5** Peel the skin off the mackerel and cut the flesh into long fingers.

**6** In a small, heavy pan, fry the pine nuts in the olive oil, until they begin to colour. Toss in the currants to plump them up, then pour them on to kitchen paper to drain. Leave to cool.

**7** Arrange the lettuce and rocket leaves in a dome in the centre of a round serving dish. Arrange the mackerel fingers around the sides of the dome, laying them gently on top of the leaves, and interspersing them with strips of tomato. Place the reserved slice of tomato on the very top of the dome.

**8** Decorate the dome with the dill fronds, placing a little sprig in the centre of the sliced tomato, and arrange the onion rings around the base.

**9** Sprinkle the pine nuts and currants over the dome and around the base. The whole effect should be like an elaborately jewelled crown.

**10** To make the dressing, mix together all the dressing ingredients in a bowl and season to taste. Pour the dressing over the salad and serve immediately, with fresh, crusty bread.

**Per portion** Energy 575kcal/2383kJ; Protein 27.2g; Carbohydrate 9.5g, of which sugars 9.5g; Fat 47.8g, of which saturates 7.6g; Cholesterol 66mg; Calcium 60mg; Fibre 2.2g; Sodium 121mg.

# MACKEREL *PILÂKI*

*PILÂKI DISHES ALL FOLLOW THE SAME COOKING METHOD, WHETHER MADE WITH MEATY BEANS, FISH OR SHELLFISH. IN ISTANBUL, THERE IS A POPULAR PILÂKI THAT IS MADE WITH MUSSELS, BUT THE MOST COMMON PILÂKI ARE THOSE MADE WITH GOOD-SIZED, FIRM-FLESHED FISH. THE CLASSIC ONE IS MADE WITH BONITO, BUT MACKEREL AND SEA BASS ARE EQUALLY GOOD.*

## SERVES FOUR TO SIX

### INGREDIENTS

2 good-sized fresh mackerel, gutted and rinsed
120ml/4fl oz/½ cup olive oil
2 onions, chopped
3–4 garlic cloves, chopped
1 mild fresh green chilli, seeded and chopped
2–3 carrots, diced
2–3 potatoes, diced
1 medium celeriac, weighing about 450g/1lb, peeled, trimmed and diced
2 large tomatoes, skinned and chopped, or 400g/14oz can chopped tomatoes, drained of juice
5ml/1 tsp sugar
2–3 bay leaves
juice of 2 lemons
1 small bunch of fresh flat leaf parsley
salt and ground black pepper

**COOK'S TIP**
The *pilâki* dishes are very distinctive in Turkey. In Istanbul or Izmir, mussel *pilâki (midye pilâki)* is much sought-after.

**1** Preheat the oven to 170°C/325°F/ Gas 3. Using a large, sharp knife, cut the fish crossways into 2cm/¾in slices, making sure that you keep it intact at the backbone.

**2** Heat the oil in a large, heavy pan. Stir in the onions, garlic and chilli and cook until soft.

**3** Add the carrots, potatoes and celeriac to the pan and cook for 1–2 minutes, then stir in the tomatoes, sugar and bay leaves.

**4** Pour in 600ml/1 pint/2½ cups water and bring the mixture to the boil.

**5** Lower the heat, cover the pan and simmer for 5–10 minutes, until the vegetables are tender but not mushy. Season with salt and pepper to taste.

**6** Spoon half the vegetables over the bottom of an ovenproof dish, then place the fish on top and spoon the remaining vegetables over them. Sprinkle with the lemon juice and lay a few sprigs of parsley on top.

**7** Cover everything with baking parchment that has been soaked in water and squeezed out, then place in the oven for 20 minutes, or until the fish is cooked.

**8** Remove the paper and parsley sprigs and serve the fish immediately, garnished with some roughly chopped parsley. Alternatively, leave the *pilâki* to cool in the dish and serve at room temperature.

**COOK'S TIP**
A dish that seems to have completely disappeared is oyster *pilâki*, which was an old Ottoman favourite.

**Per portion** Energy 270kcal/1127kJ; Protein 17.3g; Carbohydrate 22.9g, of which sugars 11.2g; Fat 12.7g, of which saturates 2.7g; Cholesterol 40mg; Calcium 76mg; Fibre 4.1g; Sodium 115mg.

# MACKEREL STUFFED WITH NUTS AND SPICES

*THIS DISH, USKUMRU DOLMASI, IS AN OTTOMAN CLASSIC. ONE OF ISTANBUL'S MOST INSPIRED DISHES, THE FISH IS SKILFULLY MASSAGED TO EMPTY IT OF FLESH WHILE KEEPING THE SKIN INTACT, SO THAT IT CAN BE STUFFED TO RESEMBLE THE WHOLE FISH ONCE MORE.*

## SERVES FOUR

### INGREDIENTS
1 large, fresh mackerel, scaled and
  thoroughly washed, but not gutted
30–45ml/2–3 tbsp olive oil
4–5 shallots, finely chopped
30ml/2 tbsp pine nuts
30ml/2 tbsp blanched almonds,
  finely slivered
45ml/3 tbsp walnuts, finely chopped
15–30ml/1–2 tbsp currants, soaked
  in warm water for 5–10 minutes
  and drained
6–8 dried apricots, finely chopped
5–10ml/1–2 tsp ground cinnamon
5ml/1 tsp ground allspice
2.5ml/½ tsp ground cloves
5ml/1 tsp *kırmızı biber*, or
  2.5ml/½ tsp chilli powder
5ml/1 tsp sugar
1 small bunch each of fresh flat leaf
  parsley and dill, finely chopped
juice of 1 lemon
plain (all-purpose) flour
sunflower oil, for shallow-frying
salt and ground black pepper
To serve
  1 bunch of fresh dill
  a few fresh flat leaf parsley sprigs
  1 lemon, cut into wedges

**1** Take a sharp knife and cut an opening just below the gills of the mackerel, making sure the head and backbone remain intact. Push your finger into the opening and remove the guts, then rinse the fish inside and out.

**2** Using a rolling pin or mallet, gently bash the fish on both sides, making sure you smash the backbone. Now, with your hands, gently massage the skin to loosen it away from the flesh – don't pummel it too hard or the skin will tear.

**3** Working from the tail end towards the head, squeeze the loosened flesh out of the opening below the gills – use a similar motion to squeezing a half-empty tube of toothpaste.

**4** Remove any bones from the loosened flesh, then rinse out the mackerel sack and set aside.

**5** Heat the oil in a frying pan, stir in the shallots and cook until soft. Add the nuts and stir until they just begin to colour. Add the currants, apricots, spices, *kırmızı biber* or chilli and sugar and mix thoroughly.

**6** Mix in the fish flesh and cook through for 2–3 minutes, then toss in the herbs and lemon juice and season to taste with salt and pepper.

**7** Lift up the empty mackerel skin and push the filling through the opening, shaking the sack a little to jiggle the filling down towards the tail.

**8** As the skin begins to fill, gently squeeze the mixture downwards to make it compact, until it looks like a plump, fresh mackerel once more.

**9** To cook the mackerel, toss it in flour and fry it in sunflower oil, or brush with a little oil and grill (broil) until the skin begins to turn brown and buckle.

**10** To serve, cut the fish crossways into thick slices and arrange on a dish in the shape of the fish. Surround with dill and parsley and serve with lemon wedges.

### COOK'S TIP
Baked or grilled (broiled), *uskumru dolması* is both impressive and delicious. Because it is quite fiddly to make, it tends to be a speciality of fish restaurants in Istanbul. However, it is well worth the effort of making it yourself at home, perhaps for a special occasion, such as a dinner party.

**Per portion** Energy 520Kcal/2154kJ; Protein 20.2g; Carbohydrate 13.7g, of which sugars 10.1g; Fat 43.1g, of which saturates 5.5g; Cholesterol 40mg; Calcium 86mg; Fibre 3.1g; Sodium 53mg.

# BAKED SARDINES WITH TOMATOES

*WITH THE HILLSIDES COVERED IN HERBS, AROMATIC FISH DISHES LIKE THIS ONE ARE A COMMON FEATURE OF THE AEGEAN AND MEDITERRANEAN COASTS. PURPLE BASIL, WHICH HAS A MILD ANISEED TASTE, IS USED FREQUENTLY, ALTHOUGH GREEN HOLY BASIL AND LEMON BASIL WORK JUST AS WELL.*

SERVES FOUR

INGREDIENTS

  8 large sardines, scaled, gutted
    and thoroughly washed
  6–8 fresh thyme sprigs
  juice of ½ lemon
  2 x 400g/14oz cans chopped
    tomatoes, drained of juice
  60–75ml/4–5 tbsp olive oil
  4 garlic cloves, smashed flat
  5ml/1 tsp sugar
  1 bunch of fresh purple basil
  salt and ground black pepper
  lemon wedges, to serve

**1** Preheat the oven to 180°C/350°F/ Gas 4.

**2** Lay the sardines side by side in an ovenproof dish, place a sprig of thyme between each one and squeeze the lemon juice over them.

**3** In a bowl, mix the tomatoes, olive oil, garlic and sugar.

**4** Season the mixture and stir in most of the basil leaves, then spoon the mixture over the sardines.

**5** Bake, uncovered, for 25 minutes. Sprinkle the remaining basil leaves over the top and serve with lemon wedges.

**Per portion** Energy 219kcal/915kJ; Protein 11.7g; Carbohydrate 7.3g, of which sugars 7.3g; Fat 16.2g, of which saturates 3.1g; Cholesterol 0mg; Calcium 57mg; Fibre 2g; Sodium 78mg.

# STUFFED SARDINES

*Izgara sardalya dolmasi is best made with good-sized plump, gutted sardines. It is a great dish for outdoor cooking on the barbecue but it can also be cooked under the grill. The recipe also works well with red mullet and small mackerel or trout.*

### SERVES FOUR

INGREDIENTS
15ml/1 tbsp currants
4 good-sized sardines
30ml/2 tbsp olive oil
6 spring onions (scallions),
  finely sliced
2–3 garlic cloves, crushed
5ml/1 tsp cumin seeds, crushed
5ml/1 tsp sumac
15ml/1 tbsp pine nuts
1 small bunch flat leaf parsley,
  leaves finely chopped
salt and ground black pepper
For basting
45ml/3 tbsp olive oil
juice of 1 lemon
5–10ml/1–2 tsp sumac

**1** Prepare the barbecue, if using. Soak four wooden skewers in cold water for 30 minutes. Soak the currants in warm water for 15 minutes, then drain them.

**2** Slit the sardines from head to tail and remove the backbone by gently massaging the area around it to loosen it. Using your fingers, carefully prise out the bone, snapping it off at each end, while keeping the fish intact. Rinse the fish and pat it dry.

**3** Heat the oil in a heavy pan, stir in the spring onions and cook until soft. Add the garlic, cumin and sumac. Stir in the pine nuts and currants, and fry until they begin to turn golden. Toss in the parsley, and season to taste with salt and pepper. Leave to cool.

**4** Heat the grill, if using. Place each sardine on a flat surface and spread the filling inside each one. Seal by threading the skewers through the soft belly flaps.

**5** Mix together the olive oil, lemon juice and sumac, and brush some of it over the sardines.

**6** Place the fish on the rack over the hot coals and cook them for 2–3 minutes each side over a medium heat, basting them with the remainder of the olive oil mixture. Alternatively grill (broil) the sardines. Serve immediately.

**Per portion** Energy 265kcal/1098kJ; Protein 16.7g; Carbohydrate 4g, of which sugars 3.1g; Fat 20.3g, of which saturates 3.6g; Cholesterol 0mg; Calcium 90mg; Fibre 0.4g; Sodium 88mg.

# Chargrilled Sardines ᴵᴺ Vine Leaves

*This is a popular summer dish, made with small sardines freshly plucked from the sea. Although they can be cooked easily under a conventional grill, there is nothing to beat the aroma and taste when the fish are cooked over a charcoal barbecue in the open air — and the tangy, charred vine leaves and tomatoes make perfect partners for the oily flesh of the fish. Serve with lemon wedges for squeezing over the hot flesh.*

SERVES THREE TO FOUR

INGREDIENTS

   12 sardines, scaled, gutted and
      thoroughly washed
   30ml/2 tbsp olive oil, plus extra
      for brushing
   juice of ½ lemon
   12 fresh or preserved vine leaves
      (*see* Cook's Tip)
   4–6 vine tomatoes, halved
      or quartered
   salt and ground black pepper
   lemon wedges, to serve
For the dresssing
   60ml/4 tbsp olive oil
   juice of 1 lemon
   15ml/1 tbsp balsamic or white
      wine vinegar
   5–10ml/1–2 tsp clear honey
   5ml/1 tsp *kırmızı biber*, or
      1 fresh red chilli, finely chopped
   a few fresh dill fronds and flat leaf
      parsley sprigs, finely chopped

**1** Prepare the barbecue for cooking half an hour before you want to eat.

**2** Put all the dressing ingredients in a medium-sized bowl, season to taste with salt and pepper, and mix well to combine thoroughly.

**3** Pat the sardines dry with kitchen paper and lay them in a flat dish. Mix 30ml/2 tbsp olive oil with the lemon juice and brush the mixture over all the sardines.

**4** Spread the vine leaves out on a flat surface and place a sardine on each leaf. Sprinkle each one with a little salt and wrap loosely in the leaf like a cigar, with the tail and head poking out.

**5** Brush each vine leaf with a little olive oil and place seam side down to keep it from unravelling.

**6** Thread the tomatoes on skewers and sprinkle with a little salt.

**7** Place the sardines and tomatoes on the prepared barbecue and cook for 2–3 minutes on each side, until the vine leaves are charred and the tomatoes are soft.

**8** Transfer the vine leaves and tomatoes to a large serving dish and drizzle with the dressing. Serve immediately, with lemon wedges for squeezing.

**VARIATION**

You can also use whole anchovies or small mackerel for this dish.

**COOK'S TIP**

Fresh vine leaves are sold in Turkish markets, and you can get them in Middle Eastern and Mediterranean stores when they are in season in the autumn. Plunged into boiling water for a minute, the bright green leaves soften and turn a deep olive colour, indicating they are ready for use. If you can't get fresh vine leaves, you can use the ones preserved in brine that are available in packets at supermarkets and delicatessens. They require soaking in water to remove the salt. Place them in a bowl, pour boiling water over them and leave to soak for about an hour. Drain and rinse under cold running water, then pat dry.

**Per portion** Energy 300kcal/1245kJ; Protein 16.5g; Carbohydrate 5.3g, of which sugars 5.3g; Fat 23.7g, of which saturates 4.5g; Cholesterol 0mg; Calcium 82mg; Fibre 1.5g; Sodium 101mg.

# SEARED TUNA WITH SAGE, PARSLEY AND DILL

*IN GENERAL, TURKS COOK THEIR FISH AND MEAT TO A POINT THAT SOME WESTERN CULTURES WOULD CONSIDER OVERCOOKED. AS BOTH ARE OFTEN MARINATED WITH SPICES AND HERBS, THIS RARELY AFFECTS THE TASTE BUT, IN THE CASE OF TUNA STEAKS, IT DOES MAR THE ENJOYMENT. SO, IN THIS RECIPE FOR IZGARA ORKINOS, THE TUNA IS SIMPLY SEARED TO ENSURE THE FLESH IS PINK INSIDE.*

### SERVES FOUR

INGREDIENTS
  60ml/4 tbsp olive oil, plus extra
    for greasing
  juice of 1 lemon
  1 small bunch fresh sage, leaves
    finely chopped or shredded
  1 small bunch flat leaf parsley,
    leaves finely chopped
  1 small bunch fresh dill fronds,
    finely chopped
  4 thick tuna steaks
  salt and ground black pepper
  1 small bunch dill fronds, to garnish

**1** In a small bowl, mix together the olive oil and lemon juice with the herbs and season it with salt and pepper. Set this dressing aside.

**2** Smear a couple of drops of olive oil over the surface of a heavy frying pan or griddle. Place it over the heat until hot. Sear the tuna steaks for 1 minute on both sides and sprinkle them with a little salt.

**3** Quickly transfer the steaks to a serving dish and spoon the dressing over them. Garnish with the dill fronds and serve immediately.

#### COOK'S TIP
Tuna can also be used to make a popular *meze* dish called *lekerda*. Marinated in a mixture of lemon juice and dill, the meltingly succulent tuna fillets are a frequent sight on the *meze* tables of Istanbul and Izmir.

**Per portion** Energy 337kcal/1407kJ; Protein 38.6g; Carbohydrate 2.7g, of which sugars 2.3g; Fat 19.2g, of which saturates 3.4g; Cholesterol 42mg; Calcium 224mg; Fibre 5g; Sodium 104mg.

# SWORDFISH, LEMON AND RED PEPPER KEBABS

*ANY FIRM-FLESHED FISH, SUCH AS TUNA, TROUT, SALMON, MONKFISH OR SEA BASS, CAN BE USED FOR KEBABS, BUT THE CLASSIC KILIÇ ŞIŞ, MADE WITH MEATY CHUNKS OF SWORDFISH, IS A FAVOURITE IN RESTAURANTS. USUALLY SERVED AS A MAIN COURSE WITH A ROCKET AND HERB SALAD, THEY ARE LIGHT AND TASTY — IDEAL FOR A SUMMER LUNCH OR A LIGHT SUPPER.*

SERVES FOUR

INGREDIENTS

- 500g/1¼lb boneless swordfish loin or steaks, cut into bitesize chunks
- 1 lemon, halved lengthways and sliced
- 1 large tomato, halved, seeded and cut into bitesize pieces
- 2 hot green peppers (*see* Cook's Tip) or 1 green (bell) pepper, seeded and cut into bitesize pieces
- a handful of bay leaves
- lemon wedges, to serve

For the marinade

- 1 onion, grated
- 1–2 garlic cloves, crushed
- juice of ½ lemon
- 30–45ml/2–3 tbsp olive oil
- 5–10ml/1–2 tsp tomato purée (paste)
- salt and ground black pepper

**2** Thread the fish chunks on to skewers, alternating with the lemon, tomato and peppers and the occasional bay leaf. If there is any marinade left, brush it over the kebabs.

**4** Serve the kebabs hot, with lemon wedges for squeezing.

**1** Mix together the marinade ingredients in a large, shallow bowl. Toss in the chunks of swordfish and set aside for about 30 minutes to marinate and absorb the flavours.

**COOK'S TIP**

In Turkish, hot green peppers are called *çarliston biber*. They are light green, and shaped like Turkish slippers. Most *çarliston biber* are sweet, and mainly used raw in *meze* and salads, but some have a hint of heat and are good for cooked dishes like the kebabs here. Look out for them in Turkish and Middle Eastern stores.

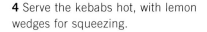

**3** Put a cast-iron griddle pan over a medium heat and leave until very hot. Place the skewers on the pan and cook for 2–3 minutes on each side until the kebab ingredients are quite charred.

**Per portion** Energy 225kcal/940kJ; Protein 23.9g; Carbohydrate 7.8g, of which sugars 7.2g; Fat 11.1g, of which saturates 2g; Cholesterol 51mg; Calcium 18mg; Fibre 1.9g; Sodium 177mg.

# SEA PERCH BAKED <u>ON A</u> TILE <u>WITH</u> POPPY SEEDS

*ALONG THE BLACK SEA COAST AND IN PARTS OF CENTRAL ANATOLIA, THE CURVED EARTHENWARE TILES, USED FOR THE ROOFS OF HOUSES, ARE USED AS PRACTICAL COOKING VESSELS. THE SHAPE OF THE TILE LENDS ITSELF IDEALLY TO CONTAINING WHOLE FISH, THE FAVOURITE BEING BLUE FISH, BUT WHOLE TROUT, SEA BASS OR SALMON CAN BE ALSO BE COOKED IN THIS WAY. FOR THIS RECIPE, KIREMITTE HAŞHAŞ LÜFER, THE FISH IS WRAPPED IN CABBAGE LEAVES. IF YOU DON'T HAVE A SUITABLE TILE YOU CAN BAKE THE FISH IN AN OVENPROOF DISH.*

**2** Place the fish in a dish and spoon the marinade all over it, inside and out. Cover and refrigerate for 2 hours.

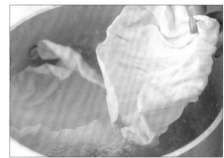

**3** Preheat the oven to 200°C/400°F/ Gas 6. Soften the cabbage leaves by plunging them into a pan of boiling water for 1 minute.

**4** If using a tile, heat it in the oven for 10 minutes, then remove with oven gloves. Brush a little oil over the surface of the tile or an ovenproof dish. Line with several cabbage leaves, then lay the fish on top, and place the remaining cabbage leaves over the top so that they totally enclose the fish.

**5** Return to the oven and bake for about 20 minutes. Remove the top cabbage leaves and pour the melted butter over the fish. Sprinkle with poppy seeds and return it to the oven for a further 10 minutes. Serve immediately with lemon to squeeze over it.

## SERVES TWO

### INGREDIENTS
1 good-sized blue fish (sea perch), or sea bass, trout or salmon, about 500g/1¼lb, gutted and cleaned
5–6 red or green cabbage leaves
50g/2oz/¼ cup butter, melted
30ml/2 tbsp poppy seeds
1 lemon, halved, to serve

For the marinade
2 large onions, grated
sea salt
30ml/2 tbsp olive oil
juice of 1 lemon
10ml/2 tsp pink peppercorns, crushed
2–3 bay leaves, crushed with your fingers

**1** To make the marinade, put the grated onion on a plate and sprinkle with salt. Leave to weep for 5 minutes. Transfer the mixture to a piece of muslin (cheesecloth) and squeeze tightly to extract the juice. Mix the juice with the olive oil and lemon juice and stir in the peppercorns and bay leaves.

**Per portion** Energy 684kcal/2840kJ; Protein 44.9g; Carbohydrate 5.4g, of which sugars 5.2g; Fat 53.8g, of which saturates 18.4g; Cholesterol 213mg; Calcium 281mg; Fibre 4.1g; Sodium 309mg.

# SEA BASS WITH RAKI

*ANISEED-FLAVOURED RAKI IS TURKEY'S NATIONAL SPIRIT AND THE PREFERRED DRINK TO ACCOMPANY MEZE AND FISH. ON OCCASION IT IS USED FOR COOKING SEAFOOD, PARTICULARLY FRIED PRAWNS AND OCTOPUS, OR WHOLE FISH, SUCH AS RED MULLET AND SEA BASS. FOR THIS DISH — RAKI SOSLU LEVREK — THE FISH IS FIRST GRILLED IN THE STANDARD WAY AND THEN DOUSED IN RAKI AND SET ALIGHT; A TRICK THAT RESTAURANT WAITERS CARRY OUT WITH GREAT PANACHE AT THE TABLE IN FRONT OF YOU. ALTERNATIVELY, YOU COULD FRY THE FISH AND FLAMBÉ IT IN THE PAN.*

## SERVES FOUR

### INGREDIENTS

2 good-sized sea bass, gutted
  and cleaned
30–45ml/2–3 tbsp olive oil
about 150ml/¼ pint/⅔ cup *raki*
2 large white radishes, grated
juice of 1 lemon
salt and ground black pepper
chopped fresh flat leaf parsley,
  to garnish

**1** First preheat the grill (broiler). Line a grill (broiling) pan with a piece of foil and place the fish on it. Brush them on both sides with the olive oil and season with salt and pepper.

**2** Place the fish under the preheated grill and cook for 6–8 minutes on each side, allowing the skin to buckle and brown. Remove the fish from the grill and pour the *raki* over them. Set the *raki* alight and flambé the fish until the flames die down.

**3** In a bowl toss the grated radish with the lemon juice and a sprinkling of salt.

**4** Divide the fish among four serving plates and garnish with a sprinkling of parsley. Serve immediately with the grated radish.

**Per portion** Energy 236kcal/984kJ; Protein 24.5g; Carbohydrate 1g, of which sugars 1g; Fat 8.7g, of which saturates 1.3g; Cholesterol 100mg; Calcium 172mg; Fibre 0.5g; Sodium 92mg.

# SEA BASS PARCELS <u>WITH</u> CINNAMON <u>AND</u> MASTIC

*TRADITIONALLY, THIS DISH, CALLED KAĞITTA LEVREK, IS COOKED WITH MASTIC, WHICH NEEDS TO BE PULVERIZED FIRST WITH A LITTLE SALT. IF THE MASTIC IS FRESH, IT WILL EMIT A DETECTABLE RESINOUS TASTE AS WELL AS AN INTERESTING TWANG TO THE OVERALL DISH.*

### SERVES FOUR

### INGREDIENTS

4 tomatoes
30ml/2 tbsp olive oil
25g/1oz/2 tbsp butter
2–3 red onions, cut in half
  lengthways and sliced along
  the grain
2 light green peppers, or 1 green
  (bell) pepper, seeded and sliced
5ml/1 tsp sugar
2 bay leaves, crushed
4 cloves, crushed
4 sea bass fillets
4 pieces of mastic, pulverized with
  a little salt
1 cinnamon stick, broken into
  4 pieces
salt and ground black pepper

### COOK'S TIP

Cooking meat and fish in foil or paper parcels ensures that the flesh is tender.

**1** Preheat the oven to 180°C/350°F/ Gas 4. Plunge the tomatoes into boiling water for 30 seconds, then refresh in cold water. Peel away the skins, remove the seeds and chop the flesh.

**2** In a heavy pan, heat the oil with the butter until it has melted. Stir in the onions and peppers, and cook until soft. Add the tomatoes, sugar, bay leaves and cloves, and cook gently for about 5 minutes. Season with salt and pepper, and leave to cool.

**3** Cut four pieces of foil large enough to enclose a fish fillet each, and spread them out on a flat surface. Spoon a little of the onion and tomato mixture on to each piece of foil, spreading it flat, and place a fish fillet on top. Sprinkle the pulverized mastic over the fillets.

**4** Spoon the remaining onion and tomato mixture over and around the fillets, and place a piece of cinnamon stick on top of each one.

**5** Wrap up the parcels into little packets, by pulling up the sides and pinching the edges tightly, leaving a little room for steam to escape. Brush some water over the parcels and place them on a baking tray. Put them in the oven for about 15–20 minutes.

**6** Place the parcels on individual plates, or on a serving dish, and open them up to let the aroma whet the appetite.

**Per portion** Energy 267kcal/1114kJ; Protein 21.7g; Carbohydrate 14.9g, of which sugars 12.5g; Fat 13.8g, of which saturates 4.6g; Cholesterol 93mg; Calcium 167mg; Fibre 3.1g; Sodium 121mg.

# CINNAMON FISHCAKES WITH CURRANTS, PINE NUTS AND HERBS

*WHETHER SERVED AS A HOT MEZE OR AS A MAIN COURSE WITH A GREEN SALAD, THESE FRESH, TASTY FISHCAKES ARE DELICIOUS FLAVOURED WITH CINNAMON AND THE UBIQUITOUS TRIAD OF HERBS — PARSLEY, MINT AND DILL. THEY ARE POPULAR THROUGHOUT THE AEGEAN AND MEDITERRANEAN REGIONS.*

## SERVES FOUR

### INGREDIENTS

450g/1lb skinless fresh white fish fillets, such as haddock or sea bass
2 slices of day-old bread, sprinkled with water and left for a few minutes, then squeezed dry
1 red onion, finely chopped
30ml/2 tbsp currants, soaked in warm water for 5–10 minutes and drained
30ml/2 tbsp pine nuts
1 small bunch each of fresh flat leaf parsley, mint and dill, finely chopped
1 egg
5–10ml/1–2 tsp tomato purée (paste) or ketchup
15ml/1 tbsp ground cinnamon
45–60ml/3–4 tbsp plain (all-purpose) flour
45–60ml/3–4 tbsp sunflower oil
salt and ground black pepper
To serve
1 small bunch of fresh flat leaf parsley
1–2 lemons or limes, cut into wedges

**1** In a bowl, break up the fish with a fork. Add the bread, onion, currants and pine nuts, toss in the herbs and mix.

**2** In another small bowl, beat the egg with the tomato purée and 10ml/2 tsp of the cinnamon. Pour the mixture over the fish and season with salt and pepper to taste, then mix with your hands and mould into small balls.

**3** Mix the flour on a plate with the remaining cinnamon. Press each ball into a flat cake and coat in the flour.

**4** Heat the oil in a wide, shallow pan and fry the fishcakes in batches for 8–10 minutes, until golden brown. Lift out and drain on kitchen paper. Serve hot on a bed of parsley, with lemon or lime wedges for squeezing.

**Per portion** Energy 317kcal/1324kJ; Protein 26.1g; Carbohydrate 17.8g, of which sugars 2.5g; Fat 16.2g, of which saturates 1.9g; Cholesterol 99mg; Calcium 79mg; Fibre 1.6g; Sodium 169mg.

# SEA BASS BAKED IN SALT

*THIS IS A RESTAURANT SPECIALITY, ESPECIALLY POPULAR ALONG THE BOSPHORUS IN ISTANBUL AND THE WATERFRONT RESTAURANTS IN IZMIR. THIS ANCIENT METHOD OF COOKING INTENSIFIES THE FRESHNESS OF THE FISH, CONJURING UP THE TASTE OF THE SEA, BUT IT DOES REQUIRE A LOT OF SALT. SERVE ON ITS OWN WITH LEMON, FRESHLY GROUND BLACK PEPPER AND A ROCKET SALAD.*

**1** Preheat the oven to 190°C/375°F/ Gas 5. Rinse the fish inside and out.

**2** Find an ovenproof dish to fit the fish and cover the bottom with a thick layer of salt, pressing it down with the heel of your hand. Place the fish on top and spoon salt over it until it is completely covered, then press down gently to compact the salt.

**3** Put the dish in the preheated oven and bake for 1 hour, until the salt has formed a hard crust.

**4** Place the dish on the table and make a show of cracking open the salt crust with a heavy object, such as a meat cleaver or a pestle.

SERVES TWO TO FOUR

INGREDIENTS

1.2kg/2½lb very fresh sea bass
  (*see* Variation), gutted, with head
  and tail left on
about 1kg/2¼lb coarse sea salt
ground black pepper and lemon
  wedges, to serve

**VARIATION**

In Turkey, blue fish (sea perch) is popular for this dish, but if you are unable to get it sea bass is a good alternative. You could also use any other firm-fleshed white fish, such as turbot or sole.

**5** Carefully peel off the top layer of salt using a knife, removing the skin of the fish with it.

**6** Serve chunks of the delicate white flesh immediately, with nothing more than a little black pepper and a squeeze of lemon.

**Per portion** Energy 175kcal/737kJ; Protein 33.8g; Carbohydrate 0g, of which sugars 0g; Fat 4.4g, of which saturates 0.7g; Cholesterol 140mg; Calcium 228mg; Fibre 0g; Sodium 1103mg.

# BAKED BONITO WITH BAY LEAVES

*MANY OF THE POPULAR FISH RESTAURANTS IN ISTANBUL AND IZMIR GRILL OR FRY FRESH FISH BUT, ON OCCASION, YOU COME ACROSS SOME DELICIOUS BAKED RECIPES WHERE THE FLESH IS SUCCULENT AND DELICATELY PERFUMED WITH HERBS AND LEMON. IN THIS RECIPE, FIRINDA PALAMUT, FRESH BAY LEAVES ARE USED BUT, IF YOU CAN'T FIND ANY, JUST USE DRIED ONES.*

## SERVES FOUR

### INGREDIENTS

4 tomatoes
2 fresh bonito, gutted, cleaned, and
   cut crossways into thick slices with
   the bone intact
2 red onions, cut in half lengthways
   and sliced
3 hot green peppers, or
   2 green chillies, seeded and
   cut in half lengthways
1 bunch flat leaf parsley,
   leaves chopped
6–8 fresh bay leaves, plus extra
   to garnish
60–75ml/4–5 tbsp olive oil
25g/1oz/2 tbsp butter
1 lemon, cut into wedges
salt and ground black pepper

**2** Arrange the fish in a shallow ovenproof earthenware dish and sprinkle them with a little salt and pepper. Arrange the onions, tomatoes and peppers over and around the fish, and sprinkle the parsley over the top. Tuck the bay leaves around the fish and pour over the olive oil.

**3** Cover the dish with foil and place it in the oven for 30 minutes. Remove the foil and dot the fish with little pieces of butter. Place the dish back in the oven and leave for a further 10–15 minutes for the fish to brown slightly.

**4** Serve hot with wedges of lemon to squeeze over the fish, and garnish each plate with a couple of fresh bay leaves.

### VARIATIONS

• This dish is delicious made with a variety of fresh fish, such as trout, salmon, sea bass or mackerel.
• Purple basil lends an interesting aniseed taste to the dish and can be used as an alternative to bay leaves, if you like.

**1** Preheat the oven to 180°C/350°F/ Gas 4. Plunge the tomatoes into boiling water for 30 seconds, then refresh in cold water. Peel away the skins, then cut the tomatoes in half and slice them.

**Per portion** Energy 281kcal/1168kJ; Protein 20.4g; Carbohydrate 11.4g, of which sugars 8.9g; Fat 17.4g, of which saturates 5g; Cholesterol 59mg; Calcium 64mg; Fibre 2.8g; Sodium 108mg.

# DEEP-FRIED RED MULLET WITH ROCKET

*GENERALLY, SMALL FISH, SUCH AS ANCHOVIES, SARDINES AND RED MULLET, ARE DEEP-FRIED OR GRILLED WHOLE AND SERVED SIMPLY WITH LEMON. RED MULLET IS THE MOST SOUGHT AFTER, FLAVOURED WITH GARLIC, SPRINKLED WITH SUMAC, AND SERVED WITH ROCKET LEAVES IN THE DISH BARBUNYA TAVASI. FOR MANY TURKS, THIS IS THE WAY TO ENJOY THE SWEET FLESH OF RED MULLET.*

### SERVES TWO TO FOUR

INGREDIENTS
- 1 bunch fresh flat leaf parsley, leaves chopped
- 15–30ml/1–2 tbsp sumac
- 4–5 garlic cloves, crushed
- 4 red mullet, gutted and cleaned
- salt
- plain (all-purpose) flour, for coating
- sunflower oil, for deep-frying
- 1 bunch fresh rocket (arugula) leaves
- 1 lemon, cut into wedges, to serve

**1** Mix the chopped parsley with half the sumac and half the crushed garlic, and stuff it into the gutted cavity of each fish. Mix the remainder of the garlic with some salt and rub it all over the outside of the fish.

**2** Roll each fish in flour, until it is completely coated.

**3** Heat enough oil in a large, heavy pan for deep-frying. Pop in the fish and fry for about 5 minutes until golden brown.

**4** Lift the fish out of the oil and drain on kitchen paper.

**5** Arrange the rocket leaves on a serving dish, as a bed for the fish, or in a decorative fan shape. Place the fish on the rocket, sprinkle with the remaining sumac, and serve with the lemon wedges to squeeze over them.

**Per portion** Energy 275kcal/1146kJ; Protein 19.4g; Carbohydrate 9.7g, of which sugars 0.9g; Fat 17.9g, of which saturates 1.7g; Cholesterol 0mg; Calcium 85mg; Fibre 0.5g; Sodium 97mg.

# BLUE FISH STEW

*THERE ARE A VARIETY OF TOMATO-BASED FISH DISHES IN THE AEGEAN AND MEDITERRANEAN REGIONS OF TURKEY, BUT THIS ONE, LÜFER YAHNISI, EPITOMIZES A BASIC HOME-COOKED STEW USING SIMPLE, TRADITIONAL INGREDIENTS: CURRANTS TO SWEETEN, CINNAMON TO SPICE AND VINEGAR TO SHARPEN. SERVE THE STEW WITH PLENTY OF CRUSTY BREAD OR A PLAIN PILAFF.*

SERVES THREE TO FOUR

INGREDIENTS
    30ml/2 tbsp currants
    30ml/2 tbsp olive oil
    15ml/1 tbsp butter
    2 onions, halved lengthways
        and sliced with the grain
    2 green (bell) peppers, seeded
        and sliced
    2–3 garlic cloves, chopped
    10ml/2 tsp ground cinnamon
    4 blue fish (sea perch) fillets,
        or sea bass or trout
    15ml/1 tbsp apple or white
        wine vinegar
    400g/14oz can plum tomatoes
    120ml/4fl oz/½ cup water
    salt and ground black pepper
    1 bunch flat leaf parsley,
        leaves chopped

**1** Soak the currants in a bowl of warm water for 15 minutes and then drain.

**2** Heat the olive oil and butter in a large, heavy pan, or a flameproof earthenware pot. Add the onions, peppers, garlic and currants, stir to mix thoroughly and cook until the onions begin to colour.

**3** Stir in the cinnamon and add the fish fillets, making sure they are coated with the onions and peppers.

**4** Add the vinegar, tomatoes and water, and bring the liquid to the boil.

**5** Reduce the heat and simmer gently for 15–20 minutes, or until the fish is completely cooked. Season to taste with salt and pepper.

**6** Serve the fish stew immediately, garnished with the flat leaf parsley, and accompanied by chunks of warm, crusty bread to mop up the sauce, or with a plain pilaff.

**Per portion** Energy 290kcal/1214kJ; Protein 22.5g; Carbohydrate 21.7g, of which sugars 19.2g; Fat 13.3g, of which saturates 3g; Cholesterol 8mg; Calcium 87mg; Fibre 4g; Sodium 96mg.

# HERB-STUFFED SQUID WITH SAFFRON

*THIS DISH IS BEST MADE WITH TENDER BABY SQUID. STUFFED WITH BULGUR WHEAT AND HERBS, AND FLAVOURED WITH SAFFRON, THIS VIBRANT-LOOKING DISH — KALAMAR DOLMASI — IS TASTY AND SATISFYING. THE COMMON TURKISH SAFFRON IS AN IMPOSTER FOR THE REAL THING, EXTRACTED FROM A VARIETY OF WILD FLOWERS RATHER THAN THE CROCUS. IT DOES LEND A VIBRANT YELLOW-ORANGE COLOUR TO DISHES, BUT IT DOESN'T HAVE ANY TASTE AND DOESN'T DISSOLVE INTO THE DISH LIKE THE REAL THING, SO YOU FEEL YOU ARE EATING DRIED PETALS. ALTHOUGH THERE IS GENUINE SAFFRON AVAILABLE IN TURKEY, IT IS MORE USUAL TO FIND THE IRANIAN VERSION IN THE MARKETS. AUTHENTIC SAFFRON IS USED HERE. SERVE WITH A GREEN SALAD.*

SERVES FOUR TO SIX

INGREDIENTS

   12 baby squid, cleaned and
      prepared with the body sacs
      left whole
   50g/2oz/⅓ cup fine bulgur wheat,
      rinsed and drained
   45ml/3 tbsp olive oil
   juice of 1 lemon
   120ml/4fl oz/½ cup white wine
   a generous pinch saffron threads
   30ml/2 tbsp tomato purée (paste)
   1 large bunch flat leaf parsley,
      leaves finely chopped
   1 large bunch mint, leaves
      finely chopped
   1 large bunch dill fronds,
      finely chopped
   2–3 garlic cloves, finely chopped
   salt and ground black pepper

**VARIATION**
Baby squid can be stuffed with the cinnamon-flavoured rice used in stuffed vegetable dishes, such as Peppers Stuffed with Aromatic Rice.

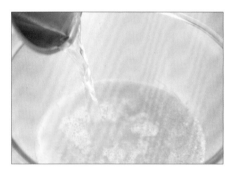

**1** Preheat the oven to 180°C/350°F/ Gas 4. Put the bulgur wheat in a bowl and pour over just enough boiling water to cover it and no more.

**2** Place a clean dish towel over the bowl and leave for about 20 minutes to absorb the liquid. Once the water has been absorbed, the quantity of bulgur wheat will double in size.

**3** In a small bowl whisk together 30ml/ 2 tbsp of the olive oil with the lemon juice, white wine and saffron. Put the mixture aside to allow the saffron to release its colour.

**COOK'S TIP**
When stuffing whole squid always be extra careful to rinse out the body sac carefully, as particles of sand can become caught inside, making them gritty and spoiling the dish.

**4** Using your fingers, rub the tomato purée into the bulgur wheat with the remaining olive oil, or combine everything well with a fork.

**5** Toss in the herbs and garlic, and mix well to combine. Season to taste with salt and pepper.

**6** Using your fingers, or a teaspoon, stuff the herby bulgur wheat into the empty body sacs and plug the hole with the tentacles.

**7** Place the stuffed squid into a shallow earthenware, or ovenproof, dish and pour over the saffron-coloured olive oil and lemon juice mixture. Place the dish in the preheated oven and bake for about 25 minutes.

**8** Serve immediately with a green salad and fresh bread.

**Per portion** Energy 201kcal/842kJ; Protein 19.7g; Carbohydrate 10.6g, of which sugars 1.2g; Fat 7.8g, of which saturates 1.3g; Cholesterol 263mg; Calcium 38mg; Fibre 1g; Sodium 144mg.

# MEDITERRANEAN SQUID <u>WITH</u> OLIVES <u>AND</u> RED WINE

*ALTHOUGH MANY MUSLIMS DO NOT DRINK ALCOHOL, THERE ARE SOME SURPRISINGLY GOOD WINES AVAILABLE IN TURKEY, AND ALONG THE MEDITERRANEAN AND AEGEAN COASTS SOME RESTAURANTS INCORPORATE WINE IN DISHES. THIS CUSTOM COULD BE DUE TO THESE LOCATIONS' PROXIMITY TO GREECE OR, PERHAPS, TO THE INFLUENCE OF WESTERN TOURISTS.*

**3** Bubble up the liquid, then lower the heat and cover the pan. Cook gently for 35–40 minutes, until most of the liquid has reduced and the squid is tender.

**4** Season the squid with salt and pepper to taste and toss in the herbs. Serve immediately, with lemon wedges.

**COOK'S TIP**
Fresh squid should smell slightly sweet. Rinse it and peel off the thin film of skin, then sever the head and trim the tentacles with a sharp knife. With your finger, pull out the backbone and reach down into the body pouch to remove the ink sac and any mushy bits. Rinse the empty pouch inside and out and pat dry. Use the pouch and trimmed head for cooking; discard the rest.

SERVES FOUR

INGREDIENTS
  30–45ml/2–3 tbsp olive oil
  2 red onions, cut in half lengthways
    and sliced along the grain
  3–4 garlic cloves, chopped
  about 750g/1lb 10oz fresh squid,
    prepared (*see* Cook's Tip) and cut
    into thick rings
  45–60ml/3–4 tbsp black olives, pitted
  5–10ml/1–2 tsp ground cinnamon
  5–10ml/1–2 tsp sugar
  300ml/½ pint/1¼ cups red wine
  2 bay leaves
  1 small bunch each of fresh flat leaf
    parsley and dill, finely chopped
  salt and ground black pepper
  lemon wedges, to serve

**1** Heat the oil in a heavy pan and cook the onions and garlic until golden.

**2** Add the squid heads and rings and toss them in the pan for 2–3 minutes, until they begin to colour. Toss in the olives, cinnamon and sugar, pour in the wine and add the bay leaves.

**Per portion** Energy 304kcal/1275kJ; Protein 30.3g; Carbohydrate 11.4g, of which sugars 6.8g; Fat 10.1g, of which saturates 1.7g; Cholesterol 422mg; Calcium 62mg; Fibre 1.7g; Sodium 468mg.

# BAKED PRAWNS WITH TOMATOES, PEPPER AND GARLIC

*THIS DISH, KARIDES GÜVEÇ, IS OFTEN SERVED AS A HOT MEZE IN THE FISH RESTAURANTS OF IZMIR AND ISTANBUL. THE MEDITERRANEAN VERSION, FOUND IN THE COASTAL REGIONS OF SOUTH-WEST TURKEY, IS FLAVOURED WITH GARLIC, RED PEPPER AND CORIANDER SEEDS. COOKED IN ONE BIG EARTHENWARE POT, GÜVEÇ, OR IN INDIVIDUAL ONES AS HERE, IT IS DELICIOUS SERVED WITH A SALAD.*

SERVES FOUR

INGREDIENTS

   30–45ml/2–3 tbsp olive oil
   1 onion, cut in half lengthways and finely sliced along the grain
   1 green (bell) pepper, seeded and finely sliced
   2–3 garlic cloves, chopped
   5–10ml/1–2 tsp coriander seeds
   5–10ml/1–2 tsp *kırmızı biber*, or 1 fresh red chilli, seeded and chopped
   5–10ml/1–2 tsp sugar
   splash of white wine vinegar
   2 x 400g/14oz cans chopped tomatoes
   1 small bunch of fresh flat leaf parsley, chopped
   500g/1¼lb fresh raw prawns (shrimp), shelled, thoroughly cleaned and drained
   about 120g/4oz *kasar peyniri*, Parmesan or a strong, dry Cheddar, grated
   salt and ground black pepper

**3** Season the sauce with salt and pepper to taste, and toss in the prawns, making sure that everything is thoroughly combined.

**4** Spoon the mixture into individual earthenware pots and sprinkle the top with the grated cheese. Bake in the oven for 25 minutes, or until the cheese is nicely browned on top.

**1** Heat the oil in a heavy pan, stir in the onion, green pepper, garlic, coriander seeds and *kırmızı biber* or chilli and cook until they begin to colour.

**2** Stir in the sugar, vinegar, tomatoes and parsley, then cook gently for about 25 minutes, until you have a chunky sauce. While the sauce is cooking, preheat the oven to 200°C/400°F/Gas 6.

**Per portion** Energy 338kcal/1413kJ; Protein 35.9g; Carbohydrate 11.2g, of which sugars 10.8g; Fat 16.9g, of which saturates 7.3g; Cholesterol 274mg; Calcium 481mg; Fibre 2.9g; Sodium 585mg.

# MUSSELS STUFFED WITH AROMATIC PILAFF AND PINE NUTS

*IN ISTANBUL, STUFFED MUSSELS ARE SOLD BY STREET VENDORS AROUND THE GOLDEN HORN, AT THE BOAT CROSSINGS OVER THE BOSPHORUS, AND IN THE MAIN BAZAARS. IN THE FISH RESTAURANTS, THEY ARE ALWAYS SERVED AT ROOM TEMPERATURE AS A POPULAR MEZE DISH.*

## SERVES FOUR

### INGREDIENTS

- 16 large fresh mussels
- 45–60ml/3–4 tbsp olive oil
- 2–3 shallots, finely chopped
- 30ml/2 tbsp pine nuts
- 30ml/2 tbsp currants, soaked in warm water for 5–10 minutes and drained
- 10ml/2 tsp ground cinnamon
- 5ml/1 tsp ground allspice
- 5–10ml/1–2 tsp sugar
- 5–10ml/1–2 tsp tomato purée (paste)
- 115g/4oz/generous ½ cup short grain or pudding rice, well rinsed and drained
- 1 small bunch each of fresh flat leaf parsley, mint and dill, finely chopped
- salt and ground black pepper
- lemon wedges and fresh flat leaf parsley sprigs, to serve

**COOK'S TIP**
Place the mussels in a bowl of cold water and scrub the shells with a stiff brush. Pull out the tough beards and cut off the barnacles with a knife. Discard any mussels that are open, or that do not close when tapped on the work surface.

**1** Clean the mussels as described in the Cook's Tip. Keep them in a bowl of cold water while you prepare the stuffing.

**2** Heat the oil in a heavy pan, stir in the shallots and cook until they soften.

**3** Add the pine nuts and currants, stir for 1–2 minutes until the pine nuts turn golden and the currants plump up, then stir in the cinnamon, allspice, sugar and tomato purée. Now add the rice, and stir until it is well coated.

**VARIATION**
A more recent creation to appear on the Istanbul culinary scene is a Turkish version of *moules marinière*. For this dish, soften 2–3 chopped shallots and a handful fresh, flat leaf parsley in a pan with 45ml/3 tbsp olive oil. Add about 16 large mussels, a squeeze of lemon juice and 200ml/7fl oz/scant 1 cup *rakı* instead of the white wine used in traditional versions. The mussels are then steamed for a few minutes until they open fully.

**4** Pour in enough water to just cover the rice. Season to taste with salt and pepper and bring to the boil. Lower the heat, partially cover the pan and simmer for 10–12 minutes, until all the water has been absorbed. Transfer the rice to a plate, leave to cool, then toss in the herbs.

**5** Using a sharp knife, prise open each mussel shell wide enough to fill with rice. Stuff a spoonful of rice into each shell, then close the shells and pack the mussels tightly into a steamer filled with water. Cover with a sheet of dampened baking parchment, put a plate on top and weigh it down with a stone – one from the garden will do – to prevent the mussels from opening during steaming.

**6** Place the lid on the steamer and bring the water to the boil. Lower the heat and steam the mussels gently for 15–20 minutes, then leave to cool a little in the pan.

**7** Serve warm on a bed of parsley, with lemon wedges for squeezing.

**Per portion** Energy 319kcal/1328kJ; Protein 13.3g; Carbohydrate 32.7g, of which sugars 7.5g; Fat 15g, of which saturates 1.9g; Cholesterol 33mg; Calcium 49mg; Fibre 0.5g; Sodium 237mg.

# MEAT AND POULTRY

*The Turks are tremendous carnivores with a preference for lamb*

*or mutton. Kebabs, in their many guises, are perhaps the most*

*ubiquitous of all meat and poultry dishes, but other notable*

*favourites include a variety of delicious Palace specialities, such as*

*the numerous meatballs, including Ladies' Thighs, and the lovely*

*Shredded Chicken with Walnuts from Circassia. Stews featuring*

*nuts or fruits, such as Chicken with Tart Green Plums and Grape*

*Syrup, lend a medieval air to a predominantly grilled-meat table.*

# LAMB SKEWERS WITH FLAT BREAD AND RED ONION

*THIS POPULAR ANATOLIAN KEBAB, ÇÖP ŞIŞ, IS TRADITIONALLY MADE WITH LAMB SCRAPS — ÇÖP MEANS RUBBISH — THAT ARE FLAVOURED WITH ONION, CUMIN AND GARLIC AND CHARGRILLED ON SWORDS OR SKEWERS. THE SMALL PIECES OF COOKED MEAT ARE THEN WRAPPED IN FRESHLY GRIDDLED FLAT BREAD WITH RED ONION, FLAT LEAF PARSLEY AND A SQUEEZE OF LEMON.*

SERVES FOUR TO SIX

INGREDIENTS
2 onions
7.5ml/1½ tsp salt
2 garlic cloves, crushed
10ml/2 tsp cumin seeds, crushed
900g/2lb boneless shoulder of
  lamb, trimmed of fat and cut into
  bitesize pieces
For the flat breads
225g/8oz/2 cups strong white
  bread flour
50g/2oz/¼ cup wholemeal
  (whole-wheat) flour
5ml/1 tsp salt
To serve
1 large red onion, cut in half
  lengthways, in half again crossways,
  and sliced along the grain
1 large bunch of fresh flat leaf
  parsley, roughly chopped
2–3 lemons, cut into wedges

**1** Grate the onions on to a plate, sprinkle with the salt and leave them to weep for about 15 minutes. Place a sieve (strainer) over a large bowl, add in the onions and press down with the back of a wooden spoon in order to extract the onion juice.

**2** Discard the onions left in the sieve, then mix the garlic and cumin seeds into the onion juice and toss in the lamb. Cover and leave to marinate for 3–4 hours.

**3** Meanwhile, prepare the dough for the flat breads. Sift the flours and salt together into a large bowl. Make a well in the middle and gradually add 200ml/7fl oz/scant 1 cup lukewarm water, drawing in the flour from the sides.

**4** Using your hands, knead the dough until firm and springy – if it is at all sticky, add more flour.

**5** Divide the dough into 24 pieces and knead each one into a ball. Place on a floured surface and cover with a damp cloth. Leave to rest for 45 minutes while you get the barbecue ready.

**6** Just before cooking, roll each ball of dough into a wide, thin circle. Dust each circle with flour so they don't stick together, and keep them covered until required with a damp dish towel to prevent them drying out.

**7** Thread the meat on to flat kebab swords or metal skewers.

**8** Cook the kebabs on the barbecue for 2–3 minutes on each side.

**9** At the same time, cook the flat breads on a hot griddle or other flat pan, flipping them over as they begin to go brown and buckle. Pile up on a plate.

**10** Slide the meat on to the flat breads. Sprinkle onion and parsley over each pile and squeeze lemon juice over the top. Wrap the breads into parcels and eat with your hands.

**Per portion** Energy 433kcal/1821kJ; Protein 34.3g; Carbohydrate 37.1g, of which sugars 4.4g; Fat 17.5g, of which saturates 7.9g; Cholesterol 114mg; Calcium 83mg; Fibre 2.5g; Sodium 460mg.

# LAMB ŞIŞ KEBAB

*THIS IS THE ULTIMATE KEBAB — CHARGRILLED MEAT SERVED ON FLAT BREAD WITH YOGURT AND TOMATOES. DESIGNED TO USE UP DAY-OLD PIDE, FOR WHICH YOU CAN SUBSTITUTE PITTA BREAD OR A PLAIN INDIAN NAAN, THE DISH IS SUCCULENT AND TASTY, AND SHOULD BE DEVOURED ON ITS OWN.*

### SERVES FOUR

INGREDIENTS
 12 plum tomatoes
 30ml/2 tbsp butter
 1 large *pide*, or 4 pitta or small
  naan, cut into bitesize chunks
 5ml/1 tsp ground sumac
 5ml/1 tsp dried oregano
 225g/8oz/1 cup thick and creamy
  natural (plain) yogurt
 salt and ground black pepper
 1 bunch of fresh flat leaf parsley,
  chopped, to garnish
For the kebabs
 500g/1¼lb/2¼ cups lean
  minced (ground) lamb
 2 onions, finely chopped
 1 fresh green chilli, seeded and
  finely chopped
 4 garlic cloves, crushed
 5ml/1 tsp *kırmızı biber*,
  or paprika
 5ml/1 tsp ground sumac
 1 bunch of fresh flat leaf parsley,
  finely chopped
For the sauce
 30ml/2 tbsp olive oil
 15ml/1 tbsp butter
 1 onion, finely chopped
 2 garlic cloves, finely chopped
 1 fresh green chilli, seeded and
  finely chopped
 5–10ml/1–2 tsp sugar
 400g/14oz can chopped tomatoes

**1** Make the kebabs. Put the lamb into a bowl with all the other ingredients and knead well to a smooth paste. Cover and chill for about 15 minutes.

**2** Meanwhile, make the sauce. Heat the oil and butter in a pan, add the onion, garlic and chilli and cook until they begin to colour. Add the sugar and tomatoes and cook, uncovered, for 30 minutes. Season and remove from the heat.

**3** Get the barbecue ready for cooking and shape the kebabs.

**4** As soon as the kebabs are shaped, cook them on the barbecue and cook for 6–8 minutes, turning once.

**5** Meanwhile, thread the whole plum tomatoes on to four skewers, place them on the barbecue and cook until they are charred.

**6** While the kebabs are cooking, melt the butter in a heavy pan, add the *pide* or other bread and cook until golden.

**7** Sprinkle with some of the sumac and oregano, then arrange on a serving dish, spreading the pieces out so they form a flat base.

**8** Spoon a little tomato sauce over the *pide* – not too much or it will go soggy – and spoon half the yogurt on top.

**9** When the kebabs are cooked on both sides, slip the meat off the skewers and cut it into bitesize pieces.

**10** Arrange the meat on the *pide* with the cooked tomatoes, sprinkle with salt and the rest of the sumac and oregano, then garnish with the chopped parsley.

**11** Serve hot, topped with dollops of the remaining sauce and yogurt.

**Per portion** Energy 642kcal/2688kJ; Protein 35.2g; Carbohydrate 52.8g, of which sugars 24.1g; Fat 33.9g, of which saturates 15.1g; Cholesterol 121mg; Calcium 253mg; Fibre 6.3g; Sodium 456mg.

# LAMB KEBAB IN PUFF PASTRY

*KEBABS IN PASTRY ARE NEITHER ANATOLIAN NOR OTTOMAN, BUT A MORE RECENT ADDITION TO THE CULINARY CULTURE OF TURKEY. OVER THE LAST CENTURY, NEW METHODS OF COOKING HAVE HAD AN IMPACT ON TRADITIONAL TECHNIQUES, AND THE EFFECT OF THIS CAN BE SEEN IN THIS DISH, TALAŞ KEBABI, WHICH REFLECTS A FRENCH INFLUENCE. YOU CAN MAKE YOUR OWN BUTTERY PUFF PASTRY FOR THIS KEBAB, OR USE THE READY-PREPARED PACKS, WHICH MAKE LIFE EASIER.*

SERVES SIX TO EIGHT

INGREDIENTS

   450g/1lb lean shoulder of lamb
   25g/1oz/2 tbsp butter
   2 onions, cut into four and sliced
   7.5ml/1½ tsp tomato purée (paste)
   10ml/2 tsp sugar
   5ml/1 tsp dried mint
   500g/1¼lb puff pastry, thawed
    if frozen
   1 egg yolk, beaten
   salt and ground black pepper

**1** Cut the shoulder of lamb into thin strips using a sharp knife.

**2** Melt the butter in a heavy pan, add the onions and cook until they have softened. Add the strips of lamb and cook for 3–4 minutes, or until most of the liquid has evaporated.

**3** Stir in the tomato purée and sugar, and pour in about 250ml/8fl oz/1 cup water. Reduce the heat, cover the pan and cook gently for about 40 minutes, or until the meat is tender.

**4** Meanwhile, preheat the oven to 180°C/350°F/Gas 4 and lightly grease a baking tray.

**5** Drain the meat over a pan to catch the cooking liquid. Reserve the cooking liquid and place the meat in a dish. Sprinkle the meat with a little salt and the dried mint. Leave to cool.

**6** On a lightly floured board, roll out the puff pastry into a rectangle. Cut out squares, about 10 x 10cm/4 x 4in square. Place a little of the cooked lamb in the centre of each square and fold over the edges to form a neat packet.

**7** Place the packets, seam-side down, in the baking tray. Brush the egg yolk over the pastry packets. Put the pastries in the oven and bake them for about 35 minutes, or until puffed up and golden brown.

**8** Heat up the reserved cooking liquid, season it and serve as a gravy with the kebabs.

**COOK'S TIP**
Smaller versions of these delicious pastry parcels make ideal appetizers or finger food at a buffet.

Per portion Energy 388kcal/1621kJ; Protein 15.6g; Carbohydrate 28.5g, of which sugars 5.1g; Fat 25g, of which saturates 4.8g; Cholesterol 75mg; Calcium 58mg; Fibre 0.7g; Sodium 266mg.

# LAMB STEW WITH ROASTED CHESTNUTS

*IN WESTERN ANATOLIA, KESTANELI KUZU IS A POPULAR STEW TO COOK AT HOME IN THE LATE AUTUMN, AND THERE IS ALSO A CLASSIC EARLY SUMMER VERSION THAT IS MADE WITH APRICOTS. EASY TO PREPARE, IT BENEFITS FROM BEING MADE IN ADVANCE. YOU CAN ROAST YOUR OWN CHESTNUTS AT HOME, OR YOU CAN BUY THEM READY-ROASTED IN CANS AND VACUUM-SEALED PACKS IN HEALTH FOOD SHOPS, SOME SUPERMARKETS AND DELICATESSENS. SERVE WITH A PLAIN PILAF AND SALAD.*

SERVES FOUR TO SIX

INGREDIENTS
- 1kg/2¼lb shoulder of lamb
- 45ml/3 tbsp olive oil
- 25g/1oz/2 tbsp butter
- 450g/1lb shallots, peeled and left whole
- 4–6 garlic cloves, smashed
- 2 cinnamon sticks
- 10ml/2 tsp allspice berries, crushed
- 15ml/1 tbsp clear honey
- 450g/1lb/4 cups roasted chestnuts, shelled
- salt and ground black pepper

**1** Trim the lamb of fat and cut the meat into chestnut-sized pieces.

**2** Heat the oil and butter in a large, heavy, flameproof earthenware pot or casserole. Stir in the shallots and fry until they turn golden brown. Transfer the shallots to a plate and set aside.

**3** Add the garlic, cinnamon sticks and allspice berries to the oil. Toss in the lamb to brown a little. Stir in the honey and pour in just enough water to cover the meat.

**4** Bring the water to the boil and reduce the heat. Cover the pot or casserole and cook gently for 45 minutes.

**5** Remove the lid and return the shallots to the pot. Add the chestnuts and cook gently for a further 10 minutes.

**6** Season to taste with salt and pepper, and serve with a plain pilaff and salad.

**VARIATION**
In the Black Sea region, a more pungent version of this stew is made using the strong, chestnut honey of the region and rancid-tasting butter.

**Per portion** Energy 760kcal/3159kJ; Protein 28.3g; Carbohydrate 34.1g, of which sugars 10.6g; Fat 57.7g, of which saturates 26.5g; Cholesterol 122mg; Calcium 62mg; Fibre 3.9g; Sodium 146mg.

# AUBERGINE MUSAKKA

*THERE ARE SEVERAL VERSIONS OF MUSAKKA IN TURKEY, AS THE WORD SIMPLY DENOTES A DISH COMPRISING MINCED MEAT AND VEGETABLES. VARIATIONS INCLUDE COURGETTES, CABBAGE AND POTATOES. THE AUBERGINE VERSION, PATLICAN MUSAKKASI, IS A CLASSIC, AND WAS PROBABLY DEVISED IN THE OTTOMAN PALACE KITCHENS, AS IT INCLUDES A MILK-BASED SAUCE, WHICH WAS SOMETIMES USED TO LEND AN AIR OF SOPHISTICATION TO DISHES. SERVE THE MUSAKKA WITH SALAD.*

SERVES FOUR TO SIX

INGREDIENTS
    4 good-sized aubergines (eggplants),
      sliced crossways
    30ml/2 tbsp currants
    sunflower oil or olive oil,
      for shallow-frying
    30ml/2 tbsp olive oil
    2 onions, chopped
    4 garlic cloves, chopped
    10ml/2 tsp sugar
    500g/1¼lb/2½ cups minced
      (ground) lamb
    25ml/1½ tbsp ground cinnamon
    10ml/2 tsp dried thyme or oregano
    5–10ml/1–2 tsp tomato purée (paste)
    salt and ground black pepper
For the sauce
    2 egg yolks
    450ml/¾ pint/scant 2 cups milk
    25ml/1½ tbsp butter
    45ml/3 tbsp plain (all-purpose) flour
    2.5ml/½ tsp freshly grated nutmeg

**1** Preheat the oven to 200°C/400°F/
Gas 6. Soak the aubergine slices in
salted water for 15–20 minutes. Soak
the currants in a bowl of warm water for
15 minutes and drain them. Drain the
aubergines and squeeze dry.

**2** Heat a layer of sunflower or olive oil in
a frying pan and fry the aubergine slices
in batches until lightly golden (you will
need to top up the oil during cooking,
as the aubergines absorb it). Drain
them on kitchen paper.

**3** Heat the 30ml/2 tbsp of olive oil in a
heavy pan. Stir in the onions and garlic
with the sugar and cook until golden.
Add the currants to plump them up and
stir in the minced lamb.

**4** Cook for 2–3 minutes, then add the
cinnamon, thyme or oregano and
tomato purée. Stir to combine and cook
for a further 2 minutes, then season to
taste with salt and pepper.

**5** Layer the aubergines and minced
meat in an earthenware or ovenproof
dish, starting and finishing with a layer
of aubergines (this can be prepared
ahead of time).

**COOK'S TIP**
A traditional musakka is designed to be
quite oily, as the oil is emitted from the
fried aubergines (eggplants), which lend
their own flavour to the overall dish.
However, if you wish to cook a less oily
version, you can brush each slice of
aubergine with a little oil and fry them
on a griddle, or grill (broil) them.

**6** To make the sauce, put the egg yolks
in a bowl. Stir in 15–30ml/1–2 tbsp of
the milk and set aside.

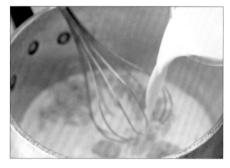

**7** Melt the butter in a pan over a
medium heat. Take the pan off the heat
and stir in the flour to make a roux.
Return the pan to the heat and pour in
the milk, whisking constantly, until the
sauce begins to thicken.

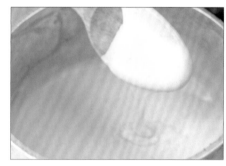

**8** Beat in the nutmeg, and season with
salt and pepper.

**9** Stir 15–30ml/1–2 tbsp of the hot
sauce into the egg yolks and then pour
them into the pan. Keep stirring until
the sauce is smooth and thick.

**10** Pour the sauce over the top layer of
aubergines and place the dish in the
preheated oven.

**11** Bake for 25–30 minutes, or until
the top of the musakka is beautifully
browned. Serve the musakka
immediately, with a salad.

**Per portion** Energy 479kcal/1993kJ; Protein 22.6g; Carbohydrate 24.4g, of which sugars 16.5g; Fat 33.1g, of which saturates 10.7g; Cholesterol 145mg; Calcium 164mg; Fibre 4.2g; Sodium 130mg.

# LAMB CUTLETS WITH GARLIC TOMATO SAUCE

*LAMB CUTLETS ARE MORE READILY AVAILABLE, BUT VEAL IS OFTEN FAVOURED BY THE WEALTHIER INHABITANTS OF ANKARA AND ISTANBUL. BUTCHERS PREPARE CUTLETS BY BASHING THEM FLAT WITH A MEAT CLEAVER. THE CUTLETS ARE THEN COOKED ON A GRIDDLE IN THEIR OWN FAT, OR A LITTLE BUTTER, AND SERVED WITH DRIED OREGANO AND WEDGES OF LEMON, OR WITH A TOMATO SAUCE.*

**3** Stir in the sugar and vinegar, then add the tomatoes and green pepper. Lower the heat, cover and simmer for about 30 minutes, until the mixture is thick and saucy. Season with salt and pepper to taste.

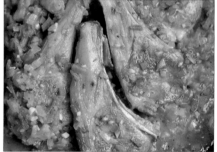

### SERVES FOUR

INGREDIENTS

   30ml/2 tbsp olive oil
   10ml/2 tsp butter
   12 lamb cutlets, trimmed and
     flattened with a cleaver – ask your
     butcher to do this
   1 onion, finely chopped
   1 fresh green chilli, seeded and
     finely chopped
   2 garlic cloves, finely chopped
   5ml/1 tsp sugar
   5–10ml/1–2 tsp white wine vinegar
   2–3 large tomatoes, skinned and
     chopped, or 400g/14oz can
     chopped tomatoes
   1 green (bell) pepper, seeded and
     finely chopped
   a sprinkling of dried oregano
   salt and ground black pepper

**1** Heat the oil and butter in a large pan and brown the cutlets on both sides.

**2** Remove from the pan, add the onion, chilli and garlic, and fry gently until the onion begins to brown.

**VARIATION**
Pan-fry the cutlets in olive oil, sprinkle with oregano and salt and serve with lemon.

**4** Return the cutlets to the pan, covering them completely in the sauce. Cook for about 15 minutes, until the meat is tender.

**5** Transfer the cutlets to a serving dish, arranging them around the edge with the bones sticking outwards. Sprinkle with oregano, spoon the sauce in the middle and serve immediately.

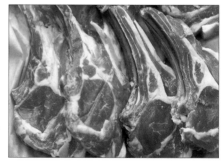

**Per portion** Energy 683kcal/2822kJ; Protein 23.2g; Carbohydrate 7.4g, of which sugars 6.9g; Fat 62.4g, of which saturates 29.2g; Cholesterol 122mg; Calcium 24mg; Fibre 1.7g; Sodium 114mg.

# LADIES' THIGHS

*WHEN YOU COME ACROSS DISHES WITH NAMES SUCH AS "YOUNG GIRLS' BREASTS", "SWEETHEART'S LIPS"
AND "LADIES' THIGHS" IT'S NOT DIFFICULT TO IMAGINE THE THOUGHT PROCESS IN THE OTTOMAN
PALACE KITCHENS. PLUMP, JUICY AND PACKED WITH FLAVOUR, THESE KADINBUDU KÖFTE ARE
DELICIOUS SERVED WITH A BUTTERY CHICKPEA PILAFF AND A FRESH GREEN SALAD.*

SERVES FOUR

INGREDIENTS

   15ml/1 tbsp olive oil
   1 onion, finely chopped
   500g/1¼lb/2½ cups lean minced
     (ground) lamb or beef
   115g/4oz/generous ½ cup long
     grain rice, cooked
   1 bunch parsley, leaves
     finely chopped
   5ml/1 tsp ground cumin
   5ml/1 tsp dried thyme
   plain (all-purpose) flour,
     for coating
   sunflower oil, for frying
   2 eggs, beaten
   salt and ground black pepper
   1 lemon, cut into wedges, to serve

**1** Heat the olive oil in a heavy pan and stir in the onions. Cook until they begin to colour.

**2** Add half the minced meat and fry over a high heat until all the liquid has evaporated. Add the cooked rice to the pan and stir well to mix.

**3** Transfer the meat and rice mixture to a bowl. Add the remainder of the raw minced meat with the parsley, cumin and thyme. Season with salt and pepper. Using a wooden spoon, combine the mixture until it is thoroughly mixed.

**COOK'S TIP**
Smaller Ladies' Thighs can be served as *meze* rather than as a main course.

**4** Take small, apricot-sized portions of the mixture in the palm of your hand and mould them into oval shapes. Flatten the ovals slightly with the heel of your hand, then dip them in the flour to coat completely.

**5** Heat enough oil for deep-frying in a pan. Dip the "thighs" into the beaten eggs and drop them into the oil. Cook in batches for about 2 minutes each side, until crisp and golden. Drain on kitchen paper and serve hot with lemon wedges.

Per portion Energy 544kcal/2261kJ; Protein 30.5g; Carbohydrate 30.2g, of which sugars 3.2g; Fat 33.6g, of which saturates 10.3g; Cholesterol 191mg; Calcium 84mg; Fibre 1.5g; Sodium 127mg.

# VINE LEAVES STUFFED WITH LAMB AND RICE

*VINE LEAVES ARE GENERALLY USED FOR WRAPPING AROUND FISH OR CHEESE, OR FOR STUFFING AND ROLLING INTO LOGS. THE BEST-KNOWN STUFFED VINE LEAVES ARE THE ONES FILLED WITH AROMATIC RICE AND SERVED COLD AS PART OF A MEZE SPREAD. IN TURKISH, THESE ARE KNOWN AS YALANCI YAPRAK DOLMASI, MEANING "FALSE STUFFED VINE LEAVES", BECAUSE THEY DO NOT CONTAIN MEAT. THE MEAT-FILLED VERSION, ETLI YAPRAK DOLMASI, IS REGARDED AS THE REAL THING, AND IS USUALLY SERVED HOT AS A MAIN COURSE WITH A DOLLOP OF NATURAL YOGURT.*

SERVES FOUR TO SIX

INGREDIENTS
  25–30 fresh or preserved vine leaves
  350g/12oz/1½ cups finely minced
    (ground) lean lamb or beef
  2 onions, finely chopped
  115g/4oz/generous ½ cup long grain
    rice, thoroughly rinsed and drained
  1 bunch each of fresh dill, flat leaf
    parsley and mint, finely chopped
  45–60ml/3–4 tbsp olive oil
  juice of 1 lemon
  salt and ground black pepper
To serve
  60–90ml/4–6 tbsp thick and creamy
    natural (plain) yogurt
  1 lemon, cut into wedges

**2** Put the lamb in a bowl and stir in the onions, rice and herbs. Season, bind with 15ml/1 tbsp of the oil and knead.

**3** Lay one of the vine leaves on a flat surface and spoon some filling at the top of the leaf. Pull this over the filling, fold in the sides, then roll into a tight log. Repeat with the remaining leaves and filling.

**5** In a bowl, mix the remaining oil with the lemon juice and 150ml/¼ pint/ ⅔ cup water, then pour over the vine leaves. The liquid should come at least halfway up the top layer, so you may need to add extra liquid.

**6** Put the pan over a medium heat. Once the liquid begins to bubble, place a plate over the leaves to stop them from unravelling, followed by a lid or foil.

**7** Lower the heat and leave the vine leaves to steam gently for 45 minutes, until the rice and meat are cooked. Serve hot, with the yogurt and lemon wedges to squeeze over.

**1** If using fresh vine leaves, bring a pan of water to the boil and plunge the fresh leaves into it for 1–2 minutes. Drain and refresh under cold running water, then drain thoroughly. Trim off the stems, and keep covered in the refrigerator for 2–3 days. If using preserved leaves, place them in a bowl and cover with boiling water. Soak for 15–20 minutes, using a fork to separate the leaves. Drain and return to the bowl with cold water. Soak for 2–3 minutes, then drain thoroughly.

**VARIATION**
You can make the same *dolma* using the leaves of a red or green cabbage.

**4** Arrange the vine leaves, seam side down, in a deep, wide pan. Pack them together in circles, making more than one layer if necessary.

Per portion Energy 276kcal/1148kJ; Protein 14.6g; Carbohydrate 23.5g, of which sugars 6.6g; Fat 13.8g, of which saturates 4.4g; Cholesterol 45mg; Calcium 88mg; Fibre 2.8g; Sodium 51mg.

# MEATBALLS WITH PINE NUTS AND CINNAMON

*THERE ARE A NUMBER OF DIFFERENT TYPES OF MEATBALL IN THE TURKISH KITCHEN. FALLING UNDER THE GENERIC NAME KÖFTE, THEY ARE GENERALLY MADE FROM LAMB OR BEEF, ALTHOUGH SOME CONTAIN CHICKEN, AND THEY ARE SHAPED INTO ROUND BALLS OR PLUMP OVALS.*

SERVES FOUR TO SIX

INGREDIENTS
- 250g/9oz/generous 1 cup lean minced (ground) lamb
- 1 onion, finely chopped
- 2 garlic cloves, crushed
- 10–15ml/2–3 tsp ground cinnamon
- 30ml/2 tbsp pine nuts
- 30ml/2 tbsp currants, soaked in warm water for 5–10 minutes and drained
- 5ml/1 tsp *kırmızı biber*, or paprika
- 2 slices of day-old white or brown bread, ground into crumbs
- 1 egg, lightly beaten
- 15ml/1 tbsp tomato ketchup
- 1 bunch each of fresh flat leaf parsley and dill
- 60ml/4 tbsp plain (all-purpose) flour
- sunflower oil, for shallow-frying
- salt and ground black pepper
- lemon wedges, to serve

**COOK'S TIP**
Other popular meatballs include *kuru köfte*, which are made with minced (ground) beef and onions and cooked in olive oil. These are particularly popular for picnics.

**1** In a large bowl, pound the minced lamb with the chopped onion, garlic and cinnamon.

**2** Knead the mixture with your hands and knock out the air, then add the pine nuts with the currants, *kırmızı biber* or paprika, breadcrumbs, egg and ketchup. Season with salt and pepper to taste.

**3** Finely chop the herbs, using a large, sharp knife reserving one or two sprigs of parsley for the garnish.

**4** Knead the herbs into the meat mixture, making sure all the ingredients are mixed well together.

**5** Take apricot-size portions of the meat mixture in your hands and roll into balls. Flatten each ball with the heel of your hand so that it resembles a thick disc, then coat lightly in the flour, shaking off any excess.

**6** Heat a thin layer of sunflower oil in a large, heavy pan. Add the meatballs and cook for 8–10 minutes, until browned on all sides.

**7** Remove the meat balls with a slotted spoon and drain on kitchen paper.

**8** Serve hot with lemon wedges and garnish with parsley.

**VARIATION**
To make quick meatballs that can be eaten on the go, omit the currants and pine nuts and add 5ml/1 tsp ground cumin and 1 chopped fresh hot chilli. Shape the mixture into small balls, cook as above for 5–6 minutes, then tuck into toasted pitta bread pockets with sliced red onion, chopped flat leaf parsley and some garlic-flavoured yogurt. Eat with your hands.

**Per portion** Energy 261kcal/1088kJ; Protein 11.4g; Carbohydrate 15.4g, of which sugars 5.2g; Fat 17.5g, of which saturates 4g; Cholesterol 64mg; Calcium 40mg; Fibre 0.7g; Sodium 129mg.

# MOTHER-IN-LAW'S MEATBALLS

*THIS IS A TRADITIONAL ANATOLIAN DISH, CALLED IÇLI KÖFTE, WHICH IS PREPARED BY THE MOTHER-IN-LAW OF A NEW BRIDE. GREAT CARE IS TAKEN OVER THE MAKING OF THE BALLS OF BULGUR WHEAT AND MINCED BEEF OR LAMB, WHICH ARE THEN HOLLOWED OUT TO FORM SHELLS FOR A SPICY, NUTTY FILLING. THEY ARE THEN PUSHED TOGETHER AND SEALED TO FORM A BALL AGAIN. THE ACT OF MAKING AND PRESENTING THESE DELICIOUS STUFFED KÖFTE IS TO SIGNIFY THAT THE LIPS OF THE NEW DAUGHTER-IN-LAW MUST NOW BE SEALED WITH DISCRETION.*

SERVES FOUR TO SIX

INGREDIENTS

   225g/8oz bulgur wheat
   225g/8oz/1 cup finely minced
    (ground) beef or lamb
   10ml/2 tsp *kırmızı biber*, or paprika
   plain (all-purpose) flour,
    for dusting
   sunflower oil, for deep-frying
   salt
   leaves from 1 large bunch parsley,
    to serve
For the filling
   15–30ml/1–2 tbsp ghee,
    or olive oil with a knob (pat)
    of butter
   1 onion, finely chopped
   4 garlic cloves, finely chopped
   50g/2oz/1/3 cup walnuts, chopped
   50g/2oz/1/3 cup blanched pistachio
    nuts, finely chopped
   5ml/1 tsp ground cumin
   5ml/1 tsp ground coriander
   5ml/1 tsp dried thyme
   115g/4oz/1/2 cup finely minced
    beef or lamb
   1 small bunch flat leaf parsley,
    finely chopped
   salt and ground black pepper

**2** Toss in the minced beef or lamb and cook for 4–5 minutes, then stir in the parsley, and season with salt and pepper. Leave the mixture to cool.

**3** Meanwhile, put the bulgur wheat into a bowl and pour in enough boiling water to just cover it. Cover the bowl and leave the bulgur wheat to absorb the water for about 25 minutes.

**4** Squeeze the bulgur wheat to make sure there is no excess water, then add the minced meat, *kırmızı biber* or paprika and salt to taste. Using your hands, knead the ingredients together thoroughly so that the mixture has a pasty consistency.

**6** Using a teaspoon, spoon a little filling into each hollow and pinch the edges of the ball together to seal.

**7** Gently squeeze the *köfte* to form a ball or a cone shape. Toss the *köfte* in a little flour to coat them lightly.

**8** Heat enough sunflower oil for deep-frying in a pan. Fry the *köfte* in batches for 3–4 minutes, or until golden brown. Drain on kitchen paper and serve hot on a bed of parsley leaves.

**COOK'S TIP**

In some parts of southern Anatolia these *köfte* are always moulded into oval shapes and slightly pointed at each end.

**1** To make the filling, melt the ghee, or olive oil and butter, in a heavy pan and stir in the onion and garlic until they begin to colour. Add the nuts, spices and thyme, and fry for 1–2 minutes.

**5** Take a small portion of the mixture in the palm of your hand and mould it into a ball. Using your thumb, hollow out an opening in the middle of the ball. Put the ball on to a flat surface. Repeat with the remainder of the mixture.

**Per portion** Energy 484kcal/2011kJ; Protein 18.2g; Carbohydrate 40.8g, of which sugars 2.8g; Fat 28.8g, of which saturates 6g; Cholesterol 40mg; Calcium 53mg; Fibre 2.2g; Sodium 89mg.

# STIR-FRIED LIVER WITH RED ONION

*THIS IS SUCH A DELICIOUS WAY TO EAT LAMB'S LIVER THAT EVEN THOSE WHO DON'T USUALLY LIKE IT WILL BE ABLE TO ENJOY IT. ARNAVUT CIĞERI, TRANSLATED AS "ALBANIAN LIVER", IT IS ONE OF THE DISHES THAT WAS ADOPTED BY THE PALACE KITCHENS AS THE OTTOMAN EMPIRE CONSUMED VAST EXPANSES OF EASTERN EUROPE. TRADITIONALLY SERVED AS A HOT OR COLD MEZE DISH WITH PLENTY OF SLICED RED ONION AND FLAT LEAF PARSLEY, IT IS ALSO A WONDERFUL DISH FOR SUPPER, SERVED WITH A SALAD AND A DOLLOP OF CREAMY YOGURT IF YOU LIKE.*

### SERVES FOUR

### INGREDIENTS

500g/1¼lb fresh lamb's liver
30ml/2 tbsp plain (all-purpose) flour
5–10ml/1–2 tsp *kırmızı biber*,
  or paprika
45–60ml/3–4 tbsp olive oil
2 garlic cloves, finely chopped
5–10ml/1–2 tsp cumin seeds
salt
1 large red onion, cut in half
  lengthways, in half again crossways,
  and sliced along the grain

To serve
a handful of fresh flat leaf parsley
1 lemon, cut into wedges

**1** Using a sharp knife, remove any skin and ducts from the liver, then cut it into thin strips or bitesize cubes.

**2** Mix the flour and *kırmızı biber* or paprika and toss the liver in it.

**3** Heat the olive oil in a heavy pan. Add the garlic and cumin seeds, season with salt and cook until the cumin gives off a nutty aroma.

**4** Toss in the strips or cubes of liver and stir-fry quickly for 2–3 minutes so that it cooks on all sides and browns slightly. Remove with a slotted spoon and drain on kichen paper.

**5** Spread the sliced red onion on a serving dish, spoon the hot liver in the middle and garnish with parsley leaves.

**6** Serve hot or cold, with the lemon wedges for squeezing.

**Per portion** Energy 298kcal/1245kJ; Protein 27g; Carbohydrate 11.8g, of which sugars 4.3g; Fat 16.3g, of which saturates 3.3g; Cholesterol 538mg; Calcium 37mg; Fibre 1.3g; Sodium 94mg.

# SPICY LIVER SAUSAGE

*THIS SPICY SAUSAGE, BUMBAR DOLMASI, IS SO POPULAR IN SOUTH-EAST ANATOLIA THAT THERE IS EVEN A BUMBAR FESTIVAL IN SIIRT. THIS TAKES PLACE IN EARLY SPRING WHEN THE FIRST WILD FLOWERS ARE PICKED IN THE MOUNTAINS. TO CELEBRATE, A SPECIAL BUMBAR IS PREPARED AND SERVED WITH A DRIED APRICOT COMPOTE (HOŞAF). IT ALSO PLAYS A ROLE IN THE MARRIAGES OF THE REGION, AS THE NEW BRIDE IS REQUIRED TO PRESENT HER MOTHER-IN-LAW WITH ANNUAL GIFTS OF HOME-COOKED BUMBAR, WHILE SHE IN TURN MUST EAT THE İÇLI KÖFTE PREPARED BY HER MOTHER-IN-LAW.*

SERVES FOUR

INGREDIENTS
    225g/8oz lamb's liver, minced
        (ground) (ask the butcher to do this)
    90g/3½oz/½ cup long grain rice,
        rinsed and drained
    5–10ml/1–2 tsp *kırmızı biber*,
        or paprika
    5ml/1 tsp ground cinnamon
    5ml/1 tsp ground cumin
    2.5ml/½ tsp ground allspice
    2.5ml/½ tsp ground black pepper
    5ml/1 tsp salt
    2 sausage skins (casings) (available
        in most butchers)
    1 bunch flat leaf parsley,
        with stalks intact, to serve
For the compote
    175g/6oz/¾ cup ready-to-eat
        dried apricots
    175g/6oz/generous ¾ cup caster
        (superfine) sugar
    juice of 1 lemon

**1** In a large bowl, mix the liver with the rice and spices. Add the salt and bind with a little water, about 15ml/1 tbsp. Mix well.

**2** Tie one end of each sausage skin in a knot, or with a piece of string. Fill them with the liver mixture (this is much easier if you have a funnel to insert into the other end of the sausage skin), and tie the ends.

**3** Place the sausages in a pan and cover with salted water. Bring the water to the boil and skim off any scum. Reduce the heat, cover the pan, and simmer for 15 minutes.

**4** Prick the sausages in several places with the sharp point of a knife and simmer for a further 15–20 minutes, or until tender.

**5** Meanwhile, prepare the compote. Put the apricots and sugar into a heavy pan and pour in enough water to cover. Heat gently and bring to the boil, stirring constantly. Reduce the heat, stir in the lemon juice, and leave to cook gently for 10 minutes. Leave to cool.

**6** Drain the sausages and return them to the pan. Cover with a clean dish towel and the lid, and leave for 15 minutes.

**7** Arrange the parsley on a serving dish and place the sausages on top. Serve with the apricot compote.

Per portion Energy 407kcal/1722kJ; Protein 15.4g; Carbohydrate 80.5g, of which sugars 61.7g; Fat 4.2g, of which saturates 1g; Cholesterol 242mg; Calcium 68mg; Fibre 2.8g; Sodium 542mg.

# CHICKEN CASSEROLE WITH OKRA AND LEMON

*THIS CLASSIC TURKISH DISH, GÜVEÇTE PILIÇLI BAMYA, IS FOUND IN VARIOUS FORMS THROUGHOUT THE MIDDLE EAST. IN THE SOUTH-EAST OF ANATOLIA, A GENEROUS DOSE OF HOT RED PEPPER IS ADDED TO GIVE A FIERY KICK, OTHERWISE IT IS USUALLY MILDLY SPICED. IT IS MOST OFTEN SERVED ON ITS OWN WITH CHUNKS OF BREAD TO MOP UP THE SAUCE, ALTHOUGH IT ALSO GOES WELL WITH A PILAFF. A SIMILAR DISH IS MADE WITH CHICKEN AND SLICED ARTICHOKE BOTTOMS.*

### SERVES FOUR

### INGREDIENTS
    30ml/2 tbsp olive oil
    30ml/2 tbsp butter
    1 small free-range chicken, trimmed
        of excess fat and cut into quarters
    2 onions, cut in half lengthways and
        finely sliced
    2–3 garlic cloves, finely chopped
    5–10ml/1–2 tsp *kırmızı biber*, or
        1 fresh red chilli, seeded and
        finely chopped
    10ml/2 tsp coriander seeds
    10ml/2 tsp dried oregano
    5–10ml/1–2 tsp sugar
    15ml/1 tbsp tomato purée (paste)
    400g/14oz can chopped tomatoes
    450g/1lb fresh okra, prepared
        as below
    juice of 1 lemon
    salt and ground black pepper
    thick and creamy natural (plain)
        yogurt, to serve

### COOK'S TIP
To retain colour and reduce sliminess when okra are cooked, prepare them as follows. Cut off the stalks, then place the okra in a bowl and sprinkle with 15ml/1 tbsp salt and 30–45ml/2–3 tbsp white wine vinegar or cider vinegar. Toss well and leave to sit for 1–2 hours. Rinse thoroughly and pat dry.

**1** Heat the oil with the butter in a wide, heavy pan or flameproof casserole. Add the chicken pieces and brown them on all sides. Remove from the pan with tongs and set aside.

**2** Add the sliced onions, chopped garlic, *kırmızı biber* or chilli, coriander seeds and oregano to the pan.

**3** Stir in the sugar and cook the mixture over a medium heat until the onions just begin to turn golden brown, then stir in the tomato purée and tomatoes and add 150ml/¼ pint/⅔ cup water. Mix to combine thoroughly.

**4** Bring the liquid to the boil, then reduce the heat and simmer gently for 2–3 minutes, to thicken the sauce. Slip in the chicken pieces and baste them all over with the sauce.

**5** Cover the pan and cook gently on top of the stove, or put the casserole in the oven at 180°C/350°F/Gas 4, and leave to cook for about 30 minutes.

**6** Sprinkle the okra over the chicken and pour the lemon juice on top. Cover the pan again and cook gently for a further 20 minutes, until the okra are tender but not soggy.

**7** Transfer the chicken pieces to a serving dish.

**8** Ensure that the okra is completely coated with the tomato sauce, season to taste with salt and pepper and spoon over and around the chicken.

**9** Serve immediately, with a bowl of yogurt on the side for spooning over the top.

**Per portion** Energy 386Kcal/1617kJ; Protein 47.3g; Carbohydrate 16g, of which sugars 13.1g; Fat 15.2g, of which saturates 5.7g; Cholesterol 139mg; Calcium 224mg; Fibre 7g; Sodium 181mg.

# CHICKEN WITH TART GREEN PLUMS AND GRAPE SYRUP

*THIS DISH, ERIKLI TAVUK, IS MADE WITH THE TART GREEN PLUMS THAT ARE POPULAR AS A SNACK DIPPED IN SALT. COOKING FRUIT WITH MEAT AND POULTRY WAS A GREAT PERSIAN TRADITION THAT FILTERED THROUGH TO THE CUISINE OF THE SELJUK TURKS IN KONYA. THE MYSTIC AND POET, MEVLANA JALAL-AL DIN RUMI, KEPT RECORDS OF RECIPES AND THE HEALING PROPERTIES OF FOOD OF THIS PERIOD.*

SERVES FOUR

INGREDIENTS

    30ml/2 tbsp olive oil with a knob
      (pat) of butter
    3–4 garlic cloves, smashed
    8 chicken thighs, skinned
    30ml/2 tbsp blanched almonds
    8–10 green plums, or other tart
      plums, stoned (pitted)
    15ml/1 tbsp grape *pekmez*
      (molasses) or honey
    salt and ground black pepper
    1 lemon, cut into wedges,
      to serve

**1** Heat the oil and butter in a heavy pan and stir in the garlic. Add the chicken thighs and cook for 2–3 minutes to brown them, then stir in the almonds.

**2** When the almonds turn golden, toss in the plums, cover the pan and cook gently for 10–15 minutes.

**3** Stir in the *pekmez* or honey, to give a hint of sweetness, and season the dish with salt and pepper.

**4** Serve the chicken dish hot or at room temperature with wedges of lemon to squeeze over it.

**VARIATION**

For a change, this dish can be made with fresh sour cherries or damsons. Tart green grapes are also occasionally added, but they must be tossed in at the end to prevent them from overcooking.

**Per portion** Energy 316kcal/1325kJ; Protein 33.7g; Carbohydrate 10g, of which sugars 9.2g; Fat 16g, of which saturates 3.6g; Cholesterol 163mg; Calcium 39mg; Fibre 1.8g; Sodium 153mg.

# CHICKEN STEW <u>WITH</u> WALNUTS <u>AND</u> POMEGRANATE JUICE

*ADAPTED FROM THE PERSIAN CLASSIC, FESINJAN, THIS DELICIOUS STEW HAS BECOME A POPULAR HOUSEHOLD DISH IN WESTERN TURKEY. TRADITIONALLY, IT WAS A PHEASANT DISH BUT MODERN VERSIONS ARE MORE OFTEN MADE WITH CHICKEN OR DUCK. GENERALLY, THE STEW, CALLED ACEM YAHNISI, IS SERVED WITH A PLAIN PILAFF AND A LEAFY SALAD.*

SERVES FOUR

INGREDIENTS

   3 pomegranates
   juice of 1 lemon
   30ml/2 tbsp ghee or butter
   2 onions, finely chopped
   1 medium chicken, jointed
   5–10ml/1–2 tsp ground cinnamon
   5ml/1 tsp sugar
   225g/8oz/1⅓ cup walnuts, crushed
   salt and ground black pepper
   a few shredded mint leaves,
     to garnish

**1** Halve the pomegranates. Extract the seeds from one of the halves and set them aside for the garnish. Squeeze the remaining pomegranate halves over a bowl to extract the juice. Add the lemon juice and mix well.

**2** Melt the butter or ghee in a heavy pan or flameproof casserole. Stir in the onions and fry until they begin to colour. Add the chicken joints to the pan and brown them lightly.

**3** Pour over the pomegranate and lemon juice and stir in the cinnamon and sugar. Season with salt and pepper.

**4** Bring the liquid to a gentle boil, then turn down the heat. Cover the pan and simmer for about 35 minutes – top up the liquid with a little water if the mixture becomes dry.

**5** Meanwhile, heat the oven to 200°C/400°F/Gas 6. Transfer to an ovenproof dish or remove the lid from the casserole, and sprinkle the walnuts over the chicken. Place in the oven and roast the walnuts on top of the chicken for about 10 minutes, or until the walnuts become golden.

**6** Transfer the chicken pieces to a serving dish. Stir the walnuts into the remaining juice in the pan and spoon them over and around the chicken. Sprinkle the reserved pomegranate seeds over the top and garnish with the shredded mint.

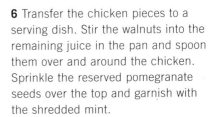

**Per portion** Energy 867kcal/3591kJ; Protein 40.6g; Carbohydrate 17.4g, of which sugars 13.8g; Fat 71.1g, of which saturates 14.6g; Cholesterol 176mg; Calcium 99mg; Fibre 4.6g; Sodium 180mg.

# SHREDDED CHICKEN WITH WALNUTS

*ÇERKEZ TAVUĞU DISH IS CIRCASSIAN (ÇERKEZ) IN ORIGIN, BUT IT WAS ADOPTED BY THE OTTOMAN PALACE CHEFS AND BECAME A CLASSIC THAT HAS SURVIVED TO THIS DAY. AT THE HEIGHT OF THE OTTOMAN EMPIRE, YOUNG CIRCASSIAN WOMEN WERE CAPTURED TO SERVE AS CONCUBINES TO THE SULTANS, WHO APPRECIATED THEIR RENOWNED BEAUTY AND FAIR FEATURES. THE TRUE CIRCASSIAN DISH HAS THREADS OF FRESH CORIANDER RUNNING THROUGH IT, BUT THE ISTANBUL VERSION IS FAMED FOR ITS PALE COLOUR, PERHAPS REMINISCENT OF THE FAIR BEAUTIES. SOMETIMES SERVED AS A MEZE DISH, ÇERKEZ TAVUĞU IS IDEAL FOR LUNCH OR SUPPER, OR FOR A BUFFET SPREAD.*

### SERVES SIX

INGREDIENTS
  1 chicken, trimmed of excess fat
  3 slices of day-old white bread,
    crusts removed
  150ml/¼ pint/⅔ cup milk
  175g/6oz/1½ cup shelled walnuts
  4–6 garlic cloves
  salt and ground black pepper
For the stock
  1 onion, quartered
  1 carrot, chopped
  2 celery sticks, chopped
  4–6 cloves
  4–6 allspice berries
  4–6 black peppercorns
  2 bay leaves
  5ml/1 tsp coriander seeds
  1 small bunch of fresh flat leaf
    parsley, stalks bruised and
    tied together
For the garnish
  30ml/2 tbsp butter
  5ml/1 tsp *kırmızı biber*,
    or paprika
  a few fresh coriander
    (cilantro) leaves

**1** Put the chicken into a deep pan with all of the ingredients for the stock. Pour in enough water to just cover the chicken and bring to the boil. Lower the heat, cover the pan and simmer the chicken for about 1 hour.

**2** Remove the chicken from the pan and leave until cool enough to handle.

**3** Meanwhile, boil the stock with the lid off for 15 minutes until reduced, then strain and season with salt and pepper.

**4** When the chicken has cooled a little, pull off the skin and discard it. Tear the chicken flesh into thin strips using two forks or your fingers and put them into a large bowl.

**5** In a small bowl, soak the bread in the milk for a few minutes until the milk is totally absorbed.

### VARIATIONS

• The *Çerkez* of eastern Anatolia often make this dish with fresh coriander (cilantro) leaves tossed through it, which adds freshness to the dish.
• A similar dish, *çerkez fasulye*, is made with green beans.

**6** Using a mortar and pestle, pound the walnuts with the garlic to form a paste, or blend them in a food processor.

**7** Beat the soaked bread into the walnut paste, then add to the chicken mixture.

**8** Beat in spoonfuls of the warm stock to the bread and walnut mixture to bind the chicken and walnut mixture until it is light and creamy.

**9** Spoon the mixture in to a serving dish, forming a smooth, rounded mound.

**10** To garnish the chicken in the Istanbul fashion, gently melt the butter over a low heat, stir in the *kırmızı biber* or paprika, then pour the mixture in a cross shape over the top of the mound.

**11** Serve the shredded chicken at room temperature, garnished with the fresh coriander leaves.

**Per portion** Energy 222kcal/937kJ; Protein 34.1g; Carbohydrate 7.6g, of which sugars 1.6g; Fat 6.4g, of which saturates 3.3g; Cholesterol 105mg; Calcium 53mg; Fibre 0.2g; Sodium 324mg.

# LEMON CHICKEN THIGHS WRAPPED IN AUBERGINE

*This elegant Ottoman dish is usually made with chicken thighs or veal fillet. Wrapping the meat in strips of fried aubergine may take a little time and effort to prepare, but the result is both impressive and tasty. Serve as a main course with a tomato and cucumber salad, or a salad of parsley, pepper and onion, and a buttery rice pilaff.*

**4** Preheat the oven to 180°C/350°F/ Gas 4. Drain the aubergines and squeeze out the excess water.

**5** Heat enough oil for deep-frying in a wok or other deep-sided pan, and deep-fry the aubergines in batches for 2–3 minutes until golden brown. Remove with a slotted spoon and drain on kitchen paper.

**6** On a board or plate, lay two strips of aubergine over one another in a cross shape, then place a chicken thigh in the middle. Tuck the thigh into a bundle and wrap the aubergine around it.

**7** Place the aubergine parcel, seam side down, in a lightly greased ovenproof dish and repeat the process with the remaining aubergine strips and chicken.

**8** Pour any remaining marinade over the parcels and sprinkle with the almonds. Cover with foil and bake for 40 minutes. Serve hot, with lemon wedges.

## SERVES FOUR

### INGREDIENTS
  juice of 2–3 lemons
  2 garlic cloves, crushed
  4–6 allspice berries, crushed
  8 chicken thighs, skinned and boned
  3–4 aubergines (eggplants)
  sunflower oil, for deep-frying
  30ml/2 tbsp toasted flaked
    (sliced) almonds
  1 lemon, cut into wedges, to serve

**1** In a shallow bowl, mix together the lemon juice, garlic and allspice berries. Toss the chicken in the mixture, rolling the pieces over in the juice to coat them thoroughly, then cover and leave to marinate in a cold place or the refrigerator for about 2 hours.

**2** Using a vegetable peeler or a small, sharp knife, peel the aubergines lengthways in stripes like a zebra.

**3** Slice the aubergines thinly lengthways using a large, sharp knife – you need 16 strips in total – then soak the slices in a bowl of salted cold water for about 30 minutes.

**Per portion** Energy 509kcal/2114kJ; Protein 34.7g; Carbohydrate 2.7g, of which sugars 2.3g; Fat 40g, of which saturates 8.4g; Cholesterol 180mg; Calcium 67mg; Fibre 2.6g; Sodium 108mg.

# ROAST WILD DUCK WITH HONEY, THYME AND ALMONDS

*WILD DUCKS ARE A COMMON SIGHT IN THE LAKES AND MARSHES OF ANATOLIA AND SOME END UP IN THE VILLAGE POT. REARED DUCKS, ON THE OTHER HAND, ARE SOLD ALONGSIDE HENS IN RURAL AND CITY MARKETS. THIS VILLAGE RECIPE, CALLED ÖRDEK FIRINDA, CAN BE MADE WITH WILD OR REARED DUCK. A TOMATO AND CUCUMBER SALAD MAKES A PERFECT ACCOMPANIMENT.*

SERVES TWO

INGREDIENTS

    1 wild duck, well hung, gutted and
       cleaned, with trimmed giblets
    15ml/1 tbsp butter
    1 bunch fresh thyme sprigs
    4 slices day-old bread, crumbled
    45ml/3 tbsp olive oil (plus an extra
       15ml/1 tbsp for roasting)
    2 garlic cloves, crushed
    10ml/2 tsp dried oregano
    45ml/3 tbsp blanched almonds
    45ml/3 tbsp wild, clear honey

**1** Soak a wooden skewer in water for 30 minutes. Preheat the oven to 230°C/450°F/Gas 8. Place the duck in an ovenproof dish, reserving the giblets, and smear the breasts in butter. Place a few sprigs of thyme into the body cavity and crumble the remainder of the leaves over the top of the duck.

**2** Put the crumbled bread into a dish and pour the oil over it, rubbing the oil into the bread.

**3** Toss in the garlic and oregano, and pack the mixture into the cavity on top of the thyme sprigs. Skewer the legs with the wooden skewer to prevent the filling from oozing out.

**4** Sprinkle the giblets and almonds around the duck and drizzle the honey and the reserved oil over the top. Place the duck in the oven and roast for about 25 minutes until the skin is browned.

**5** Serve straight from the oven with the stuffing, and accompany it with a tomato and cucumber salad.

**Per portion** Energy 776kcal/3241kJ; Protein 37g; Carbohydrate 45.9g, of which sugars 19.6g; Fat 50.8g, of which saturates 11.1g; Cholesterol 166mg; Calcium 132mg; Fibre 2.5g; Sodium 492mg.

# CHARGRILLED MARINATED QUAILS

*THIS IS A SIMPLE AND TASTY WAY OF SERVING SMALL BIRDS, SUCH AS QUAILS, POUSSINS OR GROUSE. THE SHARP, TANGY MARINADE TENDERIZES THE MEAT, AS WELL AS ENHANCING ITS FLAVOUR. IN THE TURKISH COUNTRYSIDE THE QUAILS ARE USUALLY TUCKED INTO HALF A LOAF OF BREAD WITH SOME CHOPPED RAW ONIONS, PARSLEY AND YOGURT. SERVED STRAIGHT OFF THE CHARCOAL GRILL WITH WARM FLAT BREAD AND A CRUNCHY SALAD, THEY ARE DELICIOUS FOR LUNCH OR SUPPER.*

SERVES FOUR

INGREDIENTS
  4 quails, cleaned and boned
    (ask your butcher to do this)
  juice of 4 pomegranates
    (*see* page 217)
  juice of 1 lemon
  30ml/2 tbsp olive oil
  5–10ml/1–2 tsp *kırmızı biber*,
    or 5ml/1 tsp chilli powder
  30–45ml/2–3 tbsp thick and creamy
    natural (plain) yogurt
  salt
  1 bunch of fresh flat leaf parsley
  seeds of ½ pomegranate, to garnish

**1** Soak eight wooden skewers in hot water for about 15 minutes, then drain. Thread one skewer through the wings of each bird and a second skewer through the legs to keep them together.

**2** Place the skewered birds in a wide, shallow dish. Beat the pomegranate and lemon juice with the oil and *kırmızı biber* or chilli powder, pour over the quails and rub it into the skin.

**3** Cover with foil and leave to marinate in a cold place or the refrigerator for 2–3 hours, turning the birds over from time to time.

**4** Get the barbecue ready for cooking. Lift the birds out of the marinade and pour what is left of it into a bowl. Beat the yogurt into the leftover marinade and add a little salt.

**5** Brush some of the yogurt mixture over the birds and place them on the prepared barbecue.

**6** Cook for 4–5 minutes on each side, brushing with the yogurt as they cook to form a crust.

**7** Chop some of the parsley and lay the rest on a serving dish.

**8** Place the quails on top of the parsley on the dish and garnish with the pomegranate seeds and the chopped parsley. Serve hot.

**VARIATIONS**
The same dish can be prepared with boned chicken, pigeon, partridge or grouse. Just ask your butcher to do the hard work of removing the bones for you.

**Per portion** Energy 288kcal/1207kJ; Protein 37.4g; Carbohydrate 5.8g, of which sugars 5.8g; Fat 13g, of which saturates 2.7g; Cholesterol 0mg; Calcium 84mg; Fibre 0.5g; Sodium 111mg.

# SPICY RABBIT STEW WITH SHALLOTS AND FIGS

*THERE ARE RECORDS FROM THE SELJUK AND OTTOMAN PERIODS, WHEN HUNTING WAS REGARDED AS RECREATION, OF MANY RECIPES FOR RABBIT, QUAILS, PIGEON, WILD DUCK AND DEER, BUT THE MODERN CULINARY CULTURE SADLY INCLUDES VERY LITTLE GAME. IN CENTRAL ANATOLIA, HOWEVER, YOU COME ACROSS VILLAGERS WHO STILL ENJOY HUNTING WILD RABBIT, DUCK AND QUAILS. SERVE THIS DELICIOUS STEW, TAVŞAN YAHNISI, WITH SAUTÉED POTATOES, OR A RICE OR BULGUR WHEAT PILAFF.*

### SERVES TWO TO THREE

INGREDIENTS
1 good-sized rabbit, gutted, cleaned, and jointed into 4 or 6 portions
30ml/2 tbsp ghee, or 30ml/2 tbsp olive oil with a knob (pat) butter
12 shallots, peeled and left whole
10 garlic cloves, peeled, left whole and lightly smashed
5–10ml/1–2 tsp *kırmızı biber*, or paprika
10ml/2 tsp coriander seeds
8-10 allspice berries, crushed
6 cloves, crushed
1 cinnamon stick
6–8 dried figs, halved
30ml/2 tbsp sultanas (golden raisins)
15ml/1 tbsp grape *pekmez* (molasses), or clear honey
150ml/¼ pint/⅔ cup water
salt and ground black pepper
1 bunch fresh parsley, roughly chopped, to garnish
For the marinade
30ml/2 tbsp olive oil
30ml/2 tbsp red wine vinegar
200ml/7fl oz/scant 1 cup red wine
2-3 bay leaves, crumpled

**1** Mix the marinade ingredients together. Place the rabbit joints in a shallow dish and pour the marinade over them.

**2** Cover and leave in the refrigerator for 6–8 hours, turning the joints in the marinade from time to time.

**3** Transfer the rabbit joints to a plate and reserve the marinade. Melt the ghee, or olive oil and butter, in a wide, heavy pan or flameproof earthenware dish, and brown the joints all over.

**4** Return the cooked rabbit joints to the plate and add the shallots, garlic and spices to the pan. Cook gently for 2–3 minutes, or until the shallots turn golden brown.

**5** Add the figs and sultanas and stir in the *pekmez* or clear honey.

**6** Return the rabbit joints to the pan, pour in the reserved marinade and the water, and bring the liquid to the boil. Reduce the heat, cover and cook for about 1 hour, or until the rabbit is tender.

**7** Transfer the joints to a serving dish. Bubble up the syrupy, spicy sauce and season it with salt and pepper.

**8** Spoon the sauce and shallots over and around the rabbit, garnish with some chopped parsley and serve with sautéed potatoes, or a plain rice or bulgur wheat pilaff.

**COOK'S TIP**
Crumple the bay leaves before adding them to the pan to release their flavour.

**Per portion** Energy 456kcal/1906kJ; Protein 39.4g; Carbohydrate 28g, of which sugars 23.9g; Fat 21.5g, of which saturates 5g; Cholesterol 139mg; Calcium 199mg; Fibre 4.2g; Sodium 109mg.

# SWEET SNACKS AND JAMS

*"Eat sweet, talk sweet" say the Turks, who are proud of their milk puddings, such as Classic Almond Milk Pudding, Baked Rice Pudding and Ottoman Milk Pudding, and sweet pastries, such as Baklava, Ladies' Navels and Cheese-filled Pastry in Lemon Syrup. Desserts such as these play an important role in Turkish culture, particularly at holy festivals and family celebrations, when they are greatly enjoyed as sweet snacks at any time of the day.*

# ROSE PETAL SORBET

*THE ANCIENT EGYPTIANS, ROMANS, PERSIANS AND SEAFARING ARABS ALL USED THE ROSE FOR SCENTING AND CULINARY PURPOSES. BY THE TIME IT REACHED THE OTTOMAN PALACE KITCHENS, THE PETALS HAD ALREADY BEEN USED TO MAKE ROSE WATER AND WINE. ENTRANCED BY ITS PERFUME, THE TOPKAPI PALACE CHEFS SPLASHED ROSE WATER INTO THEIR SYRUPY PASTRIES AND MILK PUDDINGS, AND INFUSED THE PRETTY PETALS IN SYRUP TO MAKE FRAGRANT JAMS AND SORBETS. THIS SORBET LOOKS LOVELY SERVED IN FROSTED GLASSES OR FINE GLASS BOWLS, DECORATED WITH FRESH OR CRYSTALLIZED ROSE PETALS.*

**2** Strain off the water, reserving the petals. Pour the water into the pan, add the sugar and bring to the boil, stirring, until the sugar has dissolved.

**3** Boil for 1–2 minutes, then lower the heat and simmer for 5–10 minutes, until the syrup thickens a little.

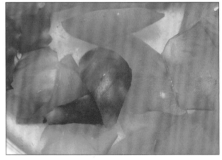

**4** Stir in the lemon juice, rose water and reserved petals, then turn off the heat and leave to cool in the pan.

**5** Once it is cool, pour the mixture into a freezer container and place in the freezer until beginning to set.

**6** Take the sorbet out of the freezer at 2–3 hour intervals and whisk to disperse the ice crystals. Alternatively, freeze in an electric sorbetière.

**7** Before serving, take the sorbet out of the freezer for 5–10 minutes, so that it softens enough to scoop.

## SERVES FOUR

### INGREDIENTS
fresh petals of 2 gloriously scented
red or pink roses, free from pesticides
225g/8oz/generous 1 cup caster
(superfine) sugar
juice of 1 lemon
15ml/1 tbsp rose water

**COOK'S TIP**
Clear, fragrant rose water is much prized in Turkish households. It is splashed on the face and hands to freshen up before or after a meal, and it is used to scent many sweet dishes.

**1** Wash the rose petals and cut off the white bases. Place in a pan with 600ml/1 pint/2½ cups water and bring to the boil. Turn off the heat, cover the pan and leave to steep for 10 minutes.

**Per portion** Energy 222kcal/946kJ; Protein 0.3g; Carbohydrate 58.8g, of which sugars 58.8g; Fat 0g, of which saturates 0g; Cholesterol 0mg; Calcium 30mg; Fibre 0g; Sodium 4mg.

# ISTANBUL CHEWY ICE CREAM

*THERE ARE MANY DELICIOUS FLAVOURS OF ICE CREAM, DONDURMA, IN TURKEY, BUT ONE THAT STANDS OUT ABOVE ALL OTHERS IS THE CLASSIC CHEWY ICE CREAM. A FEATURE OF ISTANBUL STREET LIFE AND ICE-CREAM PARLOURS, IT IS SERVED FROM VATS USING A WOODEN PADDLE. THE PINE-SCENTED TREE GUM OR MASTIC (MASTIKA) PROVIDES THE CHEWY CONSISTENCY, WHILE THE SILKY, GROUND ORCHID ROOT (SALEP) CONTRIBUTES TO ITS PEARLY WHITE COLOUR, AS WELL AS ACTING AS A THICKENING AGENT. MASTIKA AND SALEP ARE AVAILABLE IN MIDDLE EASTERN STORES.*

SERVES FOUR

INGREDIENTS
900ml/1½ pints/3¾ cups full-fat
(whole) milk
300ml/½ pint/1¼ cups double
(heavy) cream
225g/8oz/generous 1 cup sugar
45ml/3 tbsp ground *salep*
1–2 pieces of *mastika* (*see* Cook's
Tip), crushed with a little sugar

**1** Put the milk, cream and sugar into a heavy pan and bring to the boil, stirring all the time, until the sugar has dissolved. Lower the heat and simmer for 10 minutes.

**2** Put the *salep* into a bowl. Moisten it with a little cold milk, add a spoonful of the hot, sweetened milk, then transfer it to the pan, stirring all the time.

**COOK'S TIP**
Mastika is the aromatic gum from the *Pistacia lentiscus* tree that grows wild in the Mediterranean region. When sold in the markets, *mastika* is in clear crystal form, often containing a few ants that managed to get caught in the sticky gum. The aroma will indicate the strength of the resinous taste, which the crystals impart to the dish along with the chewy texture. To use the crystals, they must first be pulverized with a little sugar, using a mortar and pestle.

**3** Beat the mixture gently and stir in the *mastika*, then continue simmering for 10–15 minutes.

**4** Pour the liquid into a freezer container, cover with a dry dish towel and leave to cool.

**5** Remove the dish towel, cover the container with foil and place it in the freezer. Leave to set, beating it at intervals to disperse the ice crystals. Alternatively, churn the cooled liquid in an ice-cream maker.

**6** Before serving, allow the ice cream to sit out of the freezer for 5–10 minutes so that it becomes soft enough to scoop.

**Per portion** Energy 742Kcal/3093kJ; Protein 8.9g; Carbohydrate 70.2g, of which sugars 70.2g; Fat 49.1g, of which saturates 30.7g; Cholesterol 134mg; Calcium 332mg; Fibre 0g; Sodium 117mg.

# POACHED APRICOTS IN SCENTED SYRUP WITH BUFFALO CREAM

*A LEGACY OF THE OTTOMAN EMPIRE, THIS DISH IS SIMPLE YET SOPHISTICATED. TENDER APRICOTS ARE POACHED IN A SYRUP SCENTED WITH ORANGE BLOSSOM WATER, THEN FILLED WITH THE TURKISH BUFFALO CREAM CALLED KAYMAK. SERVED CHILLED AS A TREAT OR DESSERT, IT IS SWEET AND REFRESHING.*

SERVES FOUR

INGREDIENTS

    250g/9oz/generous 1 cup dried
      apricots, soaked in cold water for
      at least 6 hours or overnight
    200g/7oz/1 cup sugar
    juice of 1 lemon
    30ml/2 tbsp orange blossom water
    225g/8oz *kaymak* (*see* Cook's Tip)

**1** Strain the soaked apricots over a large bowl and pour the soaking water into a measuring jug (cup) up to the 250ml/8fl oz/1 cup mark (if there is not enough soaking water, make up the amount with fresh water).

**2** Pour the measured liquid into a heavy pan, add the sugar and bring to the boil, stirring all the time.

**3** When the sugar has dissolved, boil the syrup vigorously for 2–3 minutes. Lower the heat, stir in the lemon juice and orange blossom water, then slip in the apricots and poach gently for 15–20 minutes. Leave to cool.

**4** Lift an apricot out of the syrup. Pull it open with your fingers, or slit it with a small, sharp knife, and fill the opening with the *kaymak*. Place the filled apricot, cream side up, in a shallow serving dish and repeat the process with the remaining apricots and cream.

**5** Carefully spoon the syrup around the filled apricots, so the flesh of the fruit is kept moist but the cream is not submerged. Place the dish in the refrigerator to chill before serving.

**COOK'S TIP**
Made from the milk of water buffalos, *kaymak* is very thick cream, almost like clotted cream. If you cannot find it, you can fill the apricots with crème fraîche or clotted cream instead.

Per portion Energy 333kcal/1416kJ; Protein 4.6g; Carbohydrate 77.6g, of which sugars 77.6g; Fat 2.6g, of which saturates 1.4g; Cholesterol 8mg; Calcium 139mg; Fibre 4g; Sodium 36mg.

# PUMPKIN POACHED IN CLOVE-INFUSED LEMON SYRUP

*IN WINTER THE MARKETS AND STREETS ARE ALIVE WITH BUSY PUMPKIN STALLS, SELLING PUMPKIN FLESH THAT HAS BEEN LOVINGLY PREPARED ESPECIALLY FOR THIS EXQUISITE DISH. SERVE THE DESSERT ON ITS OWN OR WITH CHILLED CLOTTED CREAM OR CRÈME FRAÎCHE.*

SERVES FOUR TO SIX

INGREDIENTS
  450g/1lb sugar
  juice of 1 lemon
  6 cloves
  1kg/2¼lb pumpkin flesh, peeled,
    deseeded and cut into cubes
    or rectangular blocks

**1** Put the sugar into a deep, wide, heavy pan and pour in 250ml/8fl oz/ 1 cup water. Bring to the boil, stirring all the time, until the sugar has dissolved, then boil gently for 2–3 minutes.

**2** Lower the heat and stir in the lemon juice and cloves, then add the pumpkin and bring back to the boil. Lower the heat and put the lid on the pan.

**3** Poach the pumpkin gently in the syrup, turning the pieces over from time to time, until they are tender and a rich, gleaming orange colour. This may take 1½–2 hours, depending on the size of the pumpkin pieces.

**4** Leave the pumpkin to cool in the pan, then lift the pieces out of the syrup and place them in a serving dish. Spoon most, or all, of the syrup over the pumpkin pieces and serve at room temperature or chilled.

**Per portion** Energy 317kcal/1353kJ; Protein 1.6g; Carbohydrate 82.1g, of which sugars 81.2g; Fat 0.3g, of which saturates 0.2g; Cholesterol 0mg; Calcium 88mg; Fibre 1.7g; Sodium 5mg.

# DRIED FRUIT COMPOTE WITH ROSE WATER

*SERVED AS A WINTER DESSERT, OR AT CEREMONIAL FEASTS, HOŞAF IS A CLASSIC SWEET DISH, WHICH IS FOUND THROUGHOUT THE MIDDLE EAST. WHEN THE OTTOMANS DINED IN THE TOPKAPI PALACE, HOŞAF WAS OFTEN SPOONED OVER PLAIN RICE AS A FINAL TOUCH TO A RATHER SPLENDID MEAL. THE SYRUP CAN BE FLAVOURED WITH ROSE OR ORANGE FLOWER WATER, OR A COMBINATION OF BOTH, BUT THE ANCIENT TASTE OF SWEET-SCENTED ROSES IS THE MOST TRADITIONAL. DOUBLE CREAM OR ICE CREAM, OR A CREAMY RICE PUDDING, ALL MAKE SUPERB ACCOMPANIMENTS.*

SERVES SIX TO EIGHT

INGREDIENTS
  225g/8oz/1 cup ready-to-eat
    dried apricots
  175g/6oz/¾ cup ready-to-eat prunes
  115g/4oz/⅔ cup sultanas
    (golden raisins)
  115g/4oz/⅔ cup blanched almonds
  30ml/2 tbsp pine nuts
  45–60ml/3–4 tbsp sugar
  30–45ml/2–3 tbsp rose water
  15ml/1 tbsp orange flower water

**COOK'S TIP**
You can make this dessert as sweet as you like using sugar or scented, runny honey.

**1** Put the dried fruit and nuts into a large bowl and cover completely with water. Add the sugar according to taste, the rose water and orange flower water, and gently stir until the sugar has completely dissolved.

**2** Cover the bowl and place it in the refrigerator. Leave the fruit and nuts to soak for 48 hours, during which time the liquid will turn syrupy and golden. Serve chilled, on its own, or with cream or ice cream, or with rice pudding.

**Per portion** Energy 238kcal/1001kJ; Protein 5.4g; Carbohydrate 34.6g, of which sugars 34.2g; Fat 9.6g, of which saturates 0.7g; Cholesterol 0mg; Calcium 75mg; Fibre 4.4g; Sodium 12mg.

# BAKED FRESH FIGS

*BAKING FRUIT WITH HONEY IS AN ANCIENT COOKING METHOD, DEVISED PERHAPS WHEN LOCAL FRUIT HARVESTS WERE SO ABUNDANT THERE WAS TOO MUCH TO EAT FRESH. THIS IS A DISH MOST OFTEN MADE WITH APRICOTS OR FIGS IN RURAL HOMES, WHERE IT IS SOMETIMES SERVED AS A SWEET SNACK FOR EVERYONE TO SHARE, WITH BREAD TO MOP UP THE YOGURT AND HONEY. SPICES AND HERBS, SUCH AS ANISEED, CINNAMON, ROSEMARY AND LAVENDER, ARE OFTEN USED FOR FLAVOURING. RIPE FIGS, WITH A SWEET, PINK INTERIOR, AND AN AROMATIC HONEY ARE A PARTICULARLY DELECTABLE PAIRING.*

### SERVES FOUR

### INGREDIENTS

12 ripe figs
30ml/2 tbsp vanilla sugar
  (*see* Cook's Tip)
3–4 cinnamon sticks
45–60ml/3–4 tbsp clear honey
225g/8oz/1 cup chilled thick and
  creamy natural (plain) yogurt,
  clotted cream or *kaymak*

**1** Preheat the oven to 200°C/400°F/ Gas 6. Wash the figs and pat them dry. Using a sharp knife, cut a deep cross from the top of each fig to the bottom, keeping the skin at the bottom intact. Fan each fig out, so it looks like a flower, then place them upright in a baking dish, preferably an earthenware one.

**2** Sprinkle the vanilla sugar over each fig flower, tuck in the cinnamon sticks and drizzle with honey.

**3** Bake in the oven for 15–20 minutes, until the sugar is slightly caramelized but the honey and figs are still moist.

**4** Spoon a dollop of yogurt or cream into the middle of each fig, or serve them in bowls and let everyone help themselves to the yogurt or cream.

### COOK'S TIP

To make the vanilla sugar, split a vanilla pod (bean) lengthways in half, scrape out the seeds and mix them with 30ml/2 tbsp caster (superfine) sugar.

**Per portion** Energy 198kcal/845kJ; Protein 2.3g; Carbohydrate 48.2g, of which sugars 48.2g; Fat 1g, of which saturates 0g; Cholesterol 0mg; Calcium 155mg; Fibre 4.5g; Sodium 39mg.

# SOUR CHERRY SUMMER PUDDING

*KNOWN AS* VIŞNE TIRIDI *OR* VIŞNELI EKMEK TATLISI, *THIS IS A POPULAR SUMMER DESSERT OF BREAD SOAKED IN CHERRY COMPOTE. VIBRANT PURPLE IN COLOUR, THE PUDDING IS USUALLY SERVED WITH KAYMAK — CLOTTED CREAM — AND CAN BE MADE IN ONE LARGE DISH OR INDIVIDUAL ONES. IT IS A GREAT WAY OF USING UP DAY-OLD BREAD AND SLIGHTLY OVER-RIPE CHERRIES.*

SERVES FOUR TO SIX

### INGREDIENTS
½ loaf day-old Turkish white bread,
  or a small French baguette
250g/9oz/1½ cups fresh sour cherries
250g/9oz/1¼ cups sugar
about 550ml/18fl oz/2½ cups water
4–6 fresh sour cherries (preferably
  with stalk and leaf intact) and a few
  fresh mint leaves, to garnish
clotted cream, to serve

### COOK'S TIP
This dessert can also be made using a fresh loaf. Just toast the slices lightly before arranging them in the dish.

**1** Remove the crusts of the loaf or baguette and cut the bread into thin slices, approximately 2cm/¾in thick. Arrange the bread slices in a double layer in a shallow dish in a manner that will be easy to serve.

**2** Wash the cherries under cold running water, then drain in a colander and remove the pits.

**3** Place the pitted cherries in a deep, heavy pan with the sugar and the water, and bring to the boil, stirring from time to time.

**4** Reduce the heat and simmer the mixture for 5–6 minutes, until the cherry skins begin to crack.

**5** Pour the hot liquid and cherries over the bread, making sure it is evenly distributed, so that every piece of bread is soaked in the juice.

**6** Leave the pudding to cool and then place it in the refrigerator and leave for about 6 hours.

**7** Lift individual portions of the bread pudding out of the dish and place them on small plates. Decorate the portions with fresh sour cherries and mint leaves, and serve immediately, with clotted cream.

**Per portion** Energy 360kcal/1532kJ; Protein 6.6g; Carbohydrate 85.7g, of which sugars 50.2g; Fat 1.3g, of which saturates 0.2g; Cholesterol 0mg; Calcium 108mg; Fibre 2g; Sodium 414mg.

# CLASSIC ALMOND MILK PUDDING

*THE ORIGINS OF THIS DISH, KEŞKUL, ARE THOUGHT TO BE PERSIAN, AS BEGGARS ARE KNOWN TO HAVE GONE FROM HOUSE TO HOUSE SEEKING FOOD WITH AN OVAL BOWL, CALLED A KESHKUL. IN TURKEY, IT IS REGARDED AS ONE OF CLASSIC OTTOMAN MILK PUDDINGS AND IS ALWAYS SERVED IN INDIVIDUAL BOWLS. TRADITIONALLY, IT IS DECORATED WITH GRATED PISTACHIO NUTS, OR DESICCATED COCONUT.*

SERVES FOUR

INGREDIENTS

115g/4oz/1 cup blanched almonds
600ml/1 pint/2½ cups milk
25g/1oz rice flour
115g/4oz/generous ½ cup sugar
15–30ml/1–2 tbsp finely grated
    pistachio nuts

**1** Using a mortar and pestle, food processor or nut mill, pound or grind the almonds to a paste. Blend the paste with a little of the milk until smooth and set aside.

**2** In a small bowl, slake the rice flour with a little of the milk to form a smooth paste, the consistency of thick cream. Set the bowl aside.

**3** Pour the rest of the milk into a heavy pan. Add the sugar and bring the milk to the boil, stirring constantly. Stir 30ml/ 2 tbsp of the hot milk into the slaked rice flour and then add to the pan. Make sure you keep stirring to prevent the rice flour from cooking in clumps. Cook until the mixture coats the back of the wooden spoon.

**4** Stir in the almond paste and reduce the heat. Simmer the mixture gently for about 25 minutes, stirring from time to time, until the mixture is thick. Pour into individual bowls and leave to cool.

**5** Sprinkle the grated pistachio nuts over each bowl of *keşkul* – this is often done in a thin line across the middle of the pudding – and place the bowls in the refrigerator. Serve chilled.

**COOK'S TIP**
Another classic milk pudding is *muhallebi*, which is made in a similar way, but without the nuts, and which is flavoured with mastic and dusted with icing (confectioner's) sugar. Alternatively, it can be set in a mould, cut into blocks and served with rose water.

**Per portion** Energy 404kcal/1693kJ; Protein 12.4g; Carbohydrate 44.4g, of which sugars 38.5g; Fat 20.7g, of which saturates 3.2g; Cholesterol 9mg; Calcium 270mg; Fibre 2.5g; Sodium 91mg.

# NOAH'S DESSERT

*THIS DESSERT OF GRAINS, PULSES AND DRIED FRUIT IS REFERRED TO AS AŞURE – NOAH'S DESSERT – BECAUSE, ACCORDING TO LEGEND, HE MADE IT ON THE ARK BY COMBINING WHATEVER STORES WERE LEFT WHEN THE FLOOD SUBSIDED. IT IS ALSO THE TRADITIONAL DESSERT TO SERVE ON THE TENTH DAY OF MUHARAM, THE FIRST DAY OF THE MUSLIM CALENDAR, TO MARK THE MARTYRDOM OF THE PROPHET'S GRANDSON. IT REQUIRES A FAIR AMOUNT OF ADVANCE PREPARATION AND IS ALWAYS MADE IN LARGE QUANTITIES TO BE SHARED WITH FRIENDS AND NEIGHBOURS.*

## SERVES TEN TO TWELVE

### INGREDIENTS

50g/2oz haricot (navy) beans, soaked for at least 6 hours, or overnight, and drained

50g/2oz skinned broad (fava) beans, soaked for at least 6 hours, or overnight, and drained

50g/2oz chickpeas, soaked for at least 6 hours, or overnight, and drained

115g/4oz pot barley, with husks removed, and soaked for 24 hours in plenty of water

50g/2oz/generous ⅓ cup short grain rice, washed and drained

115g/4oz/½ cup ready-to-eat dried apricots

50g/2oz/⅓ cup sultanas (golden raisins)

50g/2oz/scant ½ cup raisins

50g/2oz/¼ cup currants

225g/8oz/generous 1 cup sugar

30ml/2 tbsp cornflour (cornstarch), or rice flour

150ml/¼ pint/⅔ cup rose water

To decorate

4–5 dried figs, sliced

4–5 ready-to-eat dried apricots, sliced

15ml/1 tbsp sultanas (golden raisins), soaked in warm water for 10 minutes, and drained

15ml/1 tbsp pine nuts

seeds of ½ pomegranate

### COOK'S TIP

Another traditional grain pudding that is thickened with cornflour (cornstarch) or arrowroot, is the rose-scented, saffron-coloured *zerde*. Persian in origin, the name derives from the Persian word *"zerd"*, meaning "yellow". This delectable dessert is prepared for weddings.

**1** Cook the beans in separate pans of fresh water until just tender. The haricot beans will required about 50 minutes; the broad beans and chickpeas about 1 hour.

**2** Transfer the barley and its soaking water to a large, deep pan and bring to the boil. Reduce the heat and simmer for about 45 minutes, or until the barley is tender, topping up the water during the cooking time if necessary.

**3** Add the cooked beans and chickpeas, and the short grain rice, and bring the liquid to the boil again. Reduce the heat and simmer for about 15 minutes.

**4** Meanwhile, place all the dried fruit in a bowl and cover with boiling water. Leave to soak for 10 minutes, then drain. Add the fruit to the pan with the beans and stir in the sugar. Continue to simmer, stirring from time to time, until the mixture thickens.

**5** Mix the cornflour or rice flour with a little water to form a creamy paste. Add 30ml/2 tbsp of the hot liquid from the pan to the paste and add it to the pan, stirring constantly. Add the rose water and continue to simmer the mixture for another 15 minutes, stirring from time to time, until the mixture is very thick.

**6** Transfer the mixture to a large serving bowl. Shake the bowl to make sure the surface is flat and leave the pudding to cool. Arrange the sliced dried figs and apricots, and the sultanas, over the top, and sprinkle the pine nuts and pomegranate seeds over the surface. Serve chilled or at room temperature.

**Per portion** Energy 289kcal/1229kJ; Protein 5.8g; Carbohydrate 65.4g, of which sugars 45.9g; Fat 2.2g, of which saturates 0.1g; Cholesterol 0mg; Calcium 98mg; Fibre 4.2g; Sodium 24mg.

# FESTIVE SEMOLINA *HELVA* WITH PINE NUTS

*HELVA SIGNIFIES GOOD FORTUNE AND IS MADE FOR EVENTS SUCH AS MOVING HOUSE OR STARTING A NEW JOB, BUT IT IS ALSO TRADITIONAL FOR A BEREAVED FAMILY TO OFFER IT TO FRIENDS WHEN SOMEONE DIES. THERE ARE MANY DIFFERENT TYPES OF HELVA, INCLUDING TAHIN HELVAS, WHICH TASTES PARTICULARLY GOOD.*

SERVES SIX TO EIGHT

INGREDIENTS
    225g/8oz/1 cup butter
    450g/1lb/scant 2¾ cups semolina
    45ml/3 tbsp pine nuts
    900ml/1½ pints/3¾ cups milk
    225g/8oz/generous 1 cup sugar
    5–10ml/1–2 tsp ground cinnamon

**COOK'S TIP**
*Helva* is made from simple ingredients, such as flour, butter, sugar and nuts, but it requires skill to get it right and is regarded by some as a culinary masterpiece.

**1** Melt the butter in a heavy pan, stir in the semolina and pine nuts and cook over a medium heat, stirring all the time, until lightly browned.

**2** Lower the heat and pour the milk into the pan. Mix well, cover the pan with a dish towel and press the lid down tightly to form a seal.

**3** Pull the flaps of the dish towel up and over the lid and simmer gently for 10–12 minutes, until the milk has been absorbed.

**4** Add the sugar and stir until it has dissolved completely. Cover the pan with the dish towel and lid again, remove from the heat and leave to stand for 1 hour.

**5** To serve, mix well with a wooden spoon and spoon into bowls, then dust with cinnamon.

Per portion Energy 568kcal/2388kJ; Protein 10.2g; Carbohydrate 78.3g, of which sugars 34.7g; Fat 26g, of which saturates 15.9g; Cholesterol 67mg; Calcium 165mg; Fibre 1.2g; Sodium 227mg.

# BAKED RICE PUDDING

*FROM THE OTTOMAN PALACE KITCHENS TO YOUR TABLE AT HOME, SÜTLAÇ IS THE BEST-EVER BAKED RICE PUDDING. SOME TRADITIONAL "PUDDING SHOPS" BURN THE TOP OF THE PUDDING TO GIVE IT A CHARRED-LOOKING SKIN, WHILE OTHERS OPT FOR A SOFTER-LOOKING, PALER PUDDING.*

SERVES FOUR TO SIX

INGREDIENTS

100g/3¾ oz/½ cup short grain
   pudding rice, rinsed thoroughly
   under running water and drained
2 litres/3½ pints/8 cups full-fat
   (whole) milk
90g/3½ oz/½ cup sugar
5–10ml/1–2 tsp vanilla extract,
   or the seeds scraped from a juicy
   vanilla pod (bean)
30ml/2 tbsp rice flour

**1** Place the pudding rice in a deep, heavy pan, pour in enough water to just cover the rice and bring to the boil.

**2** Lower the heat and simmer the mixture for 5–6 minutes, until the water has been absorbed.

**3** Pour in the milk and bring to the boil, stirring, then lower the heat and simmer until the liquid begins to thicken.

**4** Add the sugar, stirring all the time until the sugar has dissolved, then stir in the vanilla and simmer for a further 15–20 minutes.

**5** Meanwhile, preheat the oven to 200°C/400°F/Gas 6.

**COOK'S TIP**
The concept of the "pudding shop" is unique to Turkey and is devoted to the Palace milk puddings, such as *sütlaç*, *keşkül* (almond milk pudding) and *tavukgöğsü* (chicken breast pudding).

**6** In a bowl, moisten the rice flour with a little water to make a smooth paste. Stir in a spoonful of the hot liquid.

**7** Tip the rice flour mixture into the pan of rice, stirring all the time to prevent lumps forming.

**8** Once the liquid has thickened a little, transfer the mixture to a large ovenproof dish and bake in the oven for about 25 minutes, until the pudding is lightly browned on top.

**9** Remove the pudding from the oven and leave to cool, allowing a skin to form on top, then chill well in the refrigerator, preferably overnight.

**Per portion** Energy 364kcal/1520kJ; Protein 12.6g; Carbohydrate 49.7g, of which sugars 32.4g; Fat 13.1g, of which saturates 8.4g; Cholesterol 47mg; Calcium 407mg; Fibre 0.1g; Sodium 145mg.

# OTTOMAN MILK PUDDING

*FOR THE "EAT SWEET, TALK SWEET" TURKS, THERE IS ONE PUDDING ABOVE ALL OTHERS THAT THEY WILL INSIST YOU TRY. A CLASSIC OTTOMAN DISH THAT MAY EVEN HAVE HAD ITS ORIGINS IN THE LAVISH FEASTING OF THE ROMANS WHEN ANATOLIA WAS PART OF ITS EASTERN EMPIRE, THIS DESSERT EMERGED FROM THE TOPKAPI KITCHENS AS TAVUK GÖĞSÜ. SURPRISINGLY DELICIOUS, THIS MILK PUDDING IS MADE WITH CHICKEN BREAST FILLETS. OVER TIME IT HAS DEVELOPED INTO THIS DESSERT, KAZANDIBI, WHICH IS REALLY THE SAME PUDDING WITH A BURNT TOP THAT IS ROLLED INTO LOGS.*

SERVES SIX

INGREDIENTS

    1 skinless, boneless
    chicken breast
    75ml/5 tbsp rice flour
    900ml/1½ pints/3¾ cups milk
    300ml/½ pint/1¼ cups double
    (heavy) cream
    a pinch of salt
    175g/6oz/scant 1 cup sugar
    ground cinnamon, for dusting

**1** Place the chicken breast fillet in a pan with enough water to just cover it. Bring the water to the boil, lower the heat and simmer for 6–7 minutes, until the breast is tender.

**2** Drain the chicken and tear the meat into very fine threads.

**3** In a small bowl or jug (pitcher), moisten the rice flour with a little of the milk and mix to form a smooth paste that has the consistency of double cream.

**4** Pour the rest of the milk and the cream into a heavy pan, add the salt and sugar and bring the mixture to the boil, stirring all the time, until the sugar has dissolved completely.

**5** Add a few spoonfuls of the hot milk mixture to the moistened rice flour, then transfer it all to the pan and stir vigorously with a wooden spoon.

**6** Lower the heat and stir constantly until it begins to thicken. If you do not stir constantly, the mixture will stick on the bottom of the pan and burn.

**7** Gently beat in the shredded, cooked chicken and continue to simmer for about 5 minutes, until the mixture is very thick.

**8** Lightly grease a heavy frying pan and place it over the heat. When the pan is hot, transfer the pudding mixture to it and keep it over the heat for 5 minutes to brown, or burn, the bottom – check by lifting up an edge to peep beneath.

**9** Move the pan around to make sure the bottom is evenly burned, then turn off the heat and leave the pudding to cool in the pan.

**10** Using a sharp-pointed knife, cut the pudding into rectangles. Lift each rectangle out of the pan with a palette knife or metal spatula and place on a flat surface.

**11** Roll each rectangle over so that it resembles a log, and place seam side down in a serving dish.

**12** Serve chilled or at room temperature as a sweet snack or dessert, dusted with a little cinnamon.

**Per portion** Energy 504kcal/2107kJ; Protein 12.9g; Carbohydrate 48.4g, of which sugars 38.4g; Fat 29.8g, of which saturates 18.4g; Cholesterol 95mg; Calcium 224mg; Fibre 0.3g; Sodium 93mg.

# CHEESE-FILLED PASTRY IN LEMON SYRUP

*THIS DELECTABLE SWEET PASTRY, KÜNEFE, IS MADE WITH THE THIN STRANDS OF PASTRY THAT MANY VISITORS TO TURKEY REFER TO AS "SHREDDED WHEAT". DIFFICULT TO MAKE AT HOME, AS THE BATTER REQUIRES TOSSING THROUGH A STRAINER ON TO A HOT METAL SHEET OVER AN OPEN FIRE, THE PASTRY IS AVAILABLE READY PREPARED IN MOST MIDDLE EASTERN AND TURKISH FOOD STORES — LOOK FOR PACKS OF PALE STRANDS THAT LOOK LIKE VERMICELLI AND ARE CALLED KADAYIF. SOMETIMES THIS SWEET PASTRY IS SIMPLY CALLED KADAYIF BECAUSE OF THE TYPE OF PASTRY USED.*

SERVES SIX

INGREDIENTS
　225g/8oz ready-prepared *kadayif*
　　pastry, thawed if frozen, shredded
　115g/4oz clarified butter,
　　or ghee, melted
　350g/12oz *dil peyniri*,
　　or mozzarella, sliced
　15–30ml/1–2 tbsp pistachio nuts,
　　coarsely chopped
For the syrup
　225g/8oz/generous 1 cup sugar
　120ml/4fl oz/½ cup water
　juice of 1 lemon

**1** Preheat oven to 180°C/350°F/Gas 4. To make the syrup, put the sugar and water into a pan and bring it to the boil, stirring with a wooden spoon until the sugar has dissolved.

**2** Add the lemon juice, reduce the heat, and simmer for 15 minutes, until it coats the back of the wooden spoon.

**3** Turn off the heat and leave the syrup to cool. Chill it in the refrigerator until needed, if you like.

**4** Put the shredded pastry into a bowl and separate the strands.

**5** Pour the clarified butter or melted ghee over them and, using your fingers, rub it all over the strands so that they are completely coated in it.

**6** Spread half the pastry in the base of a baking tin (pan) (the Turks use a round tin about 27cm/10½in in diameter), and press it down with your fingers.

**7** Lay the slices of cheese over the top of the pastry and cover with the remainder of the pastry, pressing it down firmly and tucking it down the sides of the baking tin.

**8** Place the pastry in the oven for about 45 minutes, or until it is golden brown.

**9** Remove from the oven and leave to cool slightly for 10 minutes.

**10** Loosen the edges of the pastry with a sharp knife and pour the cold syrup over it. Sprinkle the pistachio nuts over the top.

**11** Divide the pastry into squares or segments, depending on the shape of your baking tin, and serve while it is still warm.

**COOK'S TIPS**
• The same pastry is used to make *kiz memesi kadayif* – "young girls' breasts" – a great favourite of the Ottoman Palace kitchens. Traditionally, the pastry chefs made these filled shredded pastries in special, individual, non-stick pans cooked on the stove, but the homemade version is baked in the oven.
• The cheese most commonly used for the filling is the elastic *dil peyniri*, which peels off in threads, but the blocks of hard mozzarella used for pizzas are very similar in texture and taste.

Per portion Energy 595kcal/2486kJ; Protein 13.7g; Carbohydrate 53.4g, of which sugars 39.9g; Fat 38.2g, of which saturates 18.2g; Cholesterol 75mg; Calcium 259mg; Fibre 0.2g; Sodium 478mg.

# YOGURT CAKE IN ORANGE SYRUP

*THERE ARE MANY VERSIONS OF THIS YOGURT CAKE OR DESSERT, CALLED YOĞURT TATLISI. SOME INCLUDE COCONUT, SULTANAS OR GROUND WALNUTS, SERVED AS A CAKE WITH A GLASS OF TEA, WHEREAS OTHER VERSIONS ARE SOAKED IN SYRUP AND ENJOYED AS A SWEET SNACK OR DESSERT.*

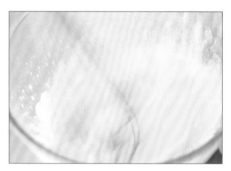

**2** In a bowl, beat the eggs with the sugar until light and fluffy. Beat in the flour, then the yogurt, lemon rind and lemon juice.

**3** Transfer the mixture to the prepared tin or dish and pop it in the oven for about 45 minutes. The cake should rise and turn golden brown on top.

**4** Meanwhile, prepare the syrup. Heat the sugar and water in a heavy pan, stirring constantly, until the sugar has dissolved. Stir in the orange juice and orange rind and bring the liquid to the boil. Reduce the heat and simmer for 10–15 minutes. Leave the syrup to cool.

**5** When the cake is ready, turn it out on to a serving dish and pour the cold syrup over it. Serve warm or at room temperature on its on, or with *kaymak* (clotted cream).

**COOK'S TIP**
The Turkish rule with all their syrupy pastries and sponges is that if the pudding is hot, the syrup should be cold, even chilled, and vice versa.

SERVES SIX

INGREDIENTS
 4 eggs
 115g/4oz/generous ½ cup sugar
 115g/4oz self-raising
  (self-rising) flour
 400g/14oz tub of thick and creamy
  natural (plain) yogurt, strained
 grated rind of 1 lemon
 juice of 1 lemon
For the syrup
 225g/8oz/generous 1 cup sugar
 120ml/4fl oz/½ cup water
 juice of 1 orange
 rind of 1 orange, finely shredded

**1** Preheat the oven to 180°C/350°F/ Gas 4. Prepare a baking tin (pan) or dish (the Turks use a round *tepsi* approximately 23cm/9in in diameter) by greasing it lightly with oil or butter.

**Per portion** Energy 415kcal/1757kJ; Protein 10.5g; Carbohydrate 75.8g, of which sugars 61.5g; Fat 10.7g, of which saturates 4.5g; Cholesterol 127mg; Calcium 217mg; Fibre 0.6g; Sodium 167mg.

# LADIES' NAVELS

*THIS CLASSIC FRIED PASTRY, KADIN GÖBEĞI, IS AN INVENTION FROM THE TOPKAPI PALACE KITCHENS. GARNISH IT WITH WHOLE OR CHOPPED PISTACHIO NUTS AND SERVE WITH KAYMAK (THICK BUFFALO CREAM), OR ANY OTHER CREAM YOU LIKE, AS A DELICIOUS HOT SNACK OR DESSERT.*

SERVES FOUR TO SIX

INGREDIENTS
   50g/2oz/¼ cup butter
   2.5ml/½ tsp salt
   175g/6oz/1½ cups plain
    (all-purpose) flour
   60g/2oz/⅓ cup semolina
   2 eggs
   sunflower oil, for deep-frying
For the syrup
   450g/1lb/scant 2¼ cups sugar
   juice of 1 lemon

**1** Make the sugar syrup. Put the sugar and 300ml/½ pint/1¼ cups water into a large, heavy pan and bring to the boil, stirring all the time. When the sugar has dissolved completely, stir in the lemon juice and lower the heat, then simmer for about 10 minutes, until the syrup has thickened a little. Remove from the heat and leave to cool.

**2** Put the butter, salt and 250ml/8fl oz/ 1 cup water in another heavy pan and bring to the boil. Remove from the heat and add the flour and semolina, beating all the time, until the mixture becomes smooth and leaves the side of the pan. Leave to cool.

**3** Beat the eggs into the cooled mixture so that it gleams. Add 15ml/1 tbsp of the cooled syrup and beat well.

**4** Pour enough oil for deep-frying into a wok or deep-sided pan. Heat until warm, then remove from the heat.

**5** Wet your hands and take an apricot-size piece of dough in your fingers. Roll it into a ball, flatten it in the palm of your hand, then use your finger to make an indentation in the middle to resemble a lady's navel.

**6** Drop the balls of dough into the pan of warmed oil. Repeat with the rest of the mixture to make about 12 navels.

**7** Place the pan back over the heat. As the oil heats up, the pastries will swell, retaining the dip in the middle. Swirl the oil, until the navels turn golden all over.

**8** Remove the navels from the oil with a slotted spoon, then toss them in the cooled syrup. Leave to soak for a few minutes, arrange in a serving dish and spoon some of the syrup over.

**Per portion** Energy 517kcal/2190kJ; Protein 6.3g; Carbohydrate 108.8g, of which sugars 78.9g; Fat 9.3g, of which saturates 4.9g; Cholesterol 81mg; Calcium 93mg; Fibre 1.1g; Sodium 80mg.

# BAKLAVA

*An Ottoman legacy, baklava is one of the greatest creations from the pastry chefs at the Topkapi Palace. Traditionally made with eight layers of pastry dough and seven layers of chopped nuts, the secret is said to be in the specially prepared, paper-thin dough made from clarified butter and the finest flour. Baklava is enjoyed as a mid-morning sweet snack with a cup of Turkish coffee, or as a mid-afternoon pick-me-up with a glass of tea.*

### SERVES TWELVE

#### INGREDIENTS
175g/6oz/¾ cup clarified or plain butter, or sunflower oil
100ml/3½fl oz/scant ½ cup sunflower oil
450g/1lb filo sheets
450g/1lb walnuts, or a mixture of walnuts, pistachios and almonds, finely chopped
5ml/1 tsp ground cinnamon
For the syrup
450g/1lb sugar
juice of 1 lemon, or 30ml/2 tbsp rose water

**1** Preheat the oven to 160°C/325°F/ Gas 3. Melt the butter and oil in a small pan, then brush a little over the bottom and sides of a 30cm/12in round or square cake tin (pan).

**2** Place a sheet of filo in the bottom and brush it with melted butter and oil. Continue until you have used half the filo sheets, brushing each one with butter and oil. Ease the sheets into the corners and trim the edges if they flop over the rim of the tin.

**3** Spread the nuts over the last buttered sheet and sprinkle with the cinnamon, then continue as before with the remaining filo sheets. Brush the top one as well, then, using a sharp knife, cut diagonal parallel lines right through all the layers to the bottom to form small diamond shapes.

**4** Bake the *baklava* in the oven for about 1 hour, until the top is golden – if it is still pale, increase the temperature for a few minutes at the end.

**5** While the *baklava* is in the oven, make the syrup. Put the sugar into a medium, heavy pan, pour in 250ml/8fl oz/1 cup water and bring the mixture to the boil, stirring constantly.

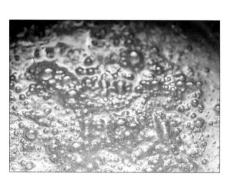

**6** When the sugar has dissolved, lower the heat and stir in the lemon juice, then simmer for 15 minutes, until the syrup thickens. Leave to cool in the pan.

**7** Remove from the oven and pour the cooled syrup over the hot pastry. Return to the oven for 2–3 minutes, then take it out and leave to cool.

**8** Once the *baklava* is cool, carefully lift the individual diamond-shaped pieces out of the tin and arrange them in a serving dish.

### COOK'S TIP
The best *baklava* is to be found in a busy, central pastry shop, where the wide selection of pastries on offer will also include the melt-in-the-mouth *sütlü* nüriye, a layered pastry filled with shaved almonds and bathed in a milky syrup; the moist, diamond-shaped *şöbiyet* filled with chopped pistachios; and the crunchy *bülbül yuvası*, a wrinkled spiral filled with nuts to resemble the nightingale's nest after which it is named.

**Per portion** Energy 973kcal/4059kJ; Protein 12.2g; Carbohydrate 89.9g, of which sugars 60.9g; Fat 65.2g, of which saturates 15.6g; Cholesterol 47mg; Calcium 139mg; Fibre 3.1g; Sodium 141mg.

# ROSE PETAL JAM

*THICK WITH DELICATE, SCENTED ROSE PETALS, GÜL REÇELI — ROSE PETAL JAM — IS ONE OF THE MOST TRADITIONAL OF THE TURKISH JAMS. SPOONED ON TO CHUNKS OF WARM, CRUSTY BREAD, OR OVER YOGURT, RICE PUDDING, CLOTTED CREAM, OR THIN SHEETS OF PASTRY, THE TASTE IS EXQUISITE. ANY SCENTED ROSE PETALS CAN BE USED, BUT THE PINK, COTTAGE-GARDEN ROSE IS PARTICULARLY GOOD. SOME MIDDLE EASTERN STORES SELL BAGS OF DRIED, SCENTED ROSE PETALS FOR JAM MAKING.*

MAKES ABOUT 750ML/1¼ PINTS/3 CUPS

INGREDIENTS
   450g/1lb fresh or dried scented
      rose petals
   about 350ml/12fl oz/1½ cups water
   450g/1lb/2¼ cups sugar
   juice of 1 lemon

**COOK'S TIP**
Rose petals used for culinary purposes must be sweetly scented and are generally pink or lilac in colour. In Turkey they are used to make jam and rose water, which is splashed into milk puddings and Turkish Delight, *lokum*.

**1** If necessary, trim and clean the petals but, if you need to rinse them, make sure they are thoroughly drained. Pour the water into a large, heavy pan. Add the rose petals and bring to the boil.

**2** Strain the petals into a bowl and return the rose-scented water to the pan. Set the strained petals aside.

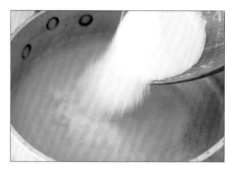

**3** Add the sugar to the rose-scented water and bring it to the boil, stirring constantly. Reduce the heat and simmer for 10 minutes, or until the liquid thickens and coats the back of a wooden spoon.

**4** Stir in the lemon juice and the strained rose petals, and simmer for a further 10 minutes.

**5** Leave the mixture to cool and thicken in the pan – it should be thick and runny, requiring a spoon for serving, not a knife.

**6** Spoon the cooled jam into sterilized jars and keep in a cool, dry place for up to 6 months.

**Per portion** Energy 1886kcal/8028kJ; Protein 14.9g; Carbohydrate 477.4g, of which sugars 477g; Fat 3.6g, of which saturates 0.5g; Cholesterol 0mg; Calcium 1004mg; Fibre 9.4g; Sodium 657mg.

# SOUR CHERRY JAM

*STUNNING IN COLOUR AND TASTE, VIŞNE REÇELI IS ONE OF TURKEY'S MOST POPULAR SUMMER JAMS. WHEN THE CHERRIES ARE IN SEASON, THE PLUMP, SWEET ONES, KIRAZ, ARE PICKED TO EAT, WHEREAS THE SOUR VARIETY, VIŞNE, ARE COVETED FOR THIS JAM AND THE SUMMER BREAD PUDDING, VIŞNELI EKMEK TATLISI. AS WITH MOST TURKISH JAMS, THIS RECIPE IS FOR A RUNNY CONSERVE, WHICH NEEDS TO BE SPOONED ON TO FRESH BREAD OR DRIZZLED OVER YOGURT.*

MAKES ABOUT 2KG/4½LB

INGREDIENTS
    1kg/2¼lb/6 cups fresh sour cherries
    1kg/2¼lb/5 cups sugar
    juice of 1 lemon

**1** Pick over the cherries and remove the stalks. (You can remove the pits, too, if you like, but this is a laborious task and few Turkish cooks bother.)

**2** Rinse and drain the cherries and put them into a large, heavy pan. Spoon the sugar over them, making sure they are all covered, and leave the cherries to weep overnight.

**3** Place the pan over the heat and bring the liquid (there will be a substantial amount of cherry juice in the pan) to the boil, stirring from time to time.

**4** Add the lemon juice, reduce the heat, and simmer for about 25 minutes, or until the liquid thickens, bearing in mind that this will be a fairly liquid jam.

**5** Leave the jam to cool in the pan and then spoon it into sterilized jars.

**6** Keep the jam in a cool, dry place, ready to enjoy with bread, or to spoon over milk and rice puddings. The jam will keep well for up to 6 months,

**COOK'S TIPS**
• Sour cherries are also boiled with sugar to make a fruit syrup, which is deep purple in colour and is used as the basis of the cool, refreshing drink, *vişne suyu*.
• If you do not remove the cherry stones (pits) you need to be careful when eating the jam or you could crack your teeth.

**Per portion** Energy 4420kcal/18840kJ; Protein 14g; Carbohydrate 1160g, of which sugars 1160g; Fat 1g, of which saturates 0g; Cholesterol 0mg; Calcium 660mg; Fibre 9g; Sodium 70mg.

# DRIED FIG JAM WITH ANISEED AND PINE NUTS

*THIS DELECTABLE HOMEMADE WINTER JAM IS MADE WITH DRIED FIGS AND PINE NUTS. IT IS FABULOUS SPREAD ON HOT, FRESH BREAD STRAIGHT FROM THE BAKER'S OVEN. LOOK FOR PLUMP, SUCCULENT DRIED FIGS WITH A SPRINGY TEXTURE — ONES THAT ARE GOOD ENOUGH TO SNACK ON — AVAILABLE IN SOME SUPERMARKETS, DELICATESSENS AND HEALTH FOOD STORES.*

MAKES ENOUGH FOR 3–4 X 450G/1LB JAM JARS

INGREDIENTS
  450g/1lb/2¼ cups sugar
  juice of 1 lemon
  5ml/1 tsp ground aniseed
  about 700g/1lb 9oz dried figs,
    coarsely chopped
  45–60ml/3–4 tbsp pine nuts

**1** Put the sugar and 600ml/1 pint/ 2½ cups water into a heavy pan and bring to the boil, stirring all the time, until the sugar has dissolved. Lower the heat and simmer for 5–10 minutes, until the syrup begins to thicken.

**2** Stir the lemon juice, aniseed and figs into the sugar syrup.

**3** Bring to the boil once more, then lower the heat again and simmer for 15–20 minutes, until the figs are tender.

**4** Add the pine nuts and simmer for a further 5 minutes. Leave the jam to cool in the pan before spooning into sterilized jars and sealing. Stored in a cool, dry place, the jam will keep for up to 6 months.

**Per portion** Energy 869kcal/3693kJ; Protein 8.4g; Carbohydrate 197.5g, of which sugars 197.5g; Fat 10.5g, of which saturates 0.5g; Cholesterol 0mg; Calcium 492mg; Fibre 13.4g; Sodium 115mg.

# PLUM TOMATO AND ALMOND JAM

*IN THE STYLE OF A CONSERVE, YOU WILL ONLY EVER COME ACROSS THIS JAM IN A TURKISH HOME, AS IT IS NOT MADE COMMERCIALLY LIKE THE WELL-KNOWN ONES MADE WITH ROSE PETALS, GREEN FIGS, SOUR CHERRIES OR QUINCE. A SUMMER JAM, MADE WITH SLIGHTLY UNRIPE OR FIRM PLUM TOMATOES, IT IS SYRUPY IN CONSISTENCY, AND SPOONED, RATHER THAN SPREAD, ON TO BREAD.*

MAKES ENOUGH FOR 2–3 X 450G/1LB
JAM JARS

INGREDIENTS
  1kg/2¼lb firm plum tomatoes
  500g/1¼ lb/2½ cups sugar
  115g/4oz/1 cup whole
    blanched almonds
  8–10 whole cloves

**1** Skin the plum tomatoes. Submerge them for a few seconds in a bowl of boiling water, then plunge them straight away into a bowl of cold water. Remove them from the water one at a time and peel off the skins with your fingers or a small knife.

**2** Place the skinned tomatoes in a heavy pan and cover with the sugar. Leave them to sit for a few hours, or overnight, to draw out some of the juices, then stir in 150ml/¼ pint/⅔ cup water. The tomatoes should be quite juicy – if not, stir in some more water, you may need up to 300ml/½ pint/ 1¼ cups.

**3** Place the pan over a low heat and stir gently with a wooden spoon until the sugar has completely dissolved.

**COOK'S TIP**
In the *güney* kitchens in the south of Turkey, plum tomatoes are often first soaked in a lime solution in order to preserve their firmness, then they are poached in a sugar syrup and served as a dessert.

**4** Bring the syrup to the boil and boil for a few minutes, skimming off any froth, then lower the heat and stir in the almonds and cloves.

**5** Simmer gently for about 25 minutes, stirring from time to time to prevent the mixture from sticking to the bottom of the pan and burning, which would spoil the flavour.

**6** Turn off the heat and leave the jam to cool in the pan before spooning into sterilized jars and sealing.

**7** Stored in a cool, dry place, the jam will keep for several months.

**Per portion** Energy 948Kcal/4016kJ; Protein 11.3g; Carbohydrate 187.1g, of which sugars 186.1g; Fat 22.4g, of which saturates 2g; Cholesterol 0mg; Calcium 204mg; Fibre 6.2g; Sodium 45mg.

# GLOSSARY

**Adı** Sage

**Adı çayı** Tea made from the branches of sun-dried sage

**Antem fıstık** Pistachio nuts

**Armut turşusu** Pickled pears

**Aşure** A fruit and grain dessert that is made to commemorate the tenth day of *Muharram*

**Ayran** A refreshing drink made with yogurt, water and salt

**Ayva** Quinces

**Badem** Almonds

**Bakliyat** Pulses (beans, peas and lentils)

**Bal** Honey

**Bal kabaği** Pumpkins

**Bamya** Okra

**Barbunya** Red mullet

**Beyaz peynir** Salty white cheese made from sheep or cow's milk that is sold in blocks, and which can be substituted with feta cheese

**Biber** Peppers

**Bildircin** Quails

**Börek** Savoury pastries and pies that originated in the Ottoman kitchens, which vary in shape and size with regional variations on the fillings

**Boza** A thick drink made from fermented bulgur wheat sprinkled with cinnamon

**Bulgur** Bulgur wheat

**Çam** Apricots

**Çay fistik** Pine nuts

**Çemen** A paste made from ground cumin, fenugreek, *kırmızı biber* and garlic, which is used to coat *pastırma*

**Ceviz** Walnuts

**Cezve** The traditional long-handled, tin-lined copper cooking vessel used for making Turkish coffee

**Çarliston biber** Mildly perfumed, slipper-shaped peppers

**Çörek** Small, ring-shaped buns

**Çoreotu** Nigella

**Dağı kekik** Thyme

**Dana** Beef

**Dereotu** Dill

**Dil peyniri** A mild-tasting cheese that can be pulled apart in stringy strips, similar to mozarella

**Dolma** A generic term for anything that is stuffed

**Domate** Tomatoes

**Elma çayi** Apple tea, made from sugar and apple-flavoured granules

**Kereviz** Celery

**Ekmek** Bread

**Enginar** Artichokes

**Ezme** A simple form of *meze*, which consists of ingredients that have the correct consistency for scooping up with bread

**Fava** Broad (fava) beans

**Fındık** Hazelnuts

**Fırın** A communal oven used for baking bread and pastries

**Ghee** Clarified butter, used for cooking

**Gül** Orange

**Günebakan** Sunflower seeds

**Güveç** An earthenware or terracotta casserole pot

**Hamsi** Anchovies

**Havuç** Carrots

**Helva** A sweetmeat made from semolina and pine nuts, which is prepared for commemorative occasions such as births, deaths, harvests and various religious festivals

**Humus** Chickpeas

**Ihlamur çayı** Tea made from the dried leaves and blossom of the linden tree, believed to aid the digestive system and fight colds

**Incir** Figs

**Ispanak** Spinach

**Kabak** Courgettes (zucchini)

**Kadayif** A type of finely shredded pastry that is used to make a range of desserts

**Kahve** Turkish coffee

**Karpuz** Watermelons

**Kaşar peynir** A hard, tangy cheese that can be grated and used in many cooked dishes

**Kavun** Melons

**Kayısı** Apricots

**Kaymak** Clotted cream made from water buffalo milk

**Kekik** Oregano

**Kereviz** Celery

**Kestane** Chestnuts

**Kiliç** Swordfish

**Kımız** A traditional fermented liquor made from the milk of mares

**Kimyon** Cumin

**Kiraz** Sweet cherries

**Kiremit** Concave roof tiles used for roasting and baking cuts of meat and fish in the communal oven

**Kırmızı biber** A ground spice made from Turkish red pepper

**Kişniş** Coriander seeds

**Köfte** Traditional meatballs made with minced (ground) meat and breadcrumbs, onions, herbs and spices; anything that is shaped into a ball before it is cooked

**Köy peyniri** A soft, creamy white cheese

**Kuyrukyağı** Fat from a sheep's tail, used in cooking

**Kuzu** Lamb

**Leblebi** Roasted chickpeas that are eaten as *meze*

**Levrek** Sea bass

**Limon** Lemons

**Lokum** Turkish Delight, a sweet (candy) flavoured with rose water

**Lufer** Blue fish (sea perch)

**Mangal** A portable charcoal stove used in traditional kitchens and on picnics

**Mantı** A type of pasta that falls between a noodle and a dumpling

**Mastika** Mastic, the aromatic gum from the *Pistacia lentiscus* tree, sold in crystal form

**Maydenoz** Flat leaf parsley

**Mercimek** Lentils

**Meze** An array of small dishes

**Nane** Mint

**Nar** Pomegranates

**Oklava** A long, thin rolling pin designed for rolling out paper-thin sheets of *yufka*

**Ördek** Duck
**Orkinos** Tuna
**Palamut** Bonito
**Pancar** Beetroot (beet)
**Pastırma** Cured, air-dried fillet of veal or beef, which is coated in *çemen*
**Patlican** Aubergines (eggplants)
**Pekmez** A fruit molasses made from a variety fruits, such as mulberries, sour cherries, sour pomegranates, carob pods and grape juice
**Pekmez helvası** Helva made with grape molasses
**Peynir** Cheese
**Pide** Soft, spongy flatbread, of which there are many varieties
**Pilâki** A method of cooking fish, mussels or beans, which involves sautéing onion, garlic, celery and carrot, then adding fish, mussels or beans, water, salt and sugar, and cooking until tender
**Pilav** A rice dish or pilaff
**Piliç** Chicken
**Pirasa** Leeks
**Pirinç** Rice
**Portakal** Orange
**Pul biber** Very spicy, finely ground *kırmızı biber*
**Rakı** An aniseed-flavoured alcoholic drink that turns cloudy when water is added
**Reçel** Jam
**Safron** Saffron
**Salatalık** Cucumbers
**Salep** A popular drink made from the ground root of an orchid
**Sardalya** Sardines

**Sarmısak** Garlic
**Semiz otu** Lamb's lettuce
**Sesam** Sesame seeds
**Sıvı tas** Standard, everyday yogurt
**Soğan** Onions
**Sucuk** A horseshoe-shaped, cured sausage made with lamb or beef and flavoured with garlic and cumin
**Şerbet** A refreshing drink made using syrups from fruits such as lemon, cherry or pomegranate
**Sumak** Sumac, a deep-red condiment with a tangy, citrus taste made from the ground, dried berries of a wild bush, *Rhus coriaria*
**Süzme** Extra-thick strained natural (plain) yogurt that is so stiff you can stand a spoon in it
**Tahin** Tahini, a fine, oily paste made from sesame seeds, used in many Turkish dishes, incuding hummus
**Tandır** A traditional beehive-shaped oven set in a pit in the earth that is used in particular for roasting meat and baking bread
**Tane** Grains
**Tarçin** Cinnamon
**Tavuk** Chicken
**Tepsi** A large tray, made from wood, copper or silver, that is raised on a wooden or copper trestle and used as a table; pan (tin) used for baking *yufka*
**Tarator** A sauce made with pounded nuts and garlic, which is served with deep-fried shellfish and steamed or fried vegetables

**Tarhana** Fermented dried curds, used for making traditional soup
**Taze fasulye** Fresh beans
**Turşu** Pickles
**Tutmaç** Traditional noodles that are cooked with meat or yogurt
**Uskumru** Mackerel
**Üzüm** Grapes
**Vanilya** Vanilla
**Vişne** Sour cherries
**Yaprak** Vine leaves
**Yeni bahar** Allspice
**Yoğurt** Yogurt
**Yufka** Paper-thin sheets of flat bread that can be filled and baked or deep-fried in a variety of ways
**Yumurta** Eggs
**Zerde** A jellied, saffron-scented rice dessert that is traditionally prepared for wedding and circumcision feasts
**Zeytin** Olives
**Zeytinyağlı** A generic term for the method of poaching vegetables, such as artichokes or (bell) peppers, in olive oil and then leaving them to cool to room temperature before serving

## AUTHOR'S ACKNOWLEDGEMENTS

Having lived, worked and travelled in Turkey frequently over the last twenty years, I feel very at home there and cook Turkish food almost every day. As always, this means I am indebted to many friendly faces, from the street markets to the hospitality I have received in many homes and, of course, my good friend, Hasan Selamet, who seeks out obscure and interesting things to eat.

At home, I would like to thank my children for being patient on our travels and for understanding the hours I work; my editor, Lucy Doncaster, who shares my enthusiasm for Turkish food and is always helpful and accommodating; and Martin Brigdale, a very talented photographer with a passion for food.

## PUBLISHER'S ACKNOWLEDGEMENTS

The publisher would like to thank Martin Brigdale for his stunning photography throughout the book, apart from the following images:
t = top; b = bottom; r = right; l = left
Alamy pages 22, 34bl; Corbis pages 6t, 6br, 7,8t, 9tl, 9b, 10t, 11tr, 13, 15b, 17, 18b, 19, 24b, 28b, 36t, 38br, 44b, 51, 54t; Lucy Doncaster pages 10bl, 10t, 16b, 30t, 36br; The Art Archive page 12.

# INDEX